VARIETIES OF JAVANESE RELIGION

AN ANTHROPOLOGICAL ACCOUNT

Java is famous for its combination of diverse cultural forms and religious beliefs. Andrew Beatty considers Javanese solutions to the problem of cultural difference, and explores the ways in which Javanese villagers make sense of their complex and multi-layered culture. Pantheist mystics, supernaturalists, orthodox Muslims, and Hindu converts at once construct contrasting faiths and create a common ground through syncretist ritual. Vividly evoking the religious life of Javanese villagers, its controversies and reconciliations, its humour and irony, its philosophical seriousness, and its formal beauty, Dr Beatty probes beyond the finished surfaces of ritual and cosmology to show the debate and compromise inherent in practical religion. This is the most comprehensive study of Javanese religion since Clifford Geertz's classic study of 1960.

ANDREW BEATTY is the author of *Society and Exchange in Nias* (1992). He has carried out over four years of field research in Nias and Java, Indonesia.

D1338894

Cambridge Studies in Social and Cultural Anthropology

111

VARIETIES OF JAVANESE RELIGION

The monograph series Cambridge Studies in Social and Cultural Anthropology publishes analytical ethnographies, comparative works, and contributions to theory. All combine an expert and critical command of ethnography and a sophisticated engagement with current theoretical debates.

A list of some other books in the series will be found at the end of the volume.

Founding Editors
Meyer Fortes, Edmund Leach, Jack Goody, Stanley Tambiah

VARIETIES OF JAVANESE RELIGION

An anthropological account

ANDREW BEATTY

CAMBRIDGE
UNIVERSITY PRESS

PUBLISHED BY THE PRESS SYNDICATE OF THE UNIVERSITY OF CAMBRIDGE
The Pitt Building, Trumpington Street, Cambridge CB2 1RP, United Kingdom

CAMBRIDGE UNIVERSITY PRESS
The Edinburgh Building, Cambridge, CB2 2RU, United Kingdom
http://www.cup.cam.ac.uk
40 West 20th Street, New York, NY 10011–4211, USA   http://www.cup.org
10 Stamford Road, Oakleigh, Melbourne 3166, Australia

First published 1999

Typeset in Times 10/13pt   [CE]

A catalogue record for this book is available from the British Library

Library of Congress Cataloguing in Publication data
Beatty, Andrew.
Varieties of Javanese religion: an anthropological account /
Andrew Beatty.
       p.   cm. – (Cambridge studies in social and cultural
anthropology: 111)
Includes bibliographical references and index.
ISBN 0 521 62444 4 (hardcover). – ISBN 0 521 62473 8 (pbk.)
1. Java (Indonesia)–Religion.   I. Title.   II. Series.
BL2120.J3B4   1999   200'.9598–dc21   98–38613   CIP

ISBN 0 521 62444 4 hardback
ISBN 0 521 62473 8 paperback

Transferred to digital printing 2004

For Mercedes, Sofía, and Daniel

Contents

Acknowledgements

The research on which this book is based was carried out with the benefit of a British Academy Postdoctoral Fellowship, which I held at the Institute of Social and Cultural Anthropology in Oxford. The British Academy also generously provided a personal research grant for fieldwork expenses. I would also like to express my thanks to the Department of Social Anthropology at Cambridge for an Evans Fellowship which gave me the opportunity to return to the field for a further project. This second period of fieldwork – though it was mainly devoted to a different subject – enabled me to make some additions and corrections to the manuscript.

A number of people have read and commented on drafts of various chapters. I am grateful to Peter Carey, Leo Howe, and Rodney Needham for their incisive comments and suggestions. I thank Robert Barnes for giving the whole manuscript a careful reading and for his advice and steadfast support over the years. Robert Hefner generously gave me the benefit of his expertise and judgement in an invaluable and detailed commentary on the manuscript. I am most grateful for his encouragement and suggestions and the great intellectual stimulus they have provided. My wife, Mercedes, has helped immeasurably in improving the book's argument and in judging the relative weight which should be given to its different elements.

Chapter 2 originally appeared in shorter form in the *Journal of the Royal Anthropological Institute* 2, 2 (1996) under the title 'Adam and Eve and Vishnu: syncretism in the Javanese slametan.' I am grateful to the editor and to the Royal Anthropological Institute for permission to use this material here.

Fieldwork was carried out under the auspices of Lembaga Ilmu

Pengetahuan Indonesia and Universitas Airlangga in Surabaya. The dean of the faculty of social science at Unair was helpful in expediting permits. In Banyuwangi, the offices of Bappeda, the *bupati*, and the *camat* and his staff in Glagah, were unfailingly helpful. I would also like to thank Pak Achmad Ismail, who was an excellent assistant in the early period of fieldwork, and Pak Sukur and Pak Hasan Ali for their help and advice. My brief stay in Krajan was made pleasant by Pak Sapuwan, Bu Sapuwan, and Pak Suwarno.

My debt to the people of Bayu is as great as my affection for them. Since I have called their village by a pseudonym, in order to spare it unwanted intrusion, I can take the liberty here of naming those to whom I am most grateful: the headman, Pak Sutris, and his wife, Bu Sulastri, for their great kindness, hospitality, and unwavering support; Pak Rayis and Bu Eti for their wisdom and friendship; Pak Daso and Ma' Daso for their loyalty and perseverance with my education; Pak Lurah Sunarto, Pak Ela and Bu Wilase, Pak Pathan, Pak Lurah Hanapi, Pak Senadi and Bi Untung, Bi Misri, Pak Suwardi and Kana, Bi Jiyah and Pak Mu'i, Mas Untung, Ma'e Yusup and Bu Suwari, Ma'e Erwin, Pak Sutam, Pak Sehan, Pak Sutris and family in Sukosari, Pak Tulik, Pak Saleh, Man Tok (a wonderful cook), Pak Serad, Pak Timbul, Pak Andi, Pak Waris: all of whom helped us in innumerable ways and enriched our lives with their friendship. I should also like to mention the boy who was a fine friend (the first among many) to our children and who I hope will one day read this book: Hadi.

Should others in Bayu eventually read this account in some form, I hope they will find it sympathetic and representative of their different views. Javanists will probably identify a four-five structure embedded in a nine; *santri* will be pleased that Islam – hence green or multicoloured! – is in the centre. Bayu, incidentally, is the name of the guardian deity of the cosmic centre.

Finally, I would like to thank my wife, Mercedes, for sharing in the joys and hardships of fieldwork. I dedicate this book to her and to our children, Sofia and Daniel.

List of plates

Glossary

Words appearing in this glossary are italicized only at first mention in the text; other foreign words are italicized throughout.

abangan	nominal Muslim
adat	custom, traditions
alus	refined, spiritual, incorporeal
barong	lion-dragon; drama of this name
buda	Hindu-Buddhist; pertaining to pre-Islamic Java
bupati	district administrator, 'regent'
buyut	great-grandparent or great-grandchild; title for spirit
cocog	fitting, apt, compatible
danyang	place spirit
desa	administrative village unit
dhukun	healer, magician
du'a	prayer
dulur	sibling, kin; one of the four personal guardian spirits
fatihah	(Arabic) opening verse of the Koran
gandrung	female entertainer/dancer
giling	windmill
hadīth	(Arabic) traditions of the Prophet
haj	the pilgrimage to Mecca
haji	title of person who has performed the pilgrimage to Mecca
kasar	coarse, material
kawruh	Javanese wisdom, Javanist lore
kejawèn	Javanism
kiyai	traditional Muslim leader, usually head of a *pesantren*

kraton	palace, court
langgar	prayer-house
lontar	literature, traditionally inscribed on palm-leaf
lurah	headman
mandi	efficacious, (magically) powerful
modin	village Islamic official
niyat	intention, required before performing prayer or ritual action
pesantren	(or *pondhok-pesantren*) Islamic boarding school
priyayi	member of nobility or elite
rasa	taste, bodily feeling, intuition, organ of consciousness
rukun	in a state of social harmony
salāt	(Arabic) prescribed Islamic prayer
sanggar	non-Islamic place of worship, shrine
sangku	zodiac beaker used in Cungking cult
santri	pious, orthodox-leaning Muslim
sedhekah	commemorative or funerary prayer meal
sembahyang	Javanese term for Islamic worship
shariah	Islamic law
slamet	well-being; secure, well, free of danger
slametan	ritual feast
tahlilan	Islamic chanting
umat	Islamic community of faithful
wakaf	Islamic foundation
wakil	delegate
wali	saint, friend of God
wayang	shadow puppet theatre

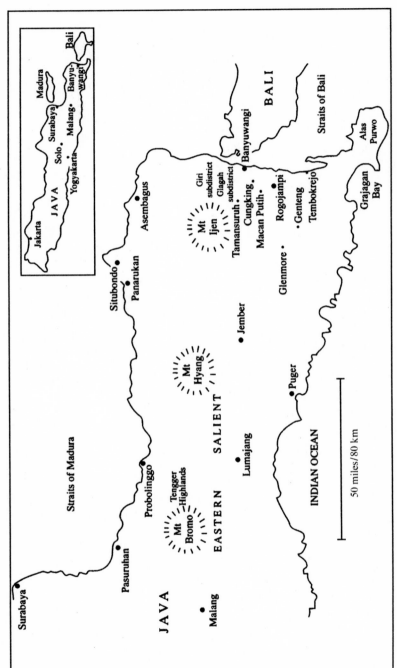

East Java

1

Introduction

This book is about religion in Java – its diverse forms, controversies, and reconciliations; more abstractly it is about cultural difference and syncretism. At a time when anthropology is increasingly preoccupied with cultural pluralism in the West, and with the challenges to personal identity, mutual tolerance, and social harmony that it presents, the example of Java reminds us that some of the more 'traditional' societies have been dealing with similar problems for quite some time. The varieties of Javanese religion are, of course, well known, thanks to a number of excellent studies. In what follows, however, my chief interest is in the *effect* of diversity upon Javanese religion. In looking at the mutual influences of Islamic piety, mysticism, Hinduism, and folk tradition upon each other, and at their different compromises with the fact of diversity, I hope to give a credible and dynamic account of how religion works in a complex society.

The setting for this book – Banyuwangi in the easternmost part of Java – is particularly appropriate to such an enterprise. In the standard view of things, the various forms of Javanese religion are unevenly distributed among village, market, court/palace, and town. Although most communities contain orthodox Muslims as well as practitioners of other tendencies (Koentjaraningrat 1985: 318), a rough spatial separation along religious and cultural lines (or a polarization within the most heterogeneous villages) has, allegedly, been characteristic of Java from the early years of the century (Jay 1963), though the sharpness of divisions has fluctuated with political developments. In rural Banyuwangi, however, typically we find pantheistic mysticism, spirit cults, and normative piety coexisting in great intimacy within a single social framework. The perennial Javanese problem – how to get on with

1

people of a different religious persuasion – is an everpresent factor in daily life.

In doing justice to this sort of complexity, anthropology still has much to learn. Fredrik Barth, writing of Bali, goes so far as to claim that 'We still do not know how to go about describing complex civilizations' (1993: 3). This is partly, no doubt, because our time-honoured methods of symbolic analysis and descriptive integration have, for the most part, grown out of the experience of living in simple societies, among people for whom, as W. Stanner memorably put it, life is a 'one possibility thing' (Bellah 1969: 272). Yet, increasingly, the 'field' – whether it be a city quarter or a once-remote tribal domain – is characterized by a loose and often paradoxical relation between religious forms and social realities. Where once our task was to reveal the depths behind apparently simple forms, we now have to grapple with diversity, inconsistency, eclecticism, even incoherence.

So how to go about it? In *Balinese worlds*, Barth sets out the case that local variation is intrinsic to 'traditional civilization' and should therefore form the object of enquiry instead of being regarded as a mere difficulty to be overcome (1993: 4). In Banyuwangi, however, as in much of rural Java, one need not stray beyond the village boundaries to find evidence of striking cultural variation: the diversity found in one small neighbourhood is replicated in other corners of the same community, and so on into the next village. As in Bali, the problem facing the anthropologist is one of variation but not (or not essentially) one of *local* variation. In rural Banyuwangi, difference is constructed within the same space, and thus with greater intensity. The pious Muslim, when he rolls out his prayer mat in public view, is all too aware of his next-door neighbour who sits on the front doorstep pointedly ignoring the call-to-prayer. The group of mystics who gather in the evenings to expatiate in loud voices on the meaning of this or that do so in allusions which seem designed to trouble, but not quite offend, more orthodox auditors on the other side of the bamboo wall. And the visitor to the local shrine during the fasting month takes a devious route with her basket of offerings, equally anxious about the blessing she seeks and the criticism she must avoid. The outcome of all this busy ritual activity, mystical speculation, and competitive piety is quite unlike the situation prevailing in neighbouring Bali. Instead of the 'disorder, multiplicity, and underdeterminedness' that Barth finds in Bali (1993: 5), and which he believes characterizes social life in general, the picture in Java (at least in the portion that concerns us here) is of a studiously crafted order, harmonization, and overdeterminedness – an intricate and elegant structure built upon a history of violence and disorder.

As we shall see, this solution to the problem of diversity calls for a certain ingenuity, both practical and intellectual, and an unremitting, though habitual, effort. It is a solution at once durable and delicate, depending on a continuing balance of interests.

In characterizing this state of affairs one hesitates to use the word 'syncretism' since this usually implies a substantial merging of types, with a loss of their separate identities: something that cannot be presumed in the Javanese case. Following Stewart (1995), however, I use this term in a more abstract sense to refer to a systematic interrelation of elements from diverse traditions, an ordered response to pluralism and cultural difference. We shall see that this interrelation need not imply or lead to fusion; the Javanese case is rather more complicated than that. Particular traditions – mystical, Islamic, folk – which are themselves hybridized, enter into further combination in ritual and religious discourse; and the nature of these higher combinations in turn affects their several constitutions. Syncretism, in this sense, refers to a dynamic, recursive process, a constant factor in cultural reproduction, rather than to a settled outcome. As Stewart (1995: 26) suggests, seen in this light it is a concept which directs our attention towards 'issues of accommodation, contest, appropriation, indigenization and a host of other dynamic intercultural processes'.

Such processes are, of course, historically situated; and syncretic forms are liable to reconfiguration and re-evaluation in the light of changing socio-political tensions (Hefner 1995; Shaw and Stewart 1994). History thus has a role in disentangling the various strands and in identifying shifts of meaning and relative power over time. But if the historical background is important, its precise relevance to the present is not always easy to establish. Javanese syncretism may have its roots in the past, but it is not simply an effect of the past, still less a concrete thing which persists through cultural inertia. Its significance lies in a combination of immediate factors (the position of Islam, the nature of the village community, norms of association, etc.) and the present arrangements would quickly unravel were these to change.

If history can take us only so far in explaining the complexity of the present, an alternative would be to explain the divisions and recombinations of Javanese religion at the level of ordinary everyday action. This is broadly the approach taken by Barth in his Balinese study. Barth's Balinese are confronted by 'a surfeit of cultural materials and ideational possibilities … from which to construct reality' (1993: 4). They are engaged in a ceaseless struggle to make sense of the flow of events and in doing so draw on diverse traditions and epistemologies. Characters in search of a culture, one might say. Javanese persons, it seems to me, do not stand outside their 'worlds' in quite the same way. Like Balinese, they move between different 'interpretative paradigms' – they may, for example, see the 'same' illness or misfortune variously in terms of sorcery, germs, fate, or a mystical imbalance (to adapt one of Barth's examples, pp. 266–7). But the triumph of one particular account over rival versions is rarely a matter of deciding which makes better sense. Abstractly considered, a ghost, a ritual mistake, or a sorceror's missile may be to blame, but when the sufferer ponders the cause of his illness it is other, non-cognitive, factors present in the situation that usually determine which paradigm he adopts. He may not have the authority to pronounce a diagnosis; or he may take into account the expectations and prejudices of his companions. Less obviously, the way the illness is experienced and presented may presume what kind of explanation is possible. Indeed, the experience may in itself constitute a kind of explanation. Diversity, in the sense of choice, may in some cases be an ethnographic illusion, an outsider's construction. The general point is that an interpretation is *part of* the world that actors construct and is inevitably subject to a range of social constraints; it is not something distinct from the world as experienced or as told.

An approach that would seek to explain cultural diversity at the level of ordinary, everyday action must always reckon with the problem of how action is culturally framed. Case histories do not provide a way round it. Far from being the eye-witness accounts of a participant, they must always rely, in part, on informants' commentaries and asides, often filtered through translation and reflecting various interpretative traditions. They draw on discourse rather than the raw data of human action.

If the nexus between culture and action is difficult to specify and perhaps (posed in these terms) chimerical, one way out of the difficulty is simply to grasp the nettle and focus explicitly on discourse and ritual – culture in its coercive and normative aspect. But this would have the reverse effect of minimizing cultural difference and masking the human variety and inventiveness which Barth rightly seeks to capture. If ethnography is to be true to experience (ours as well as others') it must deal with the paradoxical fact that, while largely constrained in what we do, and all too predictable with it, we nevertheless feel ourselves to be, in important ways, free. Indeed, a tension between freedom and constraint, at an experiential level, lies at the heart of social life. In this book I therefore try to steer a middle course between an individuals-in-action perspective and a reductive sociocentric framework. Rather than focusing on events and the interpretative paradigms in which they are cast, or on inexorable structures of power, I look at how people think their traditions, how they conceive the ideas by which they feel compelled. And I suggest that although our 'worlds' are largely constructed for us by others, and our interpretations are moulded by factors partly beyond our ken, the availability of different perspectives occasionally permits a creative space in which to manoeuvre – a space in which, minimally, we can become conscious of our predicament as social beings endowed with will. Javanese themselves allow for this possibility in what they call the 'rubbing together' of ideas in debate – a creative friction out of which arise unexpected things.

An analysis of the relation between ritual and ideology in a culturally plural setting must therefore take dominant ideas seriously *as ideas*, not merely as signs of social processes. This is, after all, to take account of what matters to our hosts as they see it. Hence, a central concern in what follows is with how ideas emerge, become accepted, and gain force among their adherents. Since we are dealing with diversity within a common structure, we must also ask why some ideas and ways are rejected, what sorts of hedges and defences are built around people's mental habits, and how people manage to conjure with differing, often contradictory, values and concepts. Such questions are germane to any social setting, of course, but they are given a peculiar salience and explicitness in a setting characterized by religious and ideological diversity. A conventional symbolic analysis or exegesis-of-the-informant's-exegesis is not really adequate to answer questions of this kind. We must move in closer to convey the *texture* of thought as well as its form and content, because style and manner register important factors such as authority, censorship, indeterminacy, and compromise.

These considerations have a bearing on the reporting of ethnography and influence the way we apprehend the material. In the present case, key topics – the definition of God from pantheistic and monotheistic perspectives, the foundation of ethics, the evaluation of rival interpretations, the locus of meaning – are presented not as settled matters, simple alternatives, but as contested issues, often in the form of argument. Only thus can one begin to appreciate the texture of cultural debate and the compelling force of particular ideas. Hence, in and among the ethnographic description will be found dialogues on the existence of the external world (is it independent of us, does it exist in the perceiving?), on the nature of the Koran as revealed or humanly invented, and even on the problems modern birth control poses for a theory of reincarnation.

A recurrent theme (reflecting a Javanese concern) is on modalities of expression: the said and the unsaid, ambiguity, suppression and irony, unequal discourses. We see how religious expression is continually given shape and emphasis – or, alternatively, is muted – by relations of power. For this reason, the wider political context – the imprint of state policy and propaganda, the dominant position of Islam, and the background of political violence – is a constant point of reference throughout the book. Indeed, home-made meanings and local solutions to the problems of diversity cannot be understood apart from cultural politics.

I have outlined the general approach adopted in this book. Let me now give an indication of its contents. Chapter 2 concerns the *slametan*, a ritual meal whose format draws on – ideally, encompasses – all the religious variants described later in the book. Centred on a synoptic ritual, this chapter serves as a thematic introduction as well as picturing what Javanese religion would look like as a whole, *if it were a whole.* Since the slametan is the central rite of popular religion, much depends on its characterization. Is it Islamic, animistic, or a relic of the Indic period of Javanese history? I examine the rival claims and explain how people of different orientation come together in ritual, and how mystical, Islamic, and indigenous traditions combine in a temporary synthesis. I show how symbols in an ideologically diverse setting work as common denominators, focusing diverse interests, and how their combination in ritual is the recipe for syncretism. The rest of the book then picks apart this synthesis: each variant is discussed with a view to how it relates to the others.

The next two chapters are about regional cults and their compromises with Islam. Chapter 3 concerns the *barong*, a popular drama in which performers are possessed by the village guardian spirit. This village spirit is the object of a complex of practices – protective rites, divination, healing – which persist in the shadow of Islam. By looking at a barong performance we can understand something of how indigenous tradition is both conceived and represented. We see how, at the climax of the show, autochthonous power erupts onto the stage, yet its significance is withheld – literally masked – from the audience. At the heart of the drama is an absence of meaning, a vacuity which draws attention both to itself and to the religious and political pressures which account for it. In pursuing the broader significance of the drama – which seems to lie in a bloody and repressed past – I trace the history of the barong troupe and show how a politically disadvantaged group has managed to retain control of a key religious institution.

Chapter 4 depicts a different kind of compromise with Islam and the modern state. The shrine of a semi-legendary sage who was adviser in the Hindu kingdom of Blambangan (the setting of modern Banyuwangi) serves as a haven of non-Islamic religiosity – a religiosity which is more or less legitimate though limited to a muted symbolic expression. In the cult of the sage can be glimpsed the predicament of modern Javanists and their poignant efforts to recover a vanished past.

A long and pivotal chapter (5) is devoted to practical Islam, that is, Islam as it is conceived and practised in contrast to and alongside the other religious variants. The pious Muslims introduced in this chapter are not the dogmatic puritans known to Javanese ethnography through the works of Geertz, Peacock, and Nakamura: stern, God-fearing types (the Javanese, that is) who cleave to their mosques and disdain contact with the irreligious masses. In rural Banyuwangi – as in much of Java – the pious have kept faith with tradition, living intermingled with the not-so-pious in what is an uncharted middle ground of Javanese religion. Contrary to the familiar picture of Islam in Java, I show village faith to be ritualistic, practice-oriented, and undogmatic – characteristics explained by the ideologically mixed setting. The emphasis of the chapter is on portraying what ordinary Muslims, as opposed to experts, make of their faith: how they conceive of merit, the purpose of worship, the nature of revelation, and so on.

Javanese mysticism, in its practical rural guise, only makes sense when set against the predominance of Islam; hence my discussion of this subject follows the chapter on Islam. Most accounts of Javanese mysticism derive from literary sources and courtly or urban informants. This is one of the first accounts to show how mysticism is embedded in rural religious life, revealing a surprising sophistication and a distinctive symbology.[1] I discuss mystical and philosophical concepts as formulated and practised by villagers, ethical ideas, and compromises with pious Muslims. I try to convey something of the wit and ingenuity of mystical debate and the peculiar ironies of the mystics' coexistence with the dominant faith. Chapter 7 continues in this vein with the story of a mystical sect based in rural Banyuwangi. I discuss links with the cult described in chapter 4 and show how the sect represents both a response to the rise of Islam and a flowering of Javanist ideas.

Chapter 8 brings us full circle. It concerns a village of mixed Muslims and Hindu converts in south Banyuwangi and shows how, among certain groups, the syncretist compromise with orthodox Islam has been broken. Faced with a narrower definition of Islam, following the 1965 coup, and greater pressure to conform to an official faith, a minority of nominal Muslims in this area (as in south-central Java and other Javanist strongholds) took the radical step of turning to Hinduism. Many others took the opposite course and opted for a strict Muslim piety (Hefner 1987). Conversion to Hinduism represented only one aspect of a wider process of cultural redefinition, as large numbers of Javanese – whether mystics, nominal Muslims, or followers of pre-Islamic faiths such as the Tengger people of East Java – were forced to question the nature of their traditional compromise with Islam (Cederroth 1995, Hefner 1985, Lyon 1980). In this chapter I outline the construction of a translocal Hinduism, its relation to Balinese Hinduism and Java's Hindu-Buddhist past, and the ingenious efforts of practitioners to ground Indian concepts in Javanese village life. I trace the background of the Hindu movement in the political upheavals and mass murder of the 1960s and identify a differential pattern of conversion (and regression to Islam) among native Banyuwangi folk and immigrants from elsewhere in Java.

The sequence of topics thus leads up to and then away from Islam, giving it a centrality which reflects its pervasiveness in Javanese concerns. Islam is not simply one option among many: it is a constant factor, albeit differently felt and appreciated according to personal history and pre-dilection. There are those who live somewhat nervously on the hitherside, within its shadow, perhaps looking up to it as an unattainable or unattractive ideal, and those (described in the latter part of the book) who claim to have gone 'beyond' it. Nevertheless, all (except of course Hindu converts) identify themselves as Muslims. Crucially, all inhabit the same social space: we are not dealing with distinct groups but with diversity in a common social and cultural framework. What I have therefore tried to capture – despite the necessity of simplifying and separating for descriptive purposes – is the interrelation between the different orientations, the sympathies and hostilities, affinities and eva-sions that help to define each variant in relation to its rivals. (It is hard to avoid the word tradition, but I am speaking of something less distinct and concrete.) In this interrelation lies the unity of the subject – and, I hope, of the book.

One publisher's reader has pointed out that 'wittingly or unwittingly' I have echoed the sequence of Clifford Geertz's classic study, *The religion of Java*, which begins with a slametan and then proceeds to analyse folk tradition, orthodox Islam, and mysticism. Clearly my reasons for adopting a similar structure, as set out above, are quite different from Geertz's. I conceive of the variant forms in rather different terms – more relationally, less identified with particular groups, and in a single social context quite unlike the disparate, semi-urban setting of Geertz's fieldwork. Unlike some of his critics, however, I agree with Geertz that Javanese religion can best be grasped from three contrasting vantage points and in adopting a similar structure (and, no doubt, certain other insights) I am happy to acknowledge a debt to a seminal work – whether wittingly or unwittingly incurred I am no longer sure.

Having sketched the plan of the book and outlined its thematic scope we can now move in closer to the field location and attempt to answer the question of where it fits in Java's cultural map.

A region in Javanese ethnography

The history of Java's great kingdoms has tended to overshadow that of its outlying regions. When we think of classical Java, what comes to mind are the early Indianized states with their great stone temples and epic statuary or the Muslim courts with their brilliant arts and ceremonies. Yet in the far east of the island existed a realm which, in its various incarnations, outlasted them all. Blambangan was the most enduring – in fact the last – Hindu-Buddhist realm in Java and the last region to fall under Dutch colonial rule.

Like a miniature Poland, its history was shaped by its unfortunate position between two powerful neighbours. To the east lay Hindu Bali; to the west, in Java, a succession of expansionist Muslim states. Its contemporary cultural make-up reflects this hybrid, contested history: a language containing Old Javanese archaisms and Balinese loan words, a dance-drama spoken in High Javanese and accompanied by a Balinese orchestra, and a polyphonic religious life with its roots in the Indic period but permeated at every level by Islam.

Banyuwangi (or Blambangan, as it once was) may not be typical of Java; but it becomes ever harder to know what should count as typical as 'new' variations crystallize against the background of earlier generalizations. The cultural yardstick which was Central Java has shrunk somewhat in recent years. And as the ethnographic and historical evidence accumulates, Java appears less and less like a singular cultural category whose exceptions can be consigned to 'enclaves'. Ricklefs (1993a: 12) has even suggested that a pan-Javanese cultural or ethnic identity may not have had much significance until late in the island's history – perhaps as late as the seventeenth century. Indeed, the very idea of 'Java' has come to be seen as an artifact of political power, born out of the competition for legitimacy between Central Javanese court culture and colonial domination (Pemberton 1994). In this struggle, the idea of a culturally unified Java, centred on the palace, emerged as a rhetorical device, eliding or encompassing local differences – an answer to the colonial imperative of divide and rule. John Pemberton suggests that this rhetoric has been taken up by the New Order regime (post-1966) which has assiduously promoted 'tradition' in order to contain diversity and relegate it to the ineffectual level of local custom. By implication, to document this diversity is to join in complicity with the regime, or at least to fall into its cultural trap. The ethnographer – so the argument goes – should, rather, swim against the tide and expose the power relations underlying the unity-in-diversity propaganda. Pemberton's point is important, though it exaggerates the effectiveness of a centrist discourse. It is now recognized that even within the framework of the classical kingdoms, with their standardizing polities of 'exemplary centres' and imitative peripheries, each province had its distinct forms, its own political and cultural dialect (Sutherland 1973–4; 1975). As Ron Hatley (1984) has pointed out, there have always been 'other Javas away from the *kraton* [palace]': regions distinguished from each other and from the courtly model by language, religion, arts, custom, 'character', even bodily posture and ways of carrying things. The difficulty for the analyst is to keep a sense of the tension between powerful cultural centres and their satellites, or, more generally, to develop an awareness of family resemblances. Yet, as Robert Hefner (1985) has shown, even the more isolated and divergent of groups, such as the Tenggerese of East Java, have maintained a centuries-old, mutually influential dialogue with the wider society. Hefner's pathbreaking study of Hindu–Muslim relations has obliged students of Java to reconsider their subject, and to recognize that the picture is not simply one of variety but of interpenetration and thematic variation.

The present work is about religion in a particular corner of Java but it is not conceived as a regional study – something which, for reasons already given, would no longer be tenable in conventional terms. Instead, it addresses themes and problems which are common to all of Java and, indeed, to much of South-east Asia. Rather than looking at regional differences and questions of local identity and ethnicity (matters of small interest to my hosts), I am concerned with broader questions of general anthropological interest as well as with the common denominators which underlie local differences. Accordingly, I shall sketch the history of Banyuwangi with the wider frame in mind.

Historical outline

There is only a slender connexion between the civilization of the old kingdom of Blambangan and the contemporary culture of Banyuwangi, the modern administrative district. If the connexion were stronger, Banyuwangi would be much less like the rest of Java than is in fact the case. Indeed, it might be said that the social history of modern Banyuwangi began around 1768 after the population of Blambangan had been all but wiped out and its civilization destroyed. A modern history would have to start with these sparse ingredients: an empty, charred landscape, a garrison of fever-stricken merchant-imperialists, and a tiny, scattered population of uprooted peasants and refugees, mostly Hindu, whose priests and leaders were either dead or in exile. Modern Banyuwangi reaches back into its fractured past across a vast emptiness.

In some of the chapters which follow I describe the fumbling efforts to span this void and recapture or reinvent the past. Given the paucity of historical evidence there is certainly scope for invention. We do not know, for example, whether the various kingdoms which called themselves Blambangan were genuinely connected. Their capitals were in places set far apart and they seem to have been ruled by unrelated dynasties. Similarly, little is known about the origin of the people now regarded as natives of Banyuwangi, the so-called Osing. Presumably, they are descendants of the remnant population of 1768, though the early chronicles do not mention such a name. Local historians suggest, plausibly enough, that the epithet was given by immigrants who would have been struck by the fact that the word for 'no' in the local dialect is *osing*, in contrast to the *ora* of standard Javanese. People who had hitherto been simply Javanese now became Osing, or Jawa Osing. But, as with much of Banyuwangi's history, this is still a matter of speculation, and the genealogy which links Blambanganer to Osing must remain conjectural until further evidence comes to light. Nevertheless, if we are to understand contemporary efforts to establish a cultural pedigree, it is with the presumed ancestors that we must begin.

Blambangan is first recorded as a province of Majapahit, Java's greatest pre-Islamic empire (Schrieke 1957: 37–43). Its first ruler, Wiraraja, had helped Raden Wijaya found his kingdom in 1292 and in return was granted Blambangan in the easternmost portion of the island, an area known in the literature as the Eastern Salient or Oosthoek. Tradition pictures Blambangan and Majapahit as inveterate rivals and opposites – a relationship epitomized in the story of Damar Wulan. In this popular drama, often performed at weddings today, Menak Jinggo, the king of Blambangan, is defeated by Damar Wulan, the refined, princely champion of Majapahit. From a local perspective a staging of the drama is a celebration of defeat, and attitudes towards the protagonists are necessarily ambivalent. Menak Jinggo, a Javanese Richard III, is portrayed as demonic and hideously disfigured; but he is also a crowd-pleaser, full of ogrish humour and vitality, while Damar Wulan, played by a boy in a flowery headdress, is effete and colourless.

Despite the rivalry between the empire's western and eastern realms (a rivalry which still excites audiences today), there was, at some level, a common culture which held sway from Majapahit in the west, through the eastern provinces, to Bali, which was incorporated in the empire in 1343. Political and cultural ties between regions were cemented by links through kinship and marriage alliance (Hägerdal 1995: 106–7). But the common thread was broken when Majapahit fell to Muslim armies early in the sixteenth century. From that moment the Eastern Salient became a cultural frontier. Blambangan, a Hindu zone beyond the pale, was a refuge for Majapahit's fleeing nobles and literati, and its rulers henceforth looked east to Bali for their allies and intimate enemies. The straits of Bali, only three miles wide at the narrowest point, were in any case less of a natural obstacle than the range of forested mountains and volcanoes that cut off Blambangan from the the heartland of Java.

The steady advance of Islam throughout the rest of the island (and the somewhat more fitful progress of colonization) widened the breach still further. Indeed, nothing speaks more clearly of the discontinuities in Javanese history – and the difficulties of an integral account – than the startling fact that, some two and a half centuries after the fall of Majapahit, Blambangan was still a viable Hindu state. Here the coming of Islam and the establishment of Dutch hegemony took a quite different turn. These two processes, which shaped the course of modern Javanese history, came together in Blambangan as nowhere else when, in 1768, the new colonial masters obliged native rulers to embrace Islam. By this act, intended to cut off Balinese influence, the Dutch redrew the cultural boundary, restoring a nominal unity with the rest of Java.

We will come back to this watershed in Blambangan's history. Very little is known about Muslim activity in the early kingdoms, and efforts at proselytization are not recorded in the chronicles, though Islam must have been familiar to inhabitants through trade contacts. There is, however, the popular story of Sheik Wali Lanang/Maulana Ishak – 'the only Javanese tale of the time of Islamization in which supernatural powers fail to produce a conversion' (Ricklefs 1993a: 308 n. 69). This holy man, who came to Blambangan to spread the new faith, was credited with ending an epidemic and as a reward was given the king's daughter. But when his missionary activities became known he was expelled from the kingdom and his infant son was cast away at sea. The child was saved and grew up to become Sunan Giri, one of Java's nine legendary Muslim saints (Lekkerkerker 1923: 1033–4).

As Islam spread eastwards through trade and conquest, for the first time more was at stake in the perennial regional wars than mere control of resources and populations. Expeditions against Blambangan in the first half of the seventeenth century by Sultan Agung, ruler of the Central Javanese state of Mataram, were coloured by the ideology of holy war (Schrieke 1957: 236). The survival of Blambangan after such attacks, in which towns were razed and thousands were captured as slaves, owed as much to its proximity to Bali as to its remoteness from the major centres of Javanese power. The Balinese kingdoms of Gèlgèl, Bulèlèng, and Mengwi, acted in turn as Blambangan's protector, sometimes its over-lord, from the mid-sixteenth century until Dutch control was established after 1767 (Arifin 1995: 314; Pigeaud and de Graaf 1976: 48). But it was only when both Javanese and Balinese parties were diverted by civil strife that Blambangan's rulers were able to reclaim their sovereignty. One such period occurred in the second half of the seventeenth century, later celebrated as a golden age (Kumar 1976: 361). Mataram was embroiled in murderous intrigues under the tyrannical Amangkurat I; Gèlgèl had ceased to be the dominant power in Bali and fell into succession wars. In the western part of Blambangan a new dynasty arose under Tawang Alun (reigned 1655–91) (Pigeaud 1932). As with other founders of Javanese realms, Tawang Alun had first withdrawn to the wilderness in quest of the magical power that legitimizes authority. After meditating for seven days, he was confronted by a huge white tiger (*macan putih*) which carried him on its back to the spot where he was to build his capital. Macan Putih, as the new city was called, though no Mataram, was clearly built to last: its fortified walls were six feet thick, twelve feet high, and measured three miles in circumference (Lekkerkerker 1923: 1041–2). The ruler of this thriving kingdom became powerful enough to raid as far west as Blitar and to trouble the bordering districts of Lumajang and Pasuruhan, where in 1680 he defeated a Dutch-led force

(Ricklefs 1993a: 75, 110). In 1676 he snubbed Mataram by cancelling his annual tributary visits and proclaimed himself an independent sovereign. We know little of his world, but some impression of the scale of its pomp (not to say, of its ruler's appetite) can be gained from the report that 270 of his 400 wives were cremated with him at his funeral.

After Tawang Alun's death in 1691 things fell apart. His sons fought over the succession and in 1697 the north Balinese principality of Bulèlèng was able to seize power. Balinese influence was henceforth dominant until Dutch intervention.

The Dutch East India Company regarded the Eastern Salient as a haven for its enemies, chief among whom was the adventurer Surapati who had carved out a domain to the northwest of Blambangan (Kumar 1976; 1979). This same domain usefully served Blambangan as a buffer zone protecting it from the claims of the old enemy in Central Java. It also kept the Dutch at arm's length. By the middle of the century, however, the situation had changed. Surapati was dead and in 1743 the Dutch gained title to the easternmost portion of Java. Surapati's followers in Pasuruhan and the Tengger highlands continued to challenge Dutch ambitions in the area for many years (Hefner 1990: 37); but what eventually prompted military action in the Oosthoek to 'cut out the whole evil growth' was the prospect of English traders gaining a foothold in Blambangan (Graaf 1949: 272). The Company was afraid that a new English entrepôt serving trade in the Far East would break their spice monopoly (Basset 1964: 214–16; Kumar 1997: 35). So, in 1767, they blockaded the straits of Bali and seized control of eastern Blambangan.

Resistance was led by Wong Agung Wilis, half brother of the last Blambangan prince. Wilis, who was a cousin of the ruler of Mengwi, used Balinese support to raise a rebellion; but the uprising was crushed with the help of Madurese troops and he was sent into exile.

The Dutch built a new colonial town at Banyuwangi, north of the old ruined capital of Blambangan. After several years of brutal rule, under which harvests were confiscated or burned, the starving population again rebelled. Their leader, Rempek, was a charismatic figure, possibly a priest, who claimed to be inspired or possessed by the spirit of Wilis (Graaf 1949: 274). Among the population he was rumoured to be Wilis's reincarnation (Wilis was, in fact, alive and in exile). Like other pretenders in Javanese history, Rempek presented himself as a world-saviour, a righteous prince sent to restore the old order (Schrieke 1957: 93; cf. Pigeaud 1932: 261). At the point of collapse of Hindu-Javanese civilization, the uprising took on a religious, nativistic tone – a moral crusade in which Sivaite holy men played a prominent role. There followed a war of attrition with terrible losses on both sides. After a siege of thirteen months the fortress at Bayu finally succumbed to epidemic and bombardment. The Dutch ordered captives to be decapitated and their heads to be hung from the treetops to spread terror among the population. Those rebels who had reportedly 'cooked and eaten' the Dutch commander were led away and drowned. Madurese troops 'vied for the women and children as their spoils. The stench of dead bodies of those who had run to the forest could be smelled from afar' (Lekkerkerker 1923: 1060). So ended a century and a half of sporadic warfare which had wiped out a civilization and devastated a once fertile and prosperous realm.

What the people of Banyuwangi make of these events today is interesting. Mostly unfamiliar with the literary chronicles or Dutch colonial historiography, they have recast the story as a popular drama in which the resistance hero is not Rempek, the 'pseudo-Wilis', but the daughter of the real Wilis, a female warrior-medium named Sayu Wiwit. The drama is played as a proto-nationalist epic. The inter-ethnic aspect of the war, the mercenary role of the Madurese, and the Balinese connexion are all minimized or ignored. In their efforts to promote an uncontroversial regional culture, local experts have simplified history as a two-sided struggle between Indonesians and imperialists. It is all but unmentionable that Sivaism was the inspiration of resistance and that the new religion, Islam, was imposed on a defeated Blambangan by the Dutch.

In fact, Dutch policy regarding Islam in the area seems to have been ambivalent. The intention in persuading the new puppet rulers to convert was evidently to undermine Balinese influence and foster relations with Javanese powers to the west (Lekkerkerker 1923: 1053). But in remote Batavia the Governor-general seems to have opposed any such move – to what effect we do not know – and directed Hindu priests and populace to be left undisturbed in religious matters (Pigeaud 1932: 253).

For whatever reasons – local administrative policy, social fragmentation, or cultural anomie – the survivors of conquest, unlike the Tenggerese in their mountain fastness to the west, were unable to maintain Hinduism as the dominant faith. We do not know how quickly or by what means Islamization advanced. But by the time Banyuwangi was fully established as a colonial enterprise an Islamic hierarchy of officials was already in place. A German physician who visited Banyuwangi early in the nineteenth century reported that there was a 'high priest' (*penghulu*) with a staff supported by salary lands, fixed payments for weddings, and a tithe of one-tenth of the peasants' harvest. In rural villages, as today, Islam was administered by an official known as the *modin* (Epp 1849: 252). This rapid incorporation of Islam into rural society presumably entailed a fair degree of popular acceptance. In the hinterland, however, there remained a shifting population of war-survivors who were loyal to the old order and still vulnerable to Balinese agitation. And pockets of Hindu-Buddhism survived well into the nine-teenth century. When the linguist, Van der Tuuk, visited the area in 1840 he found the village of Cungking, close to town, to be still Sivaite – over three centuries after the fall of Majapahit to Islam (Lekkerkerker 1923: 1030). This may seem to confirm the region as an exception in Javanese history; but similar examples of cultural overlap – of *buda* ways (as Javanese term the pre-Islamic culture) surviving intermingled with Islamic ways – can be found in many parts of Java, even in the heartland of Javanese civilization. To make the point one need only mention the royal cult of Durga (demon queen and Hindu goddess of death), which still flourishes in Solo today (Headley 1979). Similarly, in the Opak-Praga basin in Central Java, 'there are still village communities and pocket areas ... that have never been touched by Muslim influences' (Koentjaraningrat 1985: 56). I make no such claim about Banyuwangi, where Islam triumphed – at least nominally – long ago. But what such examples suggest is that Java's religious diversity cannot be adequately appreciated if we hold to a view of Islamization as a uniform process with a determinate outcome. We need a more encompassing sense of the cultural spectrum which reflects the legacy of Java's chequered history.

I take up the case of Cungking in chapter 4. For the moment we return to the aftermath of Dutch conquest. The major – self-created – problem for the colonial administration was underpopulation. Epp estimated that 60,000 people had died in the wars. Many more had fled to Bali, and fugitives continued to haunt the hills and forests to the south of the new capital. One estimate put the population in 1800 at 8,000 souls. To restore a labour supply drastic measures were needed. Women and children were barred from leaving the area; Javanese from neighbouring provinces and Chinese from Batavia were encouraged to resettle; prosti-tutes were shipped in from Semarang; Banyuwangi was made a place of banishment (Lekkerkerker 1923: 1064–5). But the population only began to revive with the settling of Madurese, drawn from their impoverished island off the north-east coast of Java. Madurese were encouraged to settle the northern part of Besuki residency and spread from there to Jember, Bondowoso, and the west of Banyuwangi. These migrants provided a labour force for the burgeoning plantation sector and eventually came to dominate the northern area (Husson 1995: 145–58). With the settling of Mandarese and Bugis fishermen as well as Chinese and Arab merchants – each *suku* in its own quarter – colonial Banyuwangi had become a model 'plural economy' (Furnivall 1939: 446–7). Other influxes of migrants to the countryside were mainly of ethnic Javanese from points west, that is, from Central Java and inland districts like Ngawi and Ponorogo in East Java. Natives of Banyuwangi call all such Javanese migrants *wong kulon(an)*, 'westerners', or *wong Mentaram*, 'Mataram people'.

It was a peaceful colonization replete with historical ironies. In 1916 migrants with putative links to the court of Yogyakarta in Central Java cleared the forest at Tembokrejo and discovered the ruins of a kraton – perhaps the palace of Menak Jinggo that their ancestors had overrun. These ruins later became the focus of a Hindu renaissance, led not by natives of Banyuwangi but by *wong kulon* (chapter 8).

The result of a century and half of immigration was an unusual ethnic mix. According to the 1930 census, 47.2 per cent of the population were born outside Banyuwangi – the highest proportion of migrants in any Javanese regency (Hugo 1980: 106). This figure does not take account of the numerous descendants of earlier migrants, and native Osing must at that time have been in a minority. Censuses carried out since Independence do not give figures on ethnic composition. However, since each group has preserved its own language or dialect, some indication of their relative strengths can be gleaned from linguistic work carried out by Indonesian researchers. According to Hasan Ali (cited in Arps 1992: 42), some 53 per cent of the regency's 1.45 million population (1990 census) are speakers of the Banyuwangi dialect, 39.5 per cent speak other Javanese dialects, and 5 per cent speak Madurese. Herusantosa (1987: 37) refers to estimates of between 30 and 50 per cent for the local dialect.

The native population of Banyuwangi has remained clustered in certain areas – the hinterland around the regency town, particularly the subdistricts (*kecamatan*) of Giri and Glagah; villages in the Kabat and Rogojampi subdistricts to the south; and, less concentrated, in Srono and Genteng. Within these areas smaller linguistic clusterings are found, and in several villages almost all the inhabitants are speakers of the Osing dialect.

Broadly, then, the north of the regency is Madurese, as are the hill plantations in the interior; the centre (except for the town, which is multi-ethnic) is Osing or Osing mixed with migrant Javanese; the south is mainly inhabited by migrant Javanese; and the coastal fishing areas are mixed.

A regional division of labour has helped preserve ethnic and cultural distinctions. As far as I know, Osing-Javanese rarely work on plantations, most inland Osing villages being inhabited by peasant farmers and sharecroppers. In contrast, plantations are overwhelmingly worked by Madurese who are often cut off from regular communication with the rest of society (Husson 1995: 218). Even today, on some private plantations such as Kaliklatak, strict rules regulate every aspect of the worker's life and limit possibilities of contact with outsiders. Migrant Javanese are more closely integrated with the native population, though – somewhat unusually – in the southern village of Krajan, described in chapter 8, the Osing form a distinct, endogamous enclave among a majority of 'westerners'. In Krajan the Osing are fishermen and the migrants are peasants.

Ethnicity – in the sense of ethnically contrastive behaviour – naturally varies in its intensity with setting. In the heavily Osing area described in this book it is simply not a matter of much concern. Although the Osing are one of the few populations in Java to bear a distinct name as opposed to a regional tag, they consider themselves to be Javanese: *Jawa Osing*. Other Javanese fully concur in this. What defines native Banyuwangi culture for outsiders is its performing arts – strongly influenced by Bali – and the dialect. There are also much-prized customs, such as marriage by abduction, and more consequential differences in social organization which distinguish Osing, in their own eyes, from other Javanese. Such differences are more a question of emphasis or tendency than of fundamentals and one would expect to find analagous, perhaps opposite, tendencies in other parts of Java. To name the most obvious 'Osing' features: (i) settlements tend to be more dense and compact than among 'westerners', with houses packed close together; (ii) local endogamy is strongly favoured, affording a depth of genealogical knowledge and a dense pattern of overlapping kin ties; (iii) a greater emphasis on kinship values than is common in Java is reflected in norms of sharing and in a ritual economy similar to, but more all-embracing than, the usual Javanese festive exchanges; (iv) in the Osing-majority villages, nearly everyone owns their own land or at least their own house-plot: traditionally, there is no distinct, inferior, class of landless boarders (Stoppelaar 1927: 21). Correspondingly, egalitarian norms enforce a certain formal equality in public behaviour. Rich and poor both dress and eat alike – surplus is spent on acquiring land rather than prestige. Compared to other Javanese, Osing regard themselves as more open and spontaneous, sociable, and coarse; also more conservative and attached to their roots.

Having accounted for ethnic distribution and digressed into ethnic stereotypes, let me now bring this brief social history up to date. Documentary information on the colonial period is sparse and people know little about the colonial system, as locally applied, beyond what they have experienced at first hand. The intricate system of offices, obligations, and carefully calculated burdens described in Stoppelaar's (1927) account awakens no memories today. To judge from what one hears in school and in casual conversation, the colonization of Indonesia happened everywhere at the same time and in the same form. Even educated people will say: 'We were ruled by the Dutch for 350 years.' It may be the case that people are more knowledgeable in the plantation area where the Dutch were more heavily involved, but the ordinary farmer recognizes only an undifferentiated *jaman londo* (Dutch period).

As elsewhere in Java, the local aristocracy was given a subordinate role within the new colonial structure. So the dynasty of Tawang Alun had a kind of afterlife, though it lacked a court and the trappings of royalty. Whereas the last four generations of rulers of Blambangan (up to 1767) were descendants of Tawang Alun through his principal wife, the dynasty of Dutch-appointed regents, who governed Banyuwangi from 1773 to 1881, stemmed from a line through Tawang Alun's secondary wife. It is this line of minor nobility which still has a shadowy corporate existence in contemporary Banyuwangi. It maintains a lineage graveyard near town, tended by an elderly scion – formerly a plantation supervisor – who also keeps the genealogies. Periodically the members of the lineage meet to take part in a savings association. But they have no significant role in the life of modern Banyuwangi.

The disappearance of court life under the colonial regime marks a crucial difference from Central Java and thus from the familiar picture of Java embodied in the ethnography. (One could say the same, of course, of vast areas of Java outside the principalities.) With the destruction of the old kingdom, the high civilization of the kraton vanished. Whereas in Central Java the ruler still commanded public loyalty and exemplified a high Javanese style, in Banyuwangi there was nothing, politically or culturally, between the village and the colonial state: no elevated urban model of manners and ideas, no unifying cultural power. While the principalities developed ever more complex codes of etiquette and artistic refinement – as they became more 'Javanese' in the face of Dutch intrusion (Pemberton 1994) – Banyuwangi, like much of the Eastern

Salient, was thrown back on the older cultural resources of the village (Hefner 1985). A trend towards differentiation and regionalism, however, was checked by the influx of migrants and the spread of Islam. In the absence of a local courtly model, the Central Javanese style – in language, dress codes, and arts – gained a certain limited acceptance as the ideal. And today the courts of Yogya and Solo are generally regarded as the repositories of Javanese learning. Islamization also narrowed the gap between Banyuwangi and the cultural heartland, though the Islam brought by the migrants was of a coarser texture than that practised in and around the courts. It was a simple, uncontemplative faith, a religion of the frontier, and its authority was dispersed among dozens of tiny, obscure *pesantren* (Islamic boarding schools) scattered throughout the countryside.

Orthodox Islam in twentieth-century Banyuwangi has retained a conservative, non-establishment cast which is closer in character to the north-coastal (*pasisir*) culture than to the hierarchical religion of the Central Javanese courts. Among the pious, the influence of prominent pesantren in the Madurese-dominated regencies to the north has steadily grown. So, too, has the influence of Nahdlatul Ulama, the largest Muslim association in Indonesia. In contrast, the modernist organization, Muhammadiyah, has only a small, mainly urban following. The position of Islam in contemporary Banyuwangi is examined in chapter 5.

It remains only to mention briefly two other developments on the religious scene since national independence was achieved after the Second World War. Alongside a drive for Islamic conformity and piety there have been two movements away from Islam, both of them impelled in part by the events of the mid-1960s when the Left in Indonesia was crushed. These are the rise of Javanist mysticism and large-scale conversions to Hinduism (see chapters 6 to 8). In the case of mysticism, one particular sect, Sangkan Paran, has put down deep roots and indirectly stimulated a re-evaluation of local tradition; in the case of Hinduism, converts have sought to restore what they see as the original and true religion of Java, and have adapted local traditions accordingly. Both movements represent a renewal of sorts, based on alternative readings of Javanese history.

Fieldwork

Fieldwork was carried out over two periods, from December 1991 to June 1993, with a further year from April 1996 to April 1997. The research for this book derives mainly from the first period. A companion volume on kinship and socialization, which stems from the second period of research, is now in preparation. This will look at the same complex of religious and cultural practices in its developmental and personal aspect.

The field location was a village of some 2,430 souls on the lower slopes of the Mount Ijen range, about six miles from town. In order to spare the village unwelcome publicity I have given it the pseudonym Bayu, incidentally commemorating Blambangan's last heroic stand at the fort of that name. I chose Bayu for several reasons: it is one of several villages in the area which are almost entirely Osing; it is reckoned to be culturally very active; and I liked, and knew I could get on with, the headman. (So it proved: he became a firm friend.) Quite by chance it turned out to be a centre of mystical activities.

Set in densely planted, gently shelving farmland, Bayu is, by local standards, a fairly prosperous agricultural settlement. Despite some recent efforts at diversification, rice remains by the far the most important crop. Accurate figures on land holdings are difficult to obtain since many people own fields and fruit groves within the borders of neighbouring villages. But the majority of villagers own or control plots of between 0.5 and 2 hectares. Landless villagers work as sharecroppers, ploughmen, or day-labourers on others' fields; or they work as builder's labourers in Banyuwangi and its surrounding villages. There is also a sprinkling of artisans, petty traders, and store-keepers such as are found in any Javanese village. Although there are a few extremely poor families and a very few rich ones (families with holdings over 10 hectares), most people describe themselves as having 'just enough' to live on. What this means is that they are decently, if modestly, lodged, enjoy a rice diet rather than poorer staples, and are able to participate fully in the many feasts and festivals of village life.

During our first stay in Bayu we lived in the house of a widow and her family. My wife, Mercedes, and our baby daughter arrived in the new year in 1992 and stayed till the end, except for two months in the middle. During their absence I stayed in Krajan, a coastal village in the subdistrict of Rogojampi to the south. My purpose was to study life in a village of mixed Osing and 'western' Javanese, and to live among converts to Hinduism.

The second period of fieldwork was in similar circumstances. This time we lived in a house belonging to the headman. We now had a son as well as a daughter, both of whom learned Javanese and lived pretty much as other village children. We took part in dozens of slametan feasts, hosted a few of our own, sponsored an all-night recitation, ushered at weddings, helped erect houses, and joined in whatever cultural, religious, and social activities seemed appropriate. It was for all of us a happy and inspiring experience and I hope something of the pleasure of living among people of such charm, generosity, and warmth comes through in this account.

A note on the language

According to Indonesian scholars there are as many as ten dialects of Javanese (Herusantosa 1987: 15; Koentjaraningrat 1985: 19–20), a fact which in itself underlines the need for a greater emphasis on Java's cultural variety. The Banyuwangi dialect is known as *cara Osing* (lit. the Osing way) or *omong Osing*, that is, 'Osing speech' or 'language'.[2] With its borrowings from Balinese (e.g. *sing*, a variant of *osing*, meaning 'no'), its numerous archaisms, and its distinctive accent, it is sufficiently different from standard Javanese to puzzle incomers, but it cannot be rated a distinct language. Indonesian scholars have suggested that it is closer than standard Javanese (which derives from south-central Java) to Old Javanese. Another peculiarity which links it with Old Java is its relatively undeveloped system of speech levels. No doubt this is one effect of the isolation of Blambangan from the Javanese heartland during the period when etiquette, vocabulary, and terms of address indicating relative status developed their present intricate form. In rural Banyu-

Plate 1 A landowner supervises his harvest

Plate 2 Villagers shelling peanuts

wangi there is a simple form of respectful Javanese called *besiki* (a term known only in a few conservative villages) or *basa*, which also applies to the standard form of High Javanese, *krama*. The basic speech level is not termed *ngoko*, as elsewhere in Java, but *cara Osing*, which suggests that *besiki* is conceived as an alien form rather than being an integral part of the dialect. Curiously, the Banyuwangi dialect inverts certain *ngoko/krama* sets. For example, the low/high words for 'black' in Osing are *cemeng/ireng*, whereas in standard Javanese they are *ireng/cemeng;* and the Osing set *lare/bocah* (child) becomes *bocah/lare* in standard Javanese. Among educated people, and especially in mixed areas, *besiki* is now being displaced by standard High Javanese. But in the more traditional areas people still use *besiki* for the prayer-like addresses at feasts and in formal encounters with parents-in-law. In other contexts within the village, ordinary demotic *cara Osing* prevails.

2

The slametan: agreeing to differ

The concept of the 'total social phenomenon', in Mauss's odd but compelling phrase, has served anthropology well, not only as a frame for thinking about the complexity of cultural forms but as a narrative device, a way of handling the transition from the exuberant and bewildering world encountered in the field to the orderly microcosm of the ethnography itself. Malinowski, it could be said, found his ethnography in the *kula*, as Bateson found his in the *naven* ceremony. If we are now less confident about the notion of totality, this is as much a matter of practical contingency as of theoretical objection: our field locations tend, increasingly, to be characterized by ideological diversity and plurality. Yet, in ritual, we still encounter powerful evocations of the whole, a semblance of totality. What are we to make of this discrepancy? Consider the Javanese case. The slametan, a ceremonial meal consisting of offerings, symbolic foods, a formal speech, and a prayer, is a very modest event by the standards of a *potlatch* or *kula*; but it has a comparable primacy within its setting and a corresponding symbolic density. Participants see it as integral to their lives as social beings and to their sense of themselves as Javanese; they regard it as the epitome of local tradition. But its 'totality' is deceptive. The slametan is a communal affair, but it defines no distinct community; it proceeds via a lengthy verbal exegesis to which all express their assent, but participants privately disagree about its meaning; and, while purporting to embody a shared perspective on mankind, God, and the world, it represents nobody's views in particular. Instead of consensus and symbolic concordance we find compromise and provisional synthesis: a temporary truce among people of radically different orientation.

It seems appropriate to begin a study of religious diversity with an event which both expresses and contains cultural difference: to begin with a sense of the whole, however insubstantial this may prove to be. In observing the various elements of Javanese tradition in combination, we can form a better idea of their individual shapes and their influences upon each other. The slametan is, moreover, the pattern of cultural compromise: the attitudes and rhetorical styles it exemplifies are, in varying degrees, carried over into the different spheres of religious life examined in the following chapters.

But as well as providing a point of entry, the slametan throws light on aspects of Javanese religion which might otherwise remain obscure and contradictory: the nature of syncretism as a social process, the relation between Islam and local tradition, and, more abstractly, the multivocality of ritual symbols. These separate theoretical issues – fascinating and problematic in themselves – are found to have an inner relation, well illustrated in the slametan.

I begin, however, with a brief theoretical comment, followed by a consideration of the place of the slametan in Javanese religion, and then turn to an analysis of the rite itself.

Ritual and ambiguity

Among the many intriguing aspects of ritual, polysemy or multivocality has proved a fertile source of theoretical debate and a continuing challenge to ethnographers. Leach (e.g. 1964: 86, 286) and Turner (1967), to name only two pioneers in this field, were both concerned in their different ways with how the ambiguity of ritual symbols related to variations and tensions in social structure. Ritual was to be seen as a 'language of argument, not a chorus of harmony' (Leach 1964: 278). Nevertheless, true to the inspiration of Durkheim, the terms of the argument were taken to be shared: they were collective representations, and what they represented was the social order (Leach 1964: 14).

Recent discussions of multivocality have placed a greater emphasis on the interplay between private, often idiosyncratic, interpretation and public constructions of ritual (Barth 1987), or on the individual's manipulation of symbolic meaning through 'implicature' or 'off record' significance (Strecker 1988). There has been a trend away from seeing ritual as 'symbolic consensus' (typically reflecting social processes) towards a greater recognition of the improvisatory, creative use of symbols and the 'fragmentation of meaning'. Humphrey and Laidlaw, to whom I owe these phrases (1994: 80), have emphasized the way in which, in a culturally complex setting, individuals draw on different sources of knowledge in construing ritual (202–4). They conclude, in terms which would have seemed startling not long ago: 'We can now see that variety, discordance, and even absence of interpretation are all integral to ritual' (264).

But there are rituals and rituals. Problems about what kinds of interpretation are legitimate, whether symbols *mean* anything (let alone many things), and whether ritual can aptly be characterized as communication (see Lewis 1980 and Sperber 1975) are diminished or at least modified when dealing with rituals in which speech is the principal medium. The Javanese slametan is exemplary in this respect. It is an extreme instance of what might be called 'ordered ambiguity'. Moreover, it has the advantage of being unusually explicit in that its multivocal elements are not simply actions or material symbols but words – words whose significance is spelled out in part during the performance. Since the burden of symbolic interpretation is shouldered by the participants themselves, the patterning of symbols is relatively conspicuous. And the social processes which give rise to this patterning (to revert to Durkheim) are, again, unusually clear: people of different orientation come together in a single ritual and manufacture consensus, or at least the appearance of it.

What has this to do with Islam and local tradition or with syncretism? As we shall see, the significance of the slametan hinges on what participants make of key terms which derive in part from Islam. Some draw orthodox conclusions; others situate the Islamic terms in a Javanese cosmology or read them as universal human symbols. Yet all appear to be saying or endorsing the same thing. This unsuspected complexity undermines efforts to determine how far the slametan – and, by extension, Javanese religion – should be regarded as Islamic. But it also, happily, illuminates a critical function of symbolism in an ideologically diverse setting; namely, its capacity to focus diverse interests and thus to compel a collective respect – to forge a unity. From this perspective, the multivocal symbol is itself revealed as an example and vehicle of syncretism.

But before turning to the rite itself, let us first review discussion of its place in Javanese religion.

The slametan in Javanese religion

Most anthropologists of Java agree that the slametan lies at the heart of Javanese religion. It is surprising, then, that there are very few detailed descriptions in the literature and perhaps only one which carries conviction as an eye-witness report. Ever since the appearance of Clifford Geertz's book, *The religion of Java* (1960), we have assumed we know what the slametan is about. As is often the case in anthropology, one well-wrought account freezes discussion for a generation. Koentjaraningrat's five-hundred-page survey of Javanese culture, which covers the literature up to 1985, devotes just six pages to the slametan (1985: 347–52) and these add little to what is already known. Indeed, it was not until Hefner's (1985) admirable study of the Hindu Tenggerese of East Java that the subject was reopened.[1] An attempt to reconsider the slametan must therefore begin with the standard discussion.

Geertz opens his book with the following claim:

At the centre of the whole Javanese religious system lies a simple, formal, undramatic, almost furtive little ritual: the slametan.   (1960: 11)

He goes on to outline the elements essential to any slametan, whether it be held for a harvest, circumcision, or Islamic feast (1960: 11–15, 40–1). The host makes a speech in High Javanese explaining the purpose of the meal to his guests, incense is burned, an Arabic prayer is recited by the guests, and the special festive food is divided and consumed in part, the remainder being taken home. Typically, the speech invokes the host's ancestors, place spirits, Muslim saints, Hindu-Javanese heroes, and Adam and Eve in a polytheistic jumble seemingly designed to scandalize Muslim purists.

Whether the slametan, in this form, is really at the centre of the whole Javanese religious system; whether there *is* in fact a whole Javanese religious system, are questions left unsettled. At any rate, Geertz blurs the issue by placing his description within a section devoted to peasant spirit beliefs, one of three variants in his total system.

One cannot get far in talking about Javanese religion without mentioning Geertz's influential typology, so a few words on this are necessary here. Geertz's view is that the Islamization of Java, begun in the thirteenth century, has been partial and variable. Pious Muslims, whom he calls *santri*, are concentrated along the northern coast, in rural areas where traditional Islamic schools are common, and among urban traders. The so-called *abangan* culture of the majority of peasants, though nominally Islamic, remains embedded in native Javanese 'animism' and ancestral tradition. The traditional, mainly urban, gentry, though also nominally Muslim, practise a form of mysticism deriving from the Hindu-Buddhist era preceding Islam in Java. These nobles-turned-bureaucrats, and those who adopt their lifestyle, are known as *priyayi*.

Later commentators have tinkered with the Geertzian terminology and found all kinds of subvarieties (Bachtiar 1973; Ricklefs 1979). Some have pointed out that the priyayi are a social class or status group, not a subculture comparable to the other two varieties; and there has been confusion about whether the terms abangan and santri should denote groups or merely categories.[2] But the debate has moved on, and one trend has been to replace Geertz's three dimensions of cultural variation with a starker dichotomy based on degree of participation in Islam (Koentjaraningrat 1985: 317; cf. Hefner 1985: 3–4, 107; 1987: 534; Stange 1986: 106). The high culture that Geertz calls priyayi and the native peasant tradition are subsumed under a single term, kejawèn (or equivalent), meaning 'Javanism' and implying an emphasis on the pre-Islamic inheritance, or at least on what is taken to be such. Kejawèn is then opposed to the Islamic piety of the santri.[3] Mark Woodward (1988; 1989), who has employed this opposition most extensively, has given the terms of debate a further twist by claiming that Javanist religion, in both its popular and mystical forms, is basically an adaptation of Sufism and therefore constitutes a local form (or forms) of Islam. The dichotomy of kejawèn and santri thus refers to a division *within* Islam. According to Woodward, the mysticism of the priyayi owes more to the theosophy of Ibn al-Arabi than to the Indic religion of pre-Islamic Java; and the cults of the saints and the slametans practised by Javanese peasants are paralleled in popular Islam elsewhere in South and South-east Asia. The scale of cultural variation is therefore not one of degrees of Islamization, but of emphasis on different *aspects* of Islam. Hence, in some sense, for Woodward too, Javanese religion is one; but the unifying factor is Islam, not, as Geertz would have it, Java.

This reclaiming of Javanese religion for Islam has something to recommend it, at least as a counterbalance to the received wisdom, and exemplifies a recent move in South-east Asian studies (e.g. Bowen 1993; Roff 1985) to redress a scholarly bias based on a liberal antipathy for Islam. Accordingly, Woodward argues that (i) 'the slametan is the product of the interpretation of Islamic texts and modes of ritual action shared by the larger (non-Javanese) Muslim community' (1988: 62); and that (ii) the slametan, at least in Central Java, is not especially or even primarily a village ritual but is modelled on the imperial cult of the court of Yogyakarta, which he sees as Sufi in inspiration (1988: 85). In other words, the form and meanings of the slametan stem from textual Islam as interpreted in the state cult. This scripturalist, top-down view of village ritual is contrary to that of Geertz, for whom the slametan (the 'core ritual' of Javanese religion) is rooted in peasant animist tradition.

There is much more to Javanese religion than slametans, but if we accept their centrality this is as good a place as any to begin a rethinking. Let us shift the scene, however, from the well-known heartland of Java to an area with a rather different history: Banyuwangi, at its eastern extremity.

The slametan in Banyuwangi resembles, in essentials, those described elsewhere in Java. There is the incense, the parade of offerings, the speech of dedication (spoken by a delegate, not the host as reported for other localities), and the prayers. Superficially, there is an impression of uniformity and simplicity, as has been noted elsewhere (Hefner 1985: 107; Jay 1969: 209). But the impression is deceptive. For the participants in this ritual, though almost uniformly peasants, hold strikingly different views of its meaning. Indeed, as religious orientations, we find all three of Geertz's variants, and combinations thereof, present in the same event. It is as if the pious trader, the animist farmer, and the mystic were seated at the same meal and obliged to talk about the very thing that divides them. What could they possibly have in common? And what keeps their passionately held differences from erupting in discord?

Description of slametan and sedhekah

Before we consider the slametan in detail it is important to note that the various terms used in the literature for the ritual meal are not, at least in Banyuwangi, synonyms. The slametan is a rite for the living, the *sedhekah* a prayer meal for the dead.[4] These events can be combined, but conceptually they are separate matters and their status within the whole syncretic complex is different. Some say that the slametan is Javanese, the sedhekah Islamic; but this is to anticipate.

In general terms, the purpose of the slametan is to create a state of well-being, security, and freedom from hindrances of both a practical and spiritual kind – a state which is called *slamet*. Although the word slamet can be used of the dead (in the sense of 'saved'), I was told on several occasions that the word slametan is inappropriate if used of funeral feasts, amounting to a solecism. Specific reasons for holding slametans include the celebration of rites of passage, housewarmings, and harvests; a wish to restore harmony after a marital or neighbour-hood quarrel, to safeguard a new motorbike or pair of oxen, to cancel the effects of a bad dream, and – among the commonest of reasons – to redeem a vow. (For example, you promise to hold a slametan if your sick child gets better.) But often there is no ostensible reason other than that one seeks the desired state of well-being.

The slametan takes place just after dark in the front room of the house. A long rectangular mat is laid out, with a set of offerings at one end, near to the inner chamber or kitchen. Cigarettes, flowers, and a packet of face powder lie on a pillow placed at the head of the mat, with other offerings to either side. On the right ('male') side is a flask of water in a bowl; on the left ('female') side a brass betel set; and in front, a small lamp, a coin, a dish containing five blobs of porridge in different colours, quids of betel, a dish of red porridge with a drop of white in the middle, and a glass of water containing red, yellow, and white petals. What kind of food is spread out along the mat depends on the occasion and purpose of the slametan. Often there is a large cone of rice, resting on briars in a basket, called the 'mound of misfortune' (*tumpeng serakat*), a chicken buried in another mound, packages of glutinous rice in tubes and diamond shapes, and so on.

Dressed soberly in sarongs and black velvet hats, men arrive from all the nearby houses, the number of guests depending on the importance and elaborateness of the slametan. When they are all seated crosslegged around the mat, the banana leaves covering the food are removed and the host fetches a small clay brazier containing glowing embers. He places it before a guest seated nearest the offerings and tells him quietly the purpose of the feast. The delegate then crumbles incense onto the embers and, as the aromatic smoke starts to rise, he addresses the other guests solemnly, beginning with the Islamic greeting. I quote one such address recorded in August 1992.

Assalamualaikum warahmatullahi wabarokatuh
Thanks to all you gentlemen who are present today to witness this act; I am merely conveying the wishes of our hosts Sukib and Sumi and family. Let the intention/slametan[5] (*ajat*) be jointly witnessed and prayed for from our sincere hearts so that it be granted. Their intention, namely, is to glorify and restore to its pristine state (*memulé*) the whole body, and to glorify their siblings born on the same day, elder sibling amniotic fluid and younger sibling placenta. May these two people, Sukib and Sumi, be guarded day and night by their siblings. The stipulations have all been fulfilled such that there is red and white porridge, acknowledging that one possesses Mother Earth and Father Power (*ibu bumi, baba kuwasa*), Father Day and Mother Night, taking the form of Mother Eve and Father Adam. May the actions of Sukib and Sumi and their family, young and old, male and female, be safeguarded northwards, southwards, eastwards, and westwards; may they be confirmed and prosper. There is five-coloured porridge: red, yellow, white, black, and green, dedicated to their four wise siblings of many colours, the fifth being oneself. There is savoury rice which Sukib and

Sumi give to their guide, the Lord Muhammad Rasulullah, may the blessing of Allah be upon him. May Sukib and Sumi receive his mercy and that of the Prophet's Companions. There are yellow *wongso* leaves, forty-four in number, for the forty-four angels guarding Sukib and Sumi day and night; hands of bananas, two each for Sukib and Sumi, for their ribs left and right, gathering to them prosperity; fragrant water so that they acknowledge the body and supplicate to the Lord Almighty. There is packaged rice acknowledging that they possess nine saints guarding the nine holes of the body; may their baffled thoughts and worries be pierced and brightened. The rice cone of misfortune, this too is part of their slametan; may the misfortune be lost and the slamet remain; let there be no hindrances north, south, east, or west, day or night, for male or female, young or old. There is betel and coconut oil so that these two people at large in the world – should they be at fault – may be forgiven by their four siblings. Let this be witnessed by the Lord and his Prophet.

The speaker, or whoever is able, then begins a short praise of Muhammad (known as *salawat*) followed by a recitation of the opening of the Koran (Fatihah) in which all join, then a specific Arabic prayer for welfare, to which all say *Amin*. In contrast to the speech of dedication which is spoken in a solemn and clear voice, the prayers are uttered quietly and quickly, often garbled.

This done, the meal begins, each person helping himself from the array of food. The host stands by, encouraging the guests to try all the dishes. He alone may not eat; it is his offering. Unlike elsewhere in Java, the guests eat to their satisfaction and there is no division of what remains. Instead, the women and children come in after the men have departed and, with much less decorum, devour the rest. But before they leave, the men are served cakes, fried bananas, and coffee, with clove cigarettes from among the offerings. Conversation is amicable and good-humoured, and when they get up to shake the host's hand, saying, 'May your wish be granted (*ajaté kabul*)', half an hour to an hour may have passed.

The pattern for a sedhekah, a prayer meal for the dead, is different. First of all, guests are senior relatives and respected elders and friends from all over the village instead of the usual circle of neighbours. One of these must be able to lead a longish sequence of prayers and chanting called *tahlilan* intended to win merit for the deceased. The tone of the event is more explicitly Islamic. The word sedhekah is recognized as deriving from the Arabic for alms, *sadaka*, although no almsgiving is involved; and the holding of commemorative feasts is said by some villagers to be authorized by *hadīth* or Traditions of the Prophet (see Woodward 1988).

Apart from the cluster of offerings at the head of the mat there are no symbolic foods in the sedhekah, simply rice with side dishes. At the end of the meal, the guests take home a bag of cooked food and sweets (not leftovers) which is called their *berkat*, blessing, a word derived from the Arabic *baraka*. Despite this usage, and contrary to what is reported from elsewhere, no blessing is felt to accrue to the guests at sedhekahs or slametans, and the food consumed is not regarded as consecrated (cf. Woodward 1988: 72, 80). Except in the case of *slametan desa* (the annual village celebration) the sole beneficiaries are the persons named in the speech of dedication.

Funeral sedhekah are held at fixed intervals after the death: on the first, third, seventh, fortieth, and one hundredth days; then after one year, two years, and a thousand days. Other sedhekah take place on the eve of the fasting month, before weddings and circumcisions, and so on. Often the sedhekah (though not a funeral sedhekah) is combined with a slametan of the kind described earlier in an effort to encompass the living and the dead in the same event. For example, after a good harvest, one 'sends prayers' to the ancestors in thanks for the land they bequeathed, and, at the same occasion, one celebrates the first fruits, 'glorifies one's body', and so on in a composite feast. The speaker must distinguish between these separate aims in the address.

A typical sedhekah dedication begins as follows:

On this, the fortieth day sedhekah of Sanuri who has returned to the realm/era of eternity (*jaman kelanggengan*), may he receive clear water, a bright path, and a perfect place, and may your prayers go with him.

In place of the slametan's rambling invocations and symbolic explication there follows a more or less elaborate request to the guests to help convey prayers and, if the sedhekah is directed to the hosts' ancestors and dead kin in general, a plea for their forgiveness for any outstanding offences in return for the ritual work.

I have described the basic sequence of speech and action in the slametan and the sedhekah. Many such feasts, of course, have more elaborate forms demanded by the occasion and are inserted into complex ritual sequences; for example, at the celebration of the seventh month of pregnancy or the erection of a house. Correspondingly, their dedications have a specific theme and refer, additionally, to symbolic foods peculiar to the occasion. But I am concerned here with general features of the slametan. What, then, can one conclude from this bare description?

One feature that strikes an anthropologist who has worked on ritual elsewhere in Indonesia is the studied explicitness of the slametan – the necessity to state clearly one's intentions and to spell out the meaning of every element. The only unexplained, uncomprehended, part is the Arabic prayer. It is important to note, also, that the guests are present not as a passive audience but as witnesses (*seksi*) validating the reiterated intentions of the host and as participants in the prayer. Their sincere assent is required and each phrase of symbolic explication is followed by a collective 'Yes'. Likewise, as Woodward notes (1988: 80), the *Amin* that follows each line of the Arabic prayer 'transforms an individual recitation into a collective prayer'. One could hardly find a more emphatic and convincing demonstration of cultural uniformity than this oath-like performance. Yet behind the show of harmony – which is felt to be real, if contrived (perhaps one should say: real *because* contrived) – each element of the event, from the moment the incense is lit to the parting handshake, has a disputed meaning. As the speech hints, but cannot elaborate, each symbol has a range of meanings which variously contradict, complement, or nest inside each other. The variant readings which comprise this symbolic ambiguity are not the quibbles of specialists over the finer points of tradition; they reflect fundamental differences of a kind we are not accustomed (not *prepared*) to expect in ritual. A few of the participants believe that a transcendent and unknowable God created man and sent down the Koran to Muhammad as his sole guide, and that man's preordained actions lead inexorably to heaven or hell. A few others disbelieve in any kind of afterlife, and question the idea of a personal God, the absolute truth of the Koran, and the divine mission of Muhammad. The remainder – perhaps a small majority, though proportions vary – believe in the continued existence of ancestors and perhaps in some form of *karma*, but not in a Muslim afterlife. But they all pronounce the same words. What, then, do they mean by them?

Sources of tradition reflected in the slametan

Before I try to answer this question let us recall, briefly, the sources of these disparate forms of knowledge. Unlike the better-known case of Central Java, the colonization of Blambangan led to the total destruction of the realm and with it the high culture of the court. A regional culture (which was still recognizably Javanese) grew up unencumbered by any superior courtly model; as in much of East Java, there was no 'ladder of distinction' (Hefner 1985: 39) connecting peasant to palace. In the religious sphere, the compromise between Islam and existing traditions was, necessarily, a matter of local solutions. There was no stately pattern to imitate, no obligation to defer to an exemplary centre. Woodward writes of Yogyakarta in Central Java (1989: 7) that 'while the state cult is based on the interpretation of Sufi doctrine, popular religion is based on the interpretation of the state cult'. It hardly needs saying that such an analysis could not apply in those many 'other Javas away from the *kraton*' (Hatley 1984).

The triangle formed by abangan, santri, and priyayi assumed a different shape in colonial Banyuwangi. The remnant priyayi, at the apex, lost their traditional function as the repository of Javanist wisdom and became cut off from the populace. Although a similar estrangement took place in much of Java during the nineteenth century, as 'priyayi culture became an intricate mockery of original Javanese values and divorced itself from the vigorous influences of the Javanese village' (Carey 1979: 104), in Banyuwangi the separation was more absolute. For its part, the Islam brought by impoverished Madurese and Javanese migrants had an altogether different character from the hierarchical, theologically sophisticated Islam of the courts. Banyuwangi's santri practised a simpler, less dogmatic faith, nurtured in rural schools and village prayer-houses. Javanist mysticism, too, became embedded in popular religion rather than remaining the preserve of a gentry or urban elite. Indeed, folk beliefs, orthodox Islam, and mysticism came to flourish alongside each other in a single setting, among rice farmers of broadly similar background.

The mystical sect which I came to know, and which I shall call Sangkan Paran (Origin and Destination: a key Javanist concept), is based in the Banyuwangi regency but has adherents, numbering a few thousand, all over East Java. The regional leader happens to live in Bayu, the village where I stayed. This village has had followers now for two generations and about one-fifth of its adult inhabitants are members. Unusually, then, for Java, this is a mystical association based in the countryside and far away from the old kingdoms. Sangkan Paran follows the teachings of an aristocratic wanderer, a paradoxical, half-legendary figure who died in 1956. One of his former incarnations, it is said, was Sèh Siti Jenar, an early Javanese saint who was executed for the same heresy as the Persian mystic, al-Hallaj (Zoetmulder 1995: 300–8). (Hallaj notoriously declared 'I am the Reality', suggesting a monism disallowed by Islamic orthodoxy (Schimmel 1975: 55, 72).) Most of the older members in Bayu were personally initiated by the founder and knew him face to face. However, the sect is not based on a personality cult around a holy man; it espouses a practical philosophy rooted in Javanese tradition. As such it translates easily into the village context, availing itself of the symbolism to hand. For the village mystics, the sect provides a philosophical justification of what they have always practised, an answer to orthodox Islam, and a means of understanding experience and one's place in the world.

These are, broadly, the dimensions of cultural variation underlying the symbolic ambiguity of the slametan. Let us now look more closely at the ritual, starting with the lighting of the incense, in order to understand how these diverse interpretations are made.

Interpretation of the slametan

Incense is referred to in the invocation as holy rice (*sekul suci*). It is what the ancestors and spirits eat along with the smells of the offerings and food, the essence (*sari*) of the feast. Some participants believe the ancestral spirits to be present at the gathering, attracted by the incense and flowers. The incense also serves as a vehicle for the words. Communication between the coarse, material (*kasar*) world and the refined, spiritual (*alus*) realm is difficult, so we convey our wishes with incense and symbolic offerings. We humans eat the material, kasar, part of the feast.

The speaker's first words are the Arabic customary greeting, directed both to the guests and the unseen spirits. He continues in Javanese, either High Javanese (*krama*) if he is able, or in the Osing dialect interlaced with phrases of village *krama*. (Most key terms in the address are common to both speech levels.) He addresses the guests as *(sa)dhérék* or *(sa)dulur*, meaning siblings or kinsmen, though most in fact are not kin. Even among pious villagers, the concept of the Islamic community of believers, the *umma*, has little significance, and the Indonesian word *umat* is hardly ever used in any village context, though it is familiar from the broadcasts of politicians and prominent Muslims. What unites the guests is a momentary fictional kinship which signifies both common background and common humanity; any notion of a community of the faithful would only draw attention to the differences among participants.

The speaker then identifies his own role, saying that he is merely passing on certain wishes as an intermediary. His disclaimer draws attention to the traditional status of his words – that they express ancient wisdom, not his own ideas. The deepest truths, it is commonly said, are timeless and cannot originate with an individual. By contrast, Islam is historically bounded and recent. While santri like to point out that

Muhammad was the last of the prophets and therefore the purveyor of the most complete and perfect revelation, in the eyes of the less devout this makes his revelation new-fangled and derivative. More mundanely, the speaker's modest disclaimer also acknowledges his role as representative of the host, theoretically a job which anyone could fill, just as anyone could say the prayer. (The coin placed among the offerings is his token reward.)

The speaker then casts his eye down the array of offerings and festive dishes and refers to them one by one, in no fixed order, giving a formulaic explanation of their meaning. There can be twenty or more items, though on average there are about a dozen. One of the purposes of the address is to enumerate and display to the spirits what is on offer; the speech is intended for them as well as for the living witnesses. The deceased are jealous of the living and are apt to frustrate and afflict them if not properly and regularly acknowledged. Hence, before the speech begins the banana-leaf coverings are removed; and witnesses or the host prompt the speaker if he leaves anything out. Each element must be individually dedicated on behalf of the hosts, specifying their names or stipulating, like the small print of an insurance policy, that male and female, young and old, and those on both sides of the family are included in the dedication of the item. Each phrase of dedication is acknowledged by the witnesses with a collective *Inggih!* (High Jav. 'Yes'). Among the mystics the naming of parts has a further purpose. To name something is to attest to its existence. Since we cannot affirm what we cannot perceive or know through intuitive feeling (*rasa*), the existence of the phenomenal world depends in some sense on our perceiving it. The enumeration of symbolic foods and the realities to which they refer is therefore, for those initiated, a kind of metaphysical contemplation of what there is.

Among the most important items are the paired red and white porridges and the dish of five-coloured porridge. A brief comment on their range of meanings will give some idea of the symbolic scope of the slametan. White and red are primary symbols in Javanese thought. In the slametan, white and red porridge represent respectively the father's semen and the mother's procreative blood, and through them Adam and Eve, our first parents. Other oppositions, such as day and night or right and left, may be linked in the address with this primordial pair. All this is explicit and agreed by everyone. The importance of filial piety, linked as it is to the sources of fortune and misfortune, can hardly be exaggerated. For many ordinary villagers filiation is the dominant theme and motivation of the slametan, with the understanding that in acknowledging one's deceased parents one safeguards oneself. A minimal slametan, in fact, consists only of the red and white porridge.

Others place the emphasis a little differently. Pious Muslims look beyond the parental symbols to Adam and Eve as historical figures, Nabi Adam being the first prophet. For the mystics, Adam is Everyman. Each man contains the seed of humanity in his sperm. Hence, *nabi* (prophet) 'means' *bibit* (seed). Adam and Eve, like our immediate parents, are mere intermediaries (*lantaran*), not the original source of life and wisdom. For the mystics, the scriptural account of creation is a humanly invented story to be mined for symbolism and fitted to what we can know directly from ourselves, the only true source of knowledge. At the risk of overschematizing, one might say that the santri reads into the symbols an Islamic cosmogony; the ordinary indifferent villager places them in a familial context; and the mystic refers everything back to the self.

The formulaic interpretations in the address thus mask divergent positions and motivations. Of these, the two extremes – that is, the mystical and the santri – are the clearest and most articulate, with the majority falling somewhere in between. It is the mystics who go furthest, by far, in developing these ideas, in smoke-filled, all-night sessions.

I will give a brief example related to the symbolism so far considered. In the teaching of the sect, Adam and Eve, or male and female, each contribute four things in conception. From the father derive the four white constituents (which need not be named here); from the mother the red. But since every act of sex does not automatically lead to conception, for life to exist there must be a third creative agent, a catalyst, and this is divine. The mystics refer to this third contributor by a variety of terms: the Hidden (*ga'ib*), Life (*urip*), Wisnu (Vishnu), or Power (*kwasa* or *kuwasa*). As they put it, 'the Arabic word is Allah', though, of course, this is not what most people understand by 'Allah'. The duality of red and white therefore implies a trinity: Adam and Eve and Wisnu. The third part of the trinity, the divine spark, is (some say: results from) the confluence of the four elements, earth, wind, fire, and water, and these elements continually renew and sustain life. The three agents in creation, Adam and Eve and Wisnu, thus each bear four constituents, making twelve, a complex whole like the four-five constellation of the multi-coloured porridge. For the sect, the figure twelve signifies a concept central to all Javanese mysticism, denoted by the phrase *sangkan paraning dumadi*: the origin and destination of being.

How much of this is spelt out in the address depends on the speaker and the audience. Some of the number sets, such as the four material elements, have a wide currency, but only those experienced in mysticism understand the interrelation between the sets. Ordinary villagers, and even santri, will sometimes refer to a concept of three-in-one, symbolized by the three coloured flowers, without being clear about what they mean by this. But whereas ordinary folk will often refer to one of the mystics for an authoritative interpretation, santri rarely do so and simply claim that it is all there in the Koran if only one knows where to look (which in fact no one does). In general, the explicit interpretation contained in the address is, to use a somewhat untropical trope, the tip of the iceberg.

From a theoretical point of view, the most interesting feature of slametan symbolism is not simply that it is polysemic in the manner of Turner's (1967) colour symbolism: we are now familiar enough with the idea of a symbol having layered and even contradictory meanings in different contexts among people who share a common ideology. I am describing something more complex: ideological diversity contained within a common frame.

A parallel case is that of the *kenduri*, or prayer-meal, of the Sumatran Gayo (Bowen 1993: 229–50). In a penetrating analysis, John Bowen shows how factional differences between modernist and traditionalist Muslims are masked or muted in the *kenduri*. As in the slametan, ritual ambiguity and multivocality are exploited – though in quite different ways – to enable people of diverse orientation to come together. In the Gayo case the risk of ideological conflict is reduced by 'a compartmentalization of the ritual [which] allows people to acknowledge some of its components and ignore others' (Bowen 1993: 241). The most controversial parts of Gayo ritual are performed privately by specialists (317). Equally important, at a *kenduri* 'no public decoding takes place, and people draw their own semiotic conclusions' (232). Community is thus maintained in spite of ideological differences.

It is the unsaid, the underinterpreted, the absence of exegesis at the event itself that permits ritual practitioners to reconstruct community on top of a wide diversity of individual opinions about what is ritually proper and practically possible.   (Bowen 1993: 318)

Likewise, among the Tengger people of East Java:

No sermon accompanies ceremony, and no one comes forth to provide 'item-by-item exegesis' of ritual symbolism. Often the priest celebrates communal rites alone ... The efficacy of ritual rarely depends upon the presence of an active congregation.   (Hefner 1985: 20)

Consequently, 'ritual social organization in Tengger buffers the liturgy from popular regard, helping to maintain two almost parallel bodies of ritual symbolism, each internally consistent and sustained in its own field' (Hefner 1985: 186; see also pp. 18, 184–8, 269). Against these characterizations (which fit many South-east Asian cases), the example presented here appears in sharp contrast – a contrast all the more striking given family resemblances among the rituals concerned. Instead of separation, specialization, and an avoidance of public speech, we find in the Banyuwangi slametan a systematic integration of very disparate ideas in a fully collective enterprise. Public exegesis forms a key part, and social compromise is achieved not merely in spite of ideological differences but by means of their combined expression in ritual.[6]

Perhaps this is clearer in my second example, the five-coloured porridge (*jenang manca warna*). In the address it refers to the *dulur papat lima badan*, literally the 'siblings-four, five-body (self)'. The four siblings are the personal guardian spirits, important in magic and protection from sorcery (see Weiss 1977). Usually only two are named: the amniotic fluid and the afterbirth, respectively elder and younger sibling to the person, and these stand for the set of four. The identity of the other two siblings is obscure or at least variable. Some people refer to the Arabic-derived *napsu* or drives; others to the blood and the umbilical cord. But these are named only to make up the number. In the slametan the *dulur* are represented, then, by a dish containing four blobs of rice porridge oriented to the cardinal points, with black to the north, red south, yellow west, and white east. In the centre is a blob of green porridge or a mixture of the other four: *manca warna*, 'multicoloured'. The centre stands, explicitly, for the person, the focus and origin of the four directions. Hence the phrase: 'siblings four, body [or self] fifth'.

In the dedication, the four-five configuration is linked to other sets, such as the material elements, and to Islamic quartets, such as the four drives, the archangels, and the Companions of the Prophet; though not to quintets such as the five daily prayers or the pillars of the faith, which lack reference to a central component.

As with the red and white porridge, a publicly agreed formula is given differential emphasis in private or esoteric interpretations. For the ordinary participant, the four spiritual siblings are primary, and are assumed, like the ancestral spirits, to have a direct influence on one's welfare. Many santri share this view, but play up the Islamic parallels when pressed in discussion. Typically, it is the mystics who go furthest in systematizing and elaborating the correspondences. For the mystics, at one level of exegesis, the four siblings represent the four faculties under the control of rasa, 'intuitive feeling' (Stange 1984: 119), located in the centre (solar plexus). Rasa is synonymous with indwelling divine life, and it is in rasa that outer and inner, man and God are united (Geertz 1960: 238–40; Gonda 1952: 158; Stange 1984; Zoetmulder 1995: 182–4).

A scheme widely shared among people of different orientation is that of microcosm and macrocosm, denoted in Javanese by the terms *jagad cilik* and *jagad gedhé*. The four-five configuration is one of the structures which links these two realms.[7] Man is composed of the four elements and returns to these at death; man is the centre from which the four directions radiate, and so on. The centre represents the whole in two senses (both explanations are offered): either as encompassing the outer components or as being their combination – hence the multicoloured blob. But, again, explicit interpretation is limited. The formal speech merely points to correspondences between various sets of four without specifying the nature of their links. Are microcosm and microcosm connected by analogy, metaphor, or identity of substance? Clearly the answers to this question sort out the sheep from the goats, doctrinally speaking. Santris would not accept the mystics' anthropocentrism – their identification of the archangels with the faculties, nor the identity of God and man in rasa, the central component; nor would the average villager accept that the ancestors are in oneself or that Adam and Eve are purely symbolic figures. But since these ideas are not spelled out in the address there is no problem.

As will be evident by now, numerology serves various ends in the slametan. Firstly, it creates a framework or structure on which interpretations of differing cast can be pinned. All agree on the importance of the four-sibling set, but some go on to link this with the four passions, others the four elements. It does not greatly matter since each set can symbolize the others. One set can be primary and in some sense real, the other derivative or merely symbolic, depending on one's point of view. The particular meanings are not exclusive. On the contrary, rather than reject a rival interpretation (so far as it is known), one fits it into one's conceptual scheme at a different level.

Another technique of explication is by a form of wordplay called *kérata basa*. Here, one takes some word or syllable and either constructs an etymology or finds in one's scheme some key word with which it rhymes. The word is then taken to have this meaning. One example already given is *nabi* (prophet). Its second syllable -bi is found (almost) in *bibit*, seed, so *nabi* 'means' (*tegesé*) seed. *Sego golong*, the packaged rice, rhymes with *bolong*, hole; thus, commonly, signifying the nine orifices of the body. The nine orifices in turn are guarded by (or, for some, merely symbolize) the nine saints credited with spreading Islam in Java. This much is common knowledge. But for the mystics these quasi-historical personages are merely symbols in turn: *waliyullah*, saint or friend of God, rhymes with and 'means' *polah* (action/doing), a key term in their ethical system. Some of the puns are widely known even though they are quite complicated and can lead on to more profound discussion. For example, the word for human being, *manungsa*, 'means' *manunggal ing rasa*: to be as one in feeling-intuition. In other words, all men are the same at the level of feeling; more profoundly, all men are united in their indwelling divine rasa.

Kérata basa, like numerology, is a way of connecting diverse realms and establishing correspondences. Perhaps one should say *recognizing* correspondences, since many of these are felt to be real, not imagined.[8] In fact, the goal of much mystical discussion is to reveal the interconnectedness of things, to realize that 'the cosmos is one community' (Pigeaud 1983: 65). Both techniques of interpretation – numerology and *kérata basa* – have the effect of synthesizing or syncretizing disparate materials by identifying common denominators. This procedure also permits a divergence of opinion and interpretation within a common ritual language.[9]

Perhaps the most extreme example of this phenomenon is the term Muhammad Rasulullah: Muhammad the Apostle of God. The mere utterance of the epithet is enough to identify the speaker as a Muslim. But what kind of Muslim? The word 'Muhammad' in Arabic script looks like, or can be perceived as, a human body lying on its side. This conceit, which features in other Javanese mystical systems as well as in classical Sufism (Schimmel 1975: 153, 225), is related by adepts to the notion that the body is a script, a 'wet book' (*kitab teles*) in contrast to the 'dry book' of the Koran. (It also fits neatly with the distinction in Islam between *nabi* (prophet) and *rasul* (apostle, bearer of a holy book).) The body's script is eternal, unlike the temporal revelation of the historical Muhammad. The script is reproduced in each generation, our bodies being the intermediaries, to be read and interpreted anew by those with a mind to it. One does not need to look outside oneself for illumination. Hence, for the mystics, the slametan, in its details and as a whole, is a meditation on the human body, the self: as microcosm, as intermediary, and as the source of knowledge. The ancestors, Adam and Eve, the four siblings, and Muhammad are all in oneself. *Rasul*, apostle, in this serious play of words, means rasa, the divine faculty of feeling-perception. So when the address closes with the words, 'May this be granted by Muhammad the Apostle of God', simple monotheists, near-polytheists, and mystics hovering somewhere between pantheism and a sceptical humanism can nod in unison.

That the slametan comprises disparate meanings is itself a matter of varying interpretation. As many authors have pointed out, Javanese grade things, including understandings, on a scale of coarse (kasar) to refined (alus) and outer (*lair*) to inner (*batin*) (Geertz 1960: 232–3). The meaning of a symbol depends on what strategic level one is adopting in discussing it. An explanation of an outward action, such as a prayer posture, in kasar or outer terms as fulfilling some scriptural obligation is true at that level; but it contains a profounder truth which is revealed through interpretative techniques of the kind described.

Santri relativize Javanist knowledge as a matter of adat or custom, something inferior to the universal truths of religion. The mystics, for their part, sometimes refer to the stages of the Sufi path. Knowledge attained in the final stage, gnosis, may be so far removed from the first stage that it appears to contradict it.[10] But esoteric knowledge is never brought into open comparison with common knowledge except among adepts. I found that pious Muslims in the village knew little of Javanist metaphysics beyond a travesty of the identification of God with man. But many of the mystics were among the more knowledgeable about Islam and could recite the prayers proficiently. This puts them at an advantage in debate and is one reason why santri are reluctant to quibble with arcane words like Wisnu that may occasionally crop up in slametans. The mystics contrast their own open-minded speculation with what they see as the narrow dogmatism of the santri. In turn, the pious tend to see mystical discussion as so much sophistry, symbol-mongering, and deviationism. The quiet, bewildered majority, caught between the two sides, is apt to defer to either as the occasion demands. But while ordinary villagers might side with the santri because they feel they ought to, they defer to the mystics because they believe them to be in possession of the truth. In this practical distinction between what is respectable or politically safe and what is ultimately true, many, perhaps the majority, of villagers tacitly accept the mystics' frame of reference.

To sum up, however sharp the disagreements may be, they are hidden in the slametan by several factors: the ambiguous phrasing of the address; a refusal to contest meanings in public; a relativism which grants a limited truth to the other's view; and a recognition of common social values and common humanity which override doctrinal differences.

I have concentrated on some of the details of the slametan dedication in order to reveal the wide variation in meaning contained in what appears to be, to quote again Geertz's characterization, 'a simple, formal, undramatic ... little ritual'. Before turning to the social context of the ritual, which again is deceptively simple, I want briefly to consider some linguistic aspects of the slametan.

The discourse of the slametan

Whether the ancestors and other spirits actually hear the address and the prayers is a matter of muted controversy, but the question bears on the nature of the discourse. In the commemorative ritual meal, the sedhekah, the ancestors are said to 'have returned to eternity' (*mulih nang jaman kelanggengan*), an ambiguous phrase which can mean reunited with God in heaven, mouldering in the graveyard, or simple extinction. Depending on one's preferred eschatology, the formal speech is therefore a direct address to disembodied spirits, a message to be passed on by intermediaries to God, or a reflexive contemplation. Since the audience is mixed, it has to be all of these things at the same time.

The significance of the invocatory speech *as a whole* is judged in relation to the prayer that follows it (cf. Bowen 1993: 230–1). For the pious, orthodox-leaning Muslim, the invocation is less important because the role of the ancestors is ancillary – they are intermediaries with God, not a source of blessing in themselves. The prayer is more powerful because it goes directly to God; moreover, Arabic is God's language.

In contrast, some Javanists regard the address itself as a prayer, and will even refer to it with the Javanese word for prayer, *donga*, as opposed to the prayer proper, for which the Arabic loan word *du'a* is reserved. The point of this usage is to stress the thematic continuity of the two sections. The Arabic prayer, usually the *du'a slamet*, is obviously thematically linked to the address, even though very few can translate it. It is also pointed out that Arabic words begin and end the whole sequence, so it forms a unity: there is the initial Arabic greeting, then the Javanese address, then the prayer.

For Javanists, Arabic words frame the more important Javanese speech, like a vessel containing and protecting a precious content. In the same way, official religion is the *wadhah* or container of the esoteric truths of Javanist philosophy.[11] The power of the vernacular words resides partly in the fact that they are pronounced clearly, understood and witnessed, in contrast to the opaque Arabic words which are merely garbled. The Javanese words of the address, moreover, are *tuwèk*, ancient and replete with wisdom and power. They pertain to mysteries – the realm of eternity, origins, and destinations.

There is another aspect to this question of verbal efficacy. Among a number of words in Javanese for power, one specifically refers to powerful speech: *mandi*. A second (cognate?) sense of the word is 'venomous'.[12] It is often said that speech in the past was mandi, meaning that – unlike today – people did what they said and that therefore their speech was authoritative. A man who told his wife that he would be staying overnight in his fieldhut would not dare to come home early; he would rather sleep outside the house. To do otherwise would be to 'incur the poison or curse of his own words' (something worse than eating his words, as we should say).

The prime example of speech which is mandi is the spell. But, as some of the more rationalistic mystics insist, any speech can be mandi; it need not be hedged about with secrecy and hocus pocus. 'If you do what you say – and how difficult this is – then your speech is mandi.' Among the mystics this is a cardinal ethical principle. It is not simply a question of keeping one's promises, but of guarding one's speech as an almost sacred vehicle of one's intentions. One man told me that if he were contemplating going to a slametan at the shrine in a nearby village he would be able to change his mind up until the point when he had told someone – perhaps a disinterested neighbour – that he was going. Then he would have to go. Once the intention has been expressed it becomes a commitment. In the slametan, too, there is much talk of intentions. The host is said not merely to be holding a slametan but to have the desire or intention (*ajat*) of holding one, now realized before assembled witnesses. The whole event, in fact, may be referred to by the word *ajat* (see note 5). By definition, then, since intention and action are fused in the slametan the words of the address are mandi, effective, and the boons hoped for from the slametan are halfway to being granted. The benefits are thus not simply requested (as in 'Give us this day our daily bread') but anticipated (rather like 'Thy kingdom come, thy will be done') in a grammatical form peculiar to the slametan address (e.g. *dikabulana, diparingana*). Indeed, the Osing word for the act of dedication is *ngabulaken*, meaning 'cause something to come true'. This captures the half-requesting/half-commanding tone of the speech. It also leaves ambiguous the identity of who is doing the causing, since this verb form can imply either that one is bringing about something oneself or that one is getting someone else (the delegate, God, the ancestors) to perform the action.

All this talk of intentions may recall to some the Islamic *niya* which precedes ritual prayer or *salāt*, and indeed Woodward (1988: 76) takes the prominence of intention as evidence of the Islamic tone of the slametan. The point of the *niya* is as an aid to concentration in worship (Padwick 1961: 50, 53). But something more is meant here. In the slametan, the expression of intention is a performative utterance which, coupled with the expression of wishes, brings about, at least symbolically, the desired result (Austin 1970; Tambiah 1985). The address thus shares some characteristics of the spell, which often begins with the phrase, 'I have the intention (Jav. *niyat*) of doing such and such', followed by the action of cutting, anointing, or whatever.

Personnel

According to reports from elsewhere in Java, it is the mosque official (modin) or some similar figure who presides at a slametan. In Banyuwangi, everything points away from a religious specialization or monopoly in the office and there is no 'ritual dependency' (Hefner 1985: 107) on the pious. The modin only presides if he happens to figure among the usual guests and if there is no one senior or more skilful in performing the address. The host's delegate is not therefore a token Muslim among the heathens, as is sometimes alleged, but is much like the other guests.[13] The speaker does not even have to be a highly respected or moral person. In any neighbourhood there are one or two men who possess the necessary knowledge and are usually called upon. One man may speak the address and another the prayer, or one person may perform the whole ceremony. Although each speaker has his personal style, certain elements are standard. The Arabic prayers – the *du'a slamet* for slametans, the *du'a kubur* for sedhekahs – are (errors aside) invariable and are learned from manuals or by repetition from a teacher.

A crucial point for the sociology of the slametan is that the content of the address is roughly the same whatever the religious orientation of the speaker. The emphasis varies but nobody imposes a private interpretation or bias in the explicit form of the speech. Neither can one elaborate at will: the formularized meanings are traditional and independent of the speaker. Just as the speaker must be neutral in composing the address, the host's choice of delegate does not usually indicate an ideological bias on his part. On the contrary, he may ask a neighbour of an opposite tendency to speak. One pious Muslim told me he would like to dispense with the address and go straight to the prayers. His next-door neighbour is a prominent mystic who regards Islam with some hostility as a 'colonization of the soul'. As a guest, on more than one occasion I witnessed each man preside at the slametan of the other. The santri would do without the address, the mystic would do without the prayer;

but each performed the whole sequence for the benefit of his host and the group of guests.

Here we come to the social significance of the slametan as distinct from its symbolic meanings. While the invocation speaks of the person and the world, saying very little of the community, the performance of slametans is recognized as having wider social benefits. Among other things, it promotes a state of *rukun* among participants (Geertz 1960: 61). Rukun, which means both social harmony and the making of such harmony, is the prime social value in village life (Mulder 1992: 40–3). In everyday affairs it is achieved by the mutual adjustment of differing interests among fellow villagers. In the slametan, rukun is enhanced by several means: first by the simple fact of taking part. Participation implies sharing the joys or sorrows of the occasion; it also requires a contribution to the costs and labour of a major feast, and ultimately a return invitation. Significantly, recruitment is impartial: guests are not chosen on the basis of group identity, personal preference, or like-mindedness; they are either neighbours or kin as the occasion demands, and one would never pass over someone unless normal relations had been completely severed. Secondly, rukun is achieved by the form of the slametan itself, which is, as we have seen, a temporary synthesis of disparate elements and ideologies. A symbolic compromise mirrors – indeed, effects – a social compromise. Syncretism is therefore to be seen in this case as a dynamic social and cultural process, not as a mere historical concretion of bits and pieces left over from Java's chequered past. The need for rukun motivates participation in the slametan; and the syncretism of the slametan transforms ideological difference into rukun.[14]

Is the slametan Islamic?

As I noted at the outset, discussion of the slametan, and of Javanese religion in general, has been preoccupied with whether or not, or to what extent, it is Islamic. It should be clear by now that this question cannot be answered simply by a description of what happens and comparison against a checklist of Islamic rules and customs. Unlike Woodward (1988: 62), I could find no one who regarded the slametan (distinct from the sedhekah) as an Islamic ritual. Anthropologists may indeed have been misled by a narrowly legalistic definition of Islam, as Woodward asserts, but then so have the Javanese themselves (cf. Federspiel 1970: 70–4). Though it obviously incorporates Islamic elements, most people regard the slametan as distinctively Javanese and pre-Islamic or even

Hindu in inspiration. Islamic terms have been appropriated and in some cases given senses wholly different from anything recognizably Muslim, or else emptied of specifically Islamic content by turning them into universal symbols. 'We all practise Islam', as one mystic told me, 'even you, because Islam means slamet, something we all seek'. Even the Javanese word for the salāt ritual prayer, *sembahyang*, is turned inside out and becomes *sembah éyang*, worship of one's ancestors (variously conceived). It seems inadequate therefore to view this kind of thinking as a local form of Islam. On the contrary, many regard Islam as a local form of 'true' knowledge. It is given a place in the total scheme of things, but there is little agreement about how important that place should be.

Woodward (1988) sees certain features of the slametan, such as humility in the host, a shared blessing, almsgiving, and invitations to the poor, as authorized by hadīth; but these are lacking in the slametan of Banyuwangi and are weakly attested elsewhere. What matters primarily for an understanding of ritual is, in any case, the significance derived by participants themselves. The putative textual origins of the slametan or its parallels in other Muslim societies have little bearing on its contemporary significance. A case in point is the slametan address, a speech act for which the Arabic-derived word *ngabulaken* (from *kabul*) is used. In Islamic law the term *kabul* is paired with *ījāb* as the formal 'acceptance' of an 'offer' made in a legal contract before witnesses (Juynboll 1953: 157).[15] Should we therefore conclude that participants conceive of the slametan as a contractual exchange with the ancestors or God? Perhaps. But the same could be said of ritual meals the world over. The classical Islamic origin, if such it is, and the legal connotations have been forgotten. Intriguingly, in standard Javanese the slametan address is called *ujub* (from Ar. *ījāb*), not *kabul*. The Osing substitution of a speech of 'acceptance' for one of 'offering' suggests a 'magical', coercive emphasis, a recasting of what was already a borrowed notion.

Evidently the Islamic nature of the ritual cannot be settled by etymology, scriptural derivation, or even the opinion of participants. For who is to say, ultimately, what counts as Islamic? There are, moreover, slametans in Banyuwangi which lack any Islamic reference. In the village of Cungking there is a popular cult of a sage associated with one of the last Hindu-Buddhist (buda) kings in Java. As we shall see in chapter 4, slametans at his shrine involve archaic buda spells instead of Arabic prayers and greetings. Further south, in the village of Krajan, Hindu converts and their Muslim neighbours regularly attend each other's slametans (see chapter 8). There is the usual incense-burning (joss-sticks for Hindus, resin for Muslims), the speech of invocation and symbolic explication, and the prayers. Naturally, one keeps a respectful silence during prayers of the opposite faith. But the formal address is remarkably similar in each case. The offerings are the same but there are differences in the glosses; for example, instead of dedicating the chicken to Muhammad, one dedicates it to Resi Wiyasa, a parallel figure who reputedly brought Hinduism to Java. Root vegetables normally dedicated to Suleiman are offered to Antaboga, the underworld serpent. But, strikingly, many of the elements remain the same for both Hindus and Muslims – the red and white symbolism and the five-coloured porridge, the three coloured flowers and fragrant water. These are, as we have seen, the essential ingredients of the slametan in Bayu.

Conclusion

Studies of multivocality in relatively closed, ideologically simple settings (notably Barth 1987 and Strecker 1988), stress the freedom of actors to manipulate meanings to their political advantage; but in a complex and diverse setting multivocality may, on the contrary, serve as a means of blending together dissonant voices and thus of orchestrating social harmony. Symbols, in this perspective, work as common denominators rather than as indexes of difference – the more ambiguous (polysemic), the more resonant and focal the symbol, and the greater its integrative power. This does not, of course, mean that the slametan is all things to all men. For a given group of celebrants it is a fairly specific embodiment of their various views: otherwise it would lose its relevance to their ultimate concerns. As Empson (1930) famously showed, ambiguity can function with some precision when employed as a stylistic device; and so it does in this case. The symbolic range of the slametan, far from being unlimited, is specified by traditional interpretative techniques and by reference to restricted sets of ideas. Social and political constraints (which are apt to change) determine which meanings shall be voiced and which shall remain implicit.

I have suggested a connexion between multivocality and syncretism. If people of different orientation are to come together, as they do in the slametan, they must create common ground, discover both what unites them and what can focus their divergent interests. This they do by means of multivocal symbols. The resulting synthesis is, as we have seen, a temporary accommodation in which participants are not required to abandon their positions and think alike. Nobody subscribes to the whole package of ideas associated with the slametan; and nobody rejects outright a rival interpretation. Moreover, underneath the differences there are commonalities – a sense of common humanity, a need for rukun, a desire to share in the occasion.

The enduring quality of the slametan no doubt derives partly from its appeal to basic Javanese values which transcend local and sectarian differences. It brings together neighbours as fellow men and women, not as fellow Muslims or Hindus. But its form – symbolically dense and comprehensive but at the same time flexible and ambiguous – has also helped it to survive and even encompass major cultural changes (cf. Lewis 1980: 8–9). The very adaptability of the slametan has made conversion from Islam to Hinduism and sometimes back again less troublesome than one might imagine. As a ritual frame adaptable to diverse faiths and ideologies, it remains at the heart of Javanese religion. As an example of religious syncretism, it shows how – and with what inventive grace – people can come to terms with their differences.

In the chapters that follow we shall come across the slametan in various contexts, public and private. In terms of its social acceptability, the ordinary, everyday slametan described above is the standard from which these depart. Alterations in the delicate balance of interests expressed in the rite, or in the degree of explicitness of some element, are always significant and are often controversial. But even in the most esoteric of religious expressions, the fundamental commitment to compromise is never fully abandoned: the lesson of the slametan is rarely forgotten.

3

The sanctuary

Introduction: the universal and the local

We have seen how profound ideological differences are both expressed and muted in the slametan. What is not said is at least as significant as what is said. And what is said, though it varies little among speakers, varies greatly in meaning. The formulaic explication of the slametan address, in its generalities, ambiguities, and wordplay, encompasses diversity and seems, superficially, to deny it. Like a carefully worded diplomatic statement, there is little anyone can quibble with and every appearance of agreement; yet, unlike a diplomatic statement perhaps, there is still a sense that something important has been said and shared. If this is ritual as consensus, it is a peculiar form of consensus which under the surface preserves contradictions and divisions.

The slametan in Bayu deals in universals, avoiding controversial names and excluding any reference to place. Rarely is there mention of the village or even neighbourhood; and, except in agricultural slametans, which are usually held in the rice fields, there is no reference to place spirits. Clearly, it would be a mistake to see the slametan as part of a 'local' religion or tradition in contrast to a dominant civilization, still less as an 'animistic' or tribal relic sheltering under the cloak of Islam.

The strain towards universality in aid of unity is achieved by burying differences in common ground and by recourse to what appear to be common denominators. (They are common only in form, not sense.) This is one solution to the problem of diversity. But it is by no means the only solution; nor does this temporary synthesis – crucial as it is – typify all ritual practice in Bayu. One can be explicit, particular, and local so long as one remains discreet. Since everyone knows, or pretends to know, what goes on in the neighbourhood, the important thing is not

51

concealment, which would be impossible, but the avoidance of open offence. Hence the pious are criticized not for praying but for making an exhibition of their piety. Likewise, non-fasters during Ramadhan excite ill will only if they smoke or eat in public.

In ritual matters, separation and avoidance are as effective as compromise in minimizing the risk of conflict. Take, for example, the magical arts of the *dhukun* or *wong tuwèk* (wise person) – healing, love magic, and divination. Normally, only persons sympathetic to these practices need come into contact with them. Others may be unsympathetic, but it is only when magic (in the guise of sorcery) appears to threaten innocent parties or the general welfare that a concerted opposition is mounted.

However, more interesting from my point of view, since it enters more conspicuously into the public domain and thus challenges the ritual-as-consensus paradigm, is the cult (if one may call it that) centred on the village shrine.[1] Despite its physical isolation and ambiguous status, the shrine impinges on the wider sphere of ritual observance. In fact, propitiation of the guardian spirit entrammels the whole slametan complex in locality, for the spirit of the shrine must be consulted and feasted before any large event; and the welfare of the village in general depends upon his protection. A set of ritual practices which departs quite radically from the 'diplomatic protocol' of the ordinary slametan thus claims an integral role in village life.

This chapter situates the spirit cult against the background of ideological diversity sketched in chapter 2, beginning with a description of the shrine and a slametan dedicated to its spirit. I try to account for the paradoxical status of the guardian spirit as ritually central but socially marginal and relate this to the play of contending discourses – Islamic, 'modern', and traditional – which govern religious life in the village. But the bulk of the chapter is concerned with the barong, a sprawling and raucous folk drama centring on a lion-dragon who is both the spirit's minion and the village mascot. At the climax of the performance the spirit himself is summoned from the shrine and manifested in a masked performer. An account of the show, its meaning and its erratic fortunes, thus serves as a commentary on the place of the spirit cult in the life of the village.

The village shrine

The shrine or sanctuary is that of Buyut Cili, who is usually referred to simply as Buyut (Great-grandfather). It lies hidden in a clump of trees on the village boundary, near the hamlet of Sukosari, about half a mile from the centre of the main settlement. A shrine has stood in the same place for generations, long before Bayu had a mosque or even a prayer house. Once it was sheltered by a sacred *suko* tree (hence the name Sukosari) marking the spot where Buyut settled and began to clear the forest.

Buyut's identity is a mystery. When I enquired about his origin I was told: 'You must ask him yourself, if you dare.' His name – a nickname – reveals nothing of rank or region. Some people say Cili is a corruption of *ngili*, meaning 'to flee'. They usually add that he was a refugee from (Muslim) Mataram who became minister in the (Hindu-Buddhist) kingdom of Macan Putih. One version has it that the cannibal king of Macan Putih lusted after Buyut's fat wife and to save her Buyut fled to the forest and settled at the spot marked by the shrine. Some say he does not speak in the Osing dialect, others assert that he is indeed a local. Whatever his origin, buda or Muslim, local or outsider, these stories place him in precolonial times, long before the village of Bayu existed. Unfortunately, written testimony is entirely lacking. A palm-leaf chronicle of his life was lost a few years ago when its owner moved house, but since no one alive today can claim to have read it one cannot be sure of its real subject. The important point, however, is that, unlike the place spirits (*danyang*) which haunt some village shrines, Buyut Cili is regarded as an historical figure – not an ancestor or even a village

Plate 3 The village shrine

founder but the powerful spirit (*wong alus*) of a former inhabitant. It would be odd, nevertheless, that an unknown pioneer or fugitive could exert such fascination over present-day villagers were it not for one thing: Buyut is a were-tiger.

That Bayu should be the lair of a were-tiger is, in itself, unremarkable in an area abounding in tiger legends and whose capital was at Macan Putih (White Tiger) – so-called after the mount of its founder. Tiger-sightings are infrequent, but nobody seems to doubt Buyut's powerful presence. One man described to me how once, when he was on his way home through the cemetery to Sukosari, his companion stopped, frozen in his tracks. There was a large tiger on the path and the other man could not be persuaded to continue until the tiger had gone. 'I didn't know what he was staring at. But that's how it is with the occult [*barang ga'ib*]: one person sees it and the other doesn't.' Since one cannot question the other's experience, such indirect knowledge reinforces belief rather than encourages scepticism. Young and old are equally convinced. A youth who was my neighbour used to sit meditating at night under a tree in the cemetery in order to 'ask Buyut for lottery numbers'. He was modestly successful, but when he repeated the attempt once too often a thunderous roar broke over his head and before taking to his heels he looked up into the gaping jaws ('more than a metre wide') of a tiger.

Sometimes Buyut appears as a dog; more often as a shaggy, white-breasted tiger with slouching head and terrifying torch-like eyes. During troubled times he patrols the village, and at lonely spots one can sometimes see flashes of light cast by his eyes. It is said that when nobody is around he walks upright. Despite his fierce appearance he has been known to partake of the rice at slametans when no one is looking.

Slametan Buyut

Slametans are held at the shrine to ask for Buyut's blessing and protection. This is particularly important in the run-up to a major feast when the host's house is vulnerable to theft and supernatural attack. I attended one such slametan sponsored by the widow of the district mosque official on the eve of her daughter's wedding. Ordinarily one would not be notified of a slametan Buyut as it is a private affair but I happened to be at the house of one of the shrine's caretakers (*juru kunci*) on the appropriate Thursday afternoon. Unlike the all-male domestic feast, a slametan Buyut always involves women, either as sponsors or participants; as in neighbouring village cults, women are not distinguished either ritually or functionally from men. In keeping with the informality and inclusiveness of the event, children sometimes tag along and join in the meal. On this occasion, apart from the sponsor, Ma' Haji, and the caretaker, only two other people came along – neighbours who had a share in the wedding preparations. These helpers – a brother and sister, both middle-aged divorcees and both outspoken non-Muslims – made up what was a very mixed gathering, quite unlike the usual slametan guest list but in a sense reflecting in caricature its doctrinal diversity.

Ma' Haji and the helpers had brought the food and offerings with them and we left for the shrine without further ado. On arrival the caretaker knelt outside the door with head bowed and hands placed together in a gesture of respect. The building itself is not usually named – one simply says that one is 'going to Buyut's' – but sometimes it is referred to as his *sanggar* (sanctuary, place of worship or meditation) or *kandhapan*. Oriented east–west, with its door facing south, it is a modest structure with a thatched roof and walls of woven bamboo strips. Inside there are two pairs of headstones a yard apart, each pair oriented north–south in the usual Muslim direction. These belong to Buyut and his consort who is known only as Buyut Wadon, Great-grandmother. Although the headstones are called *paisan* like those of a grave, Buyut Cili is thought to have dematerialized (*musna ilang*) rather than died, and the shrine is not regarded as a tomb. The main ritual focus was the headstone to the east, sometimes identified with Buyut Wadon, and this received the greater number of offerings: betel quids, leaf cigarettes, a box of matches, a small coin, a plate of rice and chicken, and sweets. The other headstone received only betel ingredients.

Crouching inside the sanctuary, the caretaker lit incense and placed the smoking brazier on the ground. The incense is made of white resin exuded by the *suko* tree, unlike the usual benzoin used in ordinary slametans. It has no other use and only the regular caretakers ('those acquainted with Buyut') have access to it. Buyut's *suko* tree no longer exists, and there are no others in the village. The caretakers claim to find the resin hidden at the bottom of Buyut's headstone or wherever else he chooses to make it appear.

After gesturing Ma' Haji to enter (the rest of us sat outside) the caretaker spoke the Islamic greeting, embracing each headstone in turn. He then appeared to answer a voice (Buyut's), heard only by himself, in a brief murmured sentence identifying the petitioner. Then he spoke a formal dedication, which I taped:

Witness the event of Ma' Haji S. Ma' Haji has a child who is to be married. In the name of *kaju, tahrut, tahyin*, speech, inclination, the deepest feeling and the centre of thought, Ma' Haji asks that Great Grandfather and Great Grandmother grant prosperity and slamet without end and Ma' Haji be given light. And Ma' Haji asks with all her heart that the one to be married be given prosperity and slamet without end; and may there be no obstacles. May Great Grandfather and Great Grandmother confirm and maintain the doings of Ma' Haji, and may she be spared misfortune. [They] are offered coloured blossoms in fragrant water, like the water of *kalkaosar* lake [in paradise?], one soul becoming one seed. May this festive occasion be granted slamet, and the blessing of our great prophet, Muhammad. *Wassalamualaikum.*

This was followed by the Islamic 'I seek refuge' formula, a dedication of the opening of the Koran to Muhammad, the fatihah itself, and finally a prayer (the *du'a slamet*) in Arabic mixed with Javanese formulas. The caretaker then sprinkled flowers between the headstones, in the manner of one visiting a grave, before emerging with Ma' Haji from the shrine. Neither of them took part in the following meal. While the rest of us ate our chicken and rice ('one cannot run out, however much one eats, at Buyut's') they sat apart, conferring about the coming wedding for which the caretaker was *tukang pager*, a sort of mystical quartermaster who oversees the provisions and wards off evil influences. Then, without further formalities, we gathered up the bowls and baskets and made our way home.

Despite certain oddities in the address, in most respects the slametan is like those held at village shrines or sacred spots elsewhere in the region. The address contains no reference to Buyut's background or special powers and he is wholly anonymous. The kinship epithet does not in itself imply that he is regarded as an ancestor; rather it is an honorific. Some of the Arabic words (left untranslated) are unusual in this context, but this particular speaker often includes them in other kinds of slametan. He cannot explain them and, as far as one can tell, their main function is to impress or mystify – as such, to signal his specialist knowledge as a *wong tuwèk*.

Regular business at the shrine is conducted on Thursdays and Sundays in the late afternoon. Apart from the usual slametans to ensure the smooth running of a circumcision, or to thank Buyut for the successful completion of a wedding, there are also personal petitions. The shrine becomes a surgery, with the caretakers ministering in turns to people with sick cows, lost valuables, failing businesses, rheumatism, and requests for good harvests. More difficult cases, involving marital jealousy or suspicion of sorcery, require Buyut's direct advice (through a medium) and take place in secret at the dead of night.

For those with a reputation to maintain there is no loss of prestige in visiting the shrine, though bad timing can be invidious. One Sunday during Ramadhan I attended with the headman. He had been suffering from a recurrent cough but decided he was better and wanted to confirm the fact by thanking Buyut. Being a modern-minded man, on the way to the shrine he joked about the visit and asked me, half-apologetically, if I thought it was a 'primitive' custom. Yes, I countered, and all the better for it. His main worry, however, was that he would run into a santri on the way, so we took the back route through the fields. (During the daylight fast it is not a good idea to be seen laden with food on your way to a feast.) As we neared the shrine we duly ran into the mosque treasurer at work in his fields. Smiling at the headman and probably enjoying his discomfiture, the old santri asked the usual polite question of greeting: 'Where are you going?' The headman simply laughed and replied, 'Pak Andrew's having a slametan', before moving on.

In fact, allowances are usually made for non-fasters. Indeed, the caretaker himself (who on this occasion was not one of the regular officiants) was fasting and could not be persuaded to join us after he had consecrated the food. After placing the head and feet of a chicken on Buyut's altar, he excused himself and left us to eat in peace.

Most petitions are of a similarly humdrum kind. The following week I accompanied another neighbour, a woman suffering from incurable boils and a spendthrift husband. She explained her complaints in a loud voice to the caretaker while her husband stood meekly by, smiling affably at other petitioners. Then the caretaker went into the shrine and made a long petition to Buyut. As we ate, others with similar worries and requests filed into the compound with their baskets of food, ready to take our place.

Sanggar/langgar: switching religious roles

The involvement of pious types like Ma' Haji, the *penghulu*'s wife, in a village cult may occasion surprise. But local canons of orthodoxy and piety pertain to the performance of obligatory Muslim rituals rather than doctrinal purity or abstention from extra-curricular activities. The question of *syrik* (Ar. *shirk*, the sin of 'association' or polytheism) is hardly ever broached in regard to the shrine, even among pious Muslims. A paramedic new to the village soon became one of Buyut's regular visitors despite his reputation as a dourly censorious *fanatik*. Indeed, it was the same man who raised hackles during Ramadhan with his megaphone broadcasts calling for Islamic renewal. Among the caretakers is a former modin (mosque official) who not only ministers to Buyut but claims to know the spells necessary for becoming a were-tiger. The present modin, though more orthodox and 'modern', has on occasion spoken to Buyut through a medium. His most recent interview concerned the origin of the Javanese turban: did Buyut, as a man of the old times, know where it came from? Was it Muslim or buda?

Modernist Islam, which decries such practices as old-fashioned and idolatrous, has so far made little progress in Bayu; and its few sympathizers, mostly incomers or the children of conservative Muslims, would not openly criticize their seniors or risk offending the sensibilities of neighbours. Only among the younger generation are reformist-style doubts and questions about inconsistency sometimes raised. As the young leader of a *langgar* (prayer-house) explained to me, it is all right to pay one's respects to Buyut, as at any sacred spot, but one may not ask his blessing: that is for God alone to grant. More objectionable still is the spirit mediumship connected with Buyut which is no better than conjuring with evil spirits. But these kinds of objections are, as yet, uncommon and rarely voiced for fear of causing offence.

Put simply, the separation of context and the remote location of the shrine allows a segregation of potentially conflicting practices and thought-worlds. (The abstinent caretaker who exits before the meal is the limiting case.) When I tackled the modin on his doctrinal inconsistency he said, 'It's like wearing different hats: when I go to the mosque I wear my *kethu* (black velvet hat); when I perform circumcision rituals I wear a trilby.' Evidently, this is not just a question of separate congregations: functional separation allows the same individual to participate in different, even contradictory, forms of religious activity. A hat for every tradition: well might the modin wonder about turbans! I mention prominent Muslim petitioners here because it makes the point better than more obviously 'syncretist' cases would. (These remarks should, incidentally, alert us to the dangers of reifying distinctions such as abangan/santri.) Even the rigid and socially insensitive paramedic is able to alternate between sanggar and langgar without, it seems, any personal difficulty or stain on his piety. As for those few who object to the shrine's existence, they need not ever visit it.

In contrast, the shrine in neighbouring Cungking (the subject of chapter 4) is centrally placed in its village and has at times proved a temptation to the vandalism of the pious. Sanggar and langgar cannot comfortably share the same space and the Cungking spirit is sometimes felt to pose a challenge to the prayer-house congregation. The Bayu shrine, though mystically central to the welfare of the community, is conveniently isolated at its periphery. Yet there remains a certain ambivalence on the part of villagers towards the shrine which makes its location not merely convenient but appropriate. Probably this ambivalence has less to do with questions of orthodoxy, which are easily circumvented, than with Buyut's paradoxical nature. Part-man, part-animal, a rice-eating were-tiger, Buyut belongs but tenuously to human society. As village guardian he is respected, but as forest predator and creature of the night he inspires terror.

There is, indeed, a dark side to the Buyut cult. Unlike the spirit of Cungking who is 'white' and wholly benevolent, the guardian of Bayu is sometimes wilful and violent. People who have approached him without caution, or who have resisted his wishes, have been driven mad or put into a frenzy. Even the controlled situation of a seance can be an alarming experience for onlookers. It is through witnessing acts of possession that villagers gain their most vivid experience of Buyut's powers and of his unruly nature. Seances with mediums are not often arranged, but every villager has witnessed the dramatic eruption of the supernatural into ordinary life that takes place at the end of the barong show when, just before dawn, the performer places on a tiger mask and, possessed by Buyut Cili, runs amok in the crowd.

There are about half a dozen men (no women, though they are not disqualified in principle) who have direct access to Buyut, either as possessed spirit mediums, caretakers able to summon, converse with, and dismiss the spirits of Buyut and his family, or as uncontrolled vehicles for these spirits. With a few exceptions, this has been a speciality of east Bayu, and in particular of one extended family, the family that holds the barong.

Barong

The barong is a mythical feline dragon found in carnivals and dramas throughout South-east Asia and the Far East. In Indonesia the most famous version is found in Bali, where the barong figures in a sacred drama of exorcism which, in its various forms, draws on local, pre-Hindu, and Hindu-Javanese elements (Belo 1949, Covarubbias 1972). The *barong kèt*, as it is called, though demonic in appearance, embodies a powerful and benevolent deity, Dewa Ayu. His opponent, the witch Rangda, is associated in mythology with Durga, the goddess of death.

There are other, cruder, kinds of barong in Bali in the shape of horses, elephants, and even giant human beings, often linked to local spirit cults; but these barongs may have little more than the name in common.

The connexion between the classical Balinese barong and Java is intriguing but difficult to specify. Barong pageants may have taken place in Java from the earliest times. Pigeaud (1960–3: IV: 175, 189) finds analogous figures in the iconography of fourteenth century Hindu Java and suggests they share a common ancestry in 'divine or demoniacal personages appearing in primeval tribal ritual pageantry and myth'. But most present-day Javanese barong have nothing in common with the sacred drama of Dewa Ayu. They figure in very different stories and superficially, at least, seem closer to the cruder, spirit-cult barongs. Only in the *réyog* of Ponorogo does a Javanese barong appear as a character in a full-scale 'historical' drama (Mahmudi 1969, Pigeaud 1938: 186). But this barong (a tiger-mask with peacock plumes worn by a man in trance) is quite different from the *barong kèt* in appearance. Travelling shows similar to the *réyog*, featuring were-creatures (usually horsemen), can be found throughout Java. These are simply entertainments, even if they purport to enlist the aid of local spirits during the trance dances.

Different in inspiration, though similar in form, are the spirit possessions organized for village rituals. In the Banyuwangi area, several villages hold annual festivals at which men go into trance and behave as animals controlled by the village guardian spirit. In Aliyan, men-buffaloes plough the first plot on which rice is planted at the start of the season. These 'village cleansings' (*bersih desa*) are, or were (since they are fast disappearing), important rituals in the life of the agricultural community. Their survival in the face of an increasingly confident and intolerant Islam depends very much on the complexion of the current village leadership. Against the wishes of many of his villagers and despite pressure from cultural bureaucrats in town, the new headman of Aliyan has banned such performances as 'trafficking with demons'.

The barong show of Bayu borrows freely from all these traditions. It is at once a popular entertainment and a sacred performance essential to the well-being of the community. Bayu is, as far as I know, the only village in Java to boast a Bali-style barong figure.[2] Like its Hinduized counterpart, as 'lord over the demons of the forest and the graveyard, [it] serves as an intermediary in combating diseases and pestilences' (Grader 1960a: 181–2). But its stage is smaller. Whereas the Balinese barong is an indigenous deity caught up in an Indic pantheon, the protagonist in a vast cosmic drama, the Javanese dragon is pet monster of a village spirit. The all-night barong show, too, suffers by comparison with its more famous rival. In place of the rich mythology that Bali once shared with Java, there is a collage of sketches drawn from local and pan-Javanese folklore. In a regional culture obsessed with symbolism, the barong show is often asserted to be quite meaningless. Only at the climax of the show does buffoonery give way to something more serious, when, amid a furious clatter of drums and cymbals, the stage curtains burst open and a were-tiger – Buyut Cili, no less – charges through the shrieking crowd.

The barong show offers us one of several frames (others being the slametan complex and spirit mediumship) through which to approach the Buyut Cili cult. On the face of it, it would seem to have the advantage of a coherent, locally devised narrative context which ought to shed some light on Cili's place in the scheme of things. If it sheds only a dim light, as seems to be the case, this is something that demands explanation. I will suggest that the reasons for its shallowness and its poverty of metaphor lie less in the dramatic form itself than in the cultural politics which frame it. The enveloping power of Islam as the official faith and the repressive politics of New Order Indonesia have effectively turned a drama into a dumbshow. The case is, nevertheless, both poignant and revealing, and it tells us much about the place of indigenous religious forms in modern Indonesia.

Plate 4 The *barong*

But before turning to these considerations let us first look at a performance, beginning with an outline of the plot, to see what, if anything, can be made of the story. There is no script and performances vary slightly in detail, so the plot summary is taken from one particular performance I witnessed.

The performance
The setting is usually a wedding or circumcision. An arena demarcated by bunting and coloured lights encloses the festivities. Usually the festive arena is set up in a houseyard or in the space enclosed by a cluster of houses. If the area is too confined, as is often the case, the bamboo walls of adjacent dwellings are simply removed, like the facades of dolls' houses, so that guest tables and long trestles laden with cakes and sweets can be placed in and among the front parlours of the neighbours. In the midst of the comings and goings of guests a space is cleared for the barong. The stage is bounded on one side by a proscenium arch with a curtained-off backstage area. Its outer rim is a human wall formed by ever-encroaching hordes of children who must periodically be driven back by the players. The gong orchestra (*panjak*) is to the side of this 'stage'.

The show – called barong after its protagonist – is in five named parts. These cannot be called 'acts' in the manner of a Western drama since they are only loosely connected and involve different sets of characters.

1. Barong
The performance begins about 9 p.m. with the hectic rattling of drums, cymbals, and gongs which is the barong's leitmotif. Against a backdrop of painted forest scenery, the barong enters, head rocking from side to side, body shivering, and feet stamping. Unlike its serpentine Balinese counterpart, this barong seems to be all head. The glaring, bulging eyes, startled expression, and wide fanged mouth could be Balinese, but there are unfamiliar features: behind the head is a red hump – a 'crown' – giving a hunched posture like a startled cat. Unlike the *barong kèt*, two sets of yellow wooden wings spread out either side of the head, framing the bright red face and adding to the impression of massiveness. In contrast, the rest of the body is plain and unadorned, like the rear half of a pantomime pony. The four legs jangle with bells as the beast bustles about, ducking and pirouetting, bulky and powerful but light on its feet. The audience is amused but a little scared as the barong rushes forward then stops suddenly, jaws clapping, with one leg raised as it stares

vacantly ahead. (The rear end, unregarded, follows as best it can.) After some minutes of these antics the percussion intensifies and the barong bustles out.

There follows a courtship dance of forest spirits performed by two boys and two girls, all turbaned. A child in a bird mask weaves among the dancers. This bird-figure, under different names, appears several times during the performance. The barong briefly reappears, dancing with his owner, a young woman called Jaripah played by a man.

Two clowns, with painted faces, now enter the empty stage from opposite sides, scratching their heads and peering about. They are lost in the forest and approach each other suspiciously.

'Are you man or beast?'
'Man.'
'What's your name?'
'I've lost it.'

A third enters and attracts their interest.

'Is it a human?'
'No, a person.'

It turns out they are the brothers Oarsman, Sailor, and Depth-tester. After further banter Jaripah re-enters and tells them she has lost her charge (the barong). They gawp at her in comic astonishment. She is

Plate 5 Scene from a *barong* performance

dressed like a *gandrung*, an erotic dancer, in tight sarong, white socks, gold bodice, and tiara.

'What are you? Male or female?' says Oarsman.
'Female', comes the falsetto reply.
'Virgin or widow?'
'Virgin.'

They dance. Oarsman invites her to his fields and asks her to fan him with her scarf.

'What will you give me if I find your barong?' asks Depth-tester.
'I'll marry you', she replies.

They, too, dance; then, carrying baskets of food they set off for the fields. On arrival, Depth-tester puts on a grass headdress and mimics the *seblang*, a trance-dance from neighbouring Olehsari. When he later finds the barong, Jaripah breaks her promise and issues a further challenge: he must now fight the barong. He slays it, then brings it back to life and claims his reward. But still she resists. Now, she says, you must fight me. They spar and grapple (a certain masculine vigour showing through Jaripah's graces) and Depth-tester is left for dead. His brothers enter to find the barong eating him. They do not recognize him but carry him off. Jaripah comes back, dancing, and tames the barong with her scarf.

2. Panji Suméra (begins around midnight)

The brothers ask permission of Mbah Gembreng, who controls the forest, to cut down trees. Mbah Gembreng, speaking from behind the forest-curtain, allows them to fell *kelor* and *dadap* trees. (The felling of *kelor* trees, which would cause misfortune, is actually prohibited by custom.) The 'contents of the forest' – ape-like demons called *buta* – enraged at seeing their home cut down, make war on the brothers and defeat them. But an aristocrat from the north coast named Panji Suméra comes to their aid and 'makes the forest safe', driving off the *buta*.

3. Marriage of spirits

The backdrop has changed. In place of the lurid forest is a town scene of concrete houses and telegraph poles. Four 'heavenly spirits' flutter in. The brothers call on Panji Suméra, now acknowledged as a kind of brother, to drive them off, making the country safe again; but they detain one of the girl-spirits. However, a *garuda* (mythical eagle; actually the 'same' bird as appeared earlier) carries her off for a moment, possibly to tell her fellow spirits that she is joining the world of humans. The bird, angry at the actions of men, then fights Panji Suméra, but he too is driven off. The girl (now renamed Yard Spirit) is later married to Oarsman, and the scene ends with wedding entertainments, including a gandrung and a Madurese song-and-dance.

4. Suwarti

Comic scenes in the life of Suwarti from birth to marriage. One day, when her trader-father is away, she is abducted by a tiger. Her guards (the ubiquitous clowns) are asleep and think the abduction is a dream. When the trader comes back he burns incense and contacts the tiger who then returns the baby.

5. Lundoyo

Pak Mantri is an irrigation official who is often away from home. One day, as he takes his leave, he warns his wives (the gandrungs of previous scenes) not to be unfaithful. Back in the forest, a dignified and sinister figure strides across the stage. He has a human face and striped tiger costume. This is Lundoyo, played by the actor who was Panji Suméra.[3] Lundoyo wants to become a man, to marry and know the world of the village; so he consults a sage who gives him the necessary spell. He then enters the village, still in his tiger stripes, and meets the retainers of Mantri (the clowns again). When he tells them he is looking for a mate, the clowns, instead of protecting Mantri's wives as they have been charged, act as panders and extol their charms. As a result of the spell Lundoyo is irresistible to women: one of the wives immediately falls for him and they go offstage together. When we next see them Lundoyo warns her that he is really a tiger; but she is now madly in love and does not believe him. (Sometimes, in performance, she is not told by Lundoyo and remains under the illusion that he is a man.)

We are now approaching the climax of the performance. The feasting is long finished and the tables lie abandoned as all those strong enough to have stayed the course huddle round for the dénouement. Many who have not attended, or who have gone home earlier, now arrive to swell the crowd. It is just before dawn.

Mantri returns and arrests his rival. Lundoyo is bound from head to foot, rolled and kicked about the floor, then caged under the drapes of a table. Mantri challenges him: if you can free yourself you can have my wife. Within a minute, unseen, Lundoyo has cast off the ropes and can be heard beating a drum within. (This always astonishes onlookers who regard the escape as miraculous.) Lundoyo claims his prize and they go off.

By now a large and excited crowd has packed the arena, pressing close on the players. Spectators begin to whistle and shout; small children cling to their mothers; tough-looking stage-hands move into position around the floor, screening off the orchestra. In the final scene Lundoyo again warns his new wife that he is a tiger and in a moment she will see the proof. He then disappears on the pretext of going to the river for a drink. While he is gone a bird enters and warns her that Lundoyo is indeed a tiger not a man. An urgent, tuneless rhythm strikes up – drums, cymbals, rattling metal plates – the barong's theme played with a vengeance. Within the curtain, incense is lit and a man is put into trance. Then, as the bird makes its escape and the barong looks on from the sidelines, the curtain flies open and a 'tiger' is unleashed, dashing into the crowd and out of the arena into the street. In the collective panic one sees only the small grimacing head, upraised and shaking violently as it strains and plunges forward. People run screaming in all directions, scrambling to safety behind tables or into the street. The tiger's handlers hang onto it, as if pulled along, and steer it away from danger. The masked head seems alive, frenzied, so that one only notices its human bearer when the handlers have brought it under control and dragged it to the floor. Nearby, another man goes into trance and begins prancing and rearing like a wild horse. Someone thoughtfully provides a bowl of water and leaves which he now begins to chomp and slurp. As it calms down, the tiger, too, claps its jaws and gobbles up a few leaves.

The moment of unmasking is almost as dangerous as the instant of possession and requires expert knowledge. The man who first summoned the spirit, impressively solemn in Javanese turban and black pantaloons, comes forward to take control. (He is none other than the shrine caretaker.) He first restrains the trancer while others lift off the mask, then wrestles with him, rolling about in the dust. Finally, he blows gently on the trancer's head and watches him come round. (A false note or missed beat in the orchestra at this point can propel him back into trance.)

There is no curtain call to round off the show and few stay to see normality restored. Already satisfied, and comparing the finale with others they have witnessed, the villagers are on their way home. As day breaks the scene is already half empty.

Problems of interpretation

What does the barong show tell people about the guardian spirit and his place in village life? Since the spirit possession is part of the drama, serving as its climax, one might expect the ensemble of scenes to provide a commentary on the activities surrounding the shrine. But this is hardly the case. Whereas the Balinese barong manifests supernatural power in a meaningful and appropriate context – the endless struggle between good and evil – the Javanese godling is presented in an inconsequential, even trivial, setting. At an explicit level, the story of Lundoyo provides a rationale for Buyut Cili's appearance, but the real significance of the spirit possession lies outside the dramatic context. The performance is really doing two different things: it has a simple (partly commercial) aim, which is to entertain; but it also has an implicit didactic one, which is to showcase the power of the village guardian. In the context of Javanese cultural politics this double nature is important: what remains implicit is safe from criticism.

At the superficial level of plot not much of significance occurs. As villagers are quick to point out, the stories are not 'about' anything, nor do the characters represent anything other than themselves. There are none of the moral dilemmas of *kéthoprak* (popular historical dramas) or the symbolic clashes of the *wayang* (shadow play). All one can point to are differences in the seriousness of the different sections and in the quality of the audience's attention. The dialogue and much of the action are improvised around invariable scenarios, but in the clown scenes the storyline gets buried under comic invention. (Not that the clowns take their comedy lightly: Oarsman visits the grave of a popular predecessor before each performance and 'asks for his humour'.) In contrast the Lundoyo section is focused and plot-driven with little opportunity for innovation; its action moves inexorably towards the tiger-possession. The first and last parts of the show – those which attract the biggest crowds – thus provide maximum contrast in tone as well as in style of performance.

There is no explicit narrative link between the main sections, though there are recurrent elements and themes which help to integrate the performance: abduction by tigers and spirits, the contest between village and forest inhabitants, the interventions of bird-figures, absent husbands and unfaithful wives, gandrung dancers and transvestites, and, not least, the overlapping of roles so that each player takes several – often similar – parts. No doubt this dreamlike doubling of themes, elements, and roles explains why spectators and even performers find it difficult to give a sequential outline of plots, even though in performance there is rarely confusion.

Lacking a manifest discursive meaning, can one point to a deeper significance embedded in the structure of the drama, a symbolic code or scheme of possibilities, as these permutations of motif seem to suggest? Putting aside, for the moment, the objections that spectators themselves acknowledge no deeper significance and that such schemes are bound to be arbitrary to a degree, it is undeniable that a structuralist analysis is suggestive.

The ensemble of scenes seems to be organized around a set of oppositions turning on that of nature versus culture (forest/village, heavens/village, spirits/humans, wild beasts/humans). As this series of pairs indicates, the natural and spiritual realms are analogous, even equated, in their opposition to the human world; nature is represented as charged with occult powers. Humans are both attracted to and repelled by this otherworld, and various relationships, successful and unsuccessful, are made across the boundary. A heavenly nymph marries a man and is reclassified as a yard spirit; a woman is seduced and preyed upon by a were-tiger. Humans can deal with the otherworld by magic – Suwarti's father burns incense and gets her back from a tiger. But the boundary is permeable both ways: another tiger, Lundoyo, similarly uses magic to enter the world of humans. The ubiquitous bird figure appears as a mediator, an envoy of the barong, weaving in and out of scenes and between the realms of spirits and humans. The barong itself, as one of the players suggested to me, can be considered as a composite of the forest denizens: he has the jaws and palm-fibre fur of the ape-demons and the wings of the bird. As such he is analogous to the Balinese barong who is Lord of the Beasts. But his name is Sri Budoyo which means Mr Culture! And he is half-domesticated, tamed by the art of the gandrung, so he belongs clearly to no single category.

Most of the action takes place *between* worlds in a paradoxical, dreamlike setting in which normal identities are ambiguous. Distinctions of gender and animality/humanity are shifting and obscured – hence the constant puzzled refrains of the clowns, 'Man or beast?', 'Male or female?' The audience is aware, too, of theatrical ambiguities – the fact that the two gandrungs are both in reality transvestites or androgynes (*wandu*) and that in former times most gandrungs were actually males offering a dubious erotic entertainment. (Buyut, culturally conservative, is said not to permit female gandrungs in his show.) The were-tiger theme in particular plays on man–beast, onstage–offstage ambiguities,

Lundoyo being an actor playing a tiger who becomes a man, who then resumes (offstage) his feline form and is substituted by a masked man-tiger. The doubling of roles further undermines a sense of fixed identity. And the action continually leads to paradox and inversion – a boatcrew finds itself adrift in a forest; a barong dies and comes back to life; humans marry spirits, and so on.

These are characteristics of a liminal world of the kind commonly enacted in rites of passage and represented in sacred dramas (Turner 1969). Though the plot is not *about* Buyut Cili, the scenarios imaginatively expand on the marginal otherworld he inhabits and the ambivalence of humans confronted by it. If the show as a whole cannot be regarded as a rite of passage (from what, to where?), like carnival it borrows the transformative techniques of ritual – masking, cross-dressing, percussion – to challenge and turn the everyday world upside down. As David Napier writes, in his fascinating study of masking (1986:16):

The presence of masks in situations relating to transition is so commonly the rule that exceptions to it are hard to find. Whether the change is from one social status to another or in the conscious states of the mask wearers or of their audiences, again and again mask users or their observers or both attest to some change in conjunction with a mask's presence ... these various transitions are recognized through alterations in point of view and through the ambiguities – the illusions and appearances – to which those alterations give rise.

Our problem, shortly, will be to question what kind of transition is being effected or mimed. For the moment, I want to draw attention to the most important transition in the performance.

In the finale the inversions and transformations multiply and reverberate, seemingly pressing towards some sort of conclusion as Lundoyo returns to his tiger form and Buyut Cili breaks loose. But the dénouement, a literal unravelling, is less a resolution of preceding concerns than yet another inversion, this time of the popular theme of the suitor's challenge. Natural justice demands the restoration of Mantri's wives, but this does not happen. With the unsatisfying triumph of usurper over cuckold the narrative gives place to what is evidently the real climax of the performance, when the threads of the story are simply blown away in a final explosion of energy. Stage conventions – character and dialogue, the suspension of disbelief, the enclosed world of the stage – are abandoned at this point and the performance moves into a different register, with the transition marked abruptly by fierce percussion and the approach of dawn (see Needham 1967). It is inappropriate, therefore, to ask what happens to the wife or the bird at the end, as if the spirit possession were bounded within the same dramatic form; and when I did ask, not surprisingly, I drew a blank. For the same reason, no one seems to have thought out the interconnexions between characters in the drama and the spirits. Mantri's wives, Siti Sendari and Siti Ambari, are in 'reality' the wife and daughter of Buyut Cili. But no one draws a parallel between Mantri (a Malay-speaking outsider) and Buyut; nor does anyone imagine that Buyut, in tiger form, is reclaiming his wife from Mantri. This would be to confuse artifice and reality in a way unintended by the performers. In fact, the story is constructed in such a way that Buyut's violent intrusion is dramatically justified, indeed expected; but once it happens the context changes and so too does the stance of spectators – they are no longer an audience of guests watching actors in an enclosed arena, but villagers confronting their guardian spirit (this is the 'alteration in point of view' to which Napier refers). This much is evident, too, in the fact that many of the onlookers at the end are not among those who came earlier as guests. For these, and for guests who return at dawn, the spirit possession is a self-contained event.[4]

The barong as performance

Having identified this shift of perspective as the key to understanding the significance of the barong show *as spectators experience it*, I want to look further at how the shift is effected. In order to go beyond a structural, 'textual' analysis, we need, first, to make a distinction between pro-duction – what goes into the show – and performance, which is the event in all its dimensions, comprising the production, interaction with the audience, and the nature of the occasion as a whole. As we have seen, an attempt to reduce the performance to the production, or to treat it as a bounded text with its own conventions and inner structure can only take us so far.

Like many other Javanese entertainments, the show is watched in snatches and does not rely on a cumulative effect. Nobody sits through the whole performance. Since guests only stay long enough to eat, pay their respects, and make a contribution, they see only a small part of the show, if indeed they take any notice of it at all. Only the host family and sundry helpers remain throughout the night, but they are usually too busy to take more than a passing interest. And even the most avid barong-goers (mostly small boys) doze off during the *longueurs* of the small hours. The festive context of the performance thus favours an episodic structure.

The dramaturgical differences between sections which I have highlighted reflect different dramatic intentions and evaluations of the content, and these respond to a range of expectations in the audience. Much of the action takes place in an imaginary forest, Alas Driboyo, peopled by sprites and monsters with no local significance. Such scenes are familiar from other forms of popular theatre and evoke only a casual interest. But the last section commands a different kind of attention from participants and spectators alike. With Lundoyo we leave the fantasy world of the travelling show and enter the sacred geography of the region: a twilight world of signs and portents, built out of personal encounters with the occult, stories of haunted spots, and historical legend. Lundoyo is thought to be a tiger spirit in Buyut Cili's circle who inhabits Alas Purwo, the forest at the eastern tip of Java and scene of the final action. Alas Purwo originally covered the whole area and is steeped in symbolic and historical significance. During my stay there were several pilgrimages to the forest to visit Hindu sites and meditate in caves. One of these caves is believed to be inhabited by Lundoyo.

If the painted scenery merges with the outside world – perhaps one should say the *inner* world, the sacred inscape of Blambangan and Alas Purwo – the action, too, borrows from and spills over into the world beyond the stage. (Literally, since the tiger runs out of the arena into the street – the only such exit in the show.) The climax of the performance, the spirit possession, is a real event, however one explains it, not a fiction. It deals with perceived realities outside the dramatic context. The transition from fantasy to supernatural reality thus also marks a change in dramatic technique from make-believe to *make believe*. The spirit of Buyut Cili is summoned from his shrine and enters the performer as the mask is attached. After all the play-acting and doubling, the distinction between performer and role vanishes: this is Buyut Cili playing himself. The personality of the trancer is suppressed, his body becoming a mere 'vessel' for the spirit which not only possesses him but transforms him (*jalma*) into another being. This is why, ideally, he should be a simple soul, 'vacant', with no resistance to supernatural invasion. Evidence of possession (*kasurupan*) is confirmed by certain signs. The trancer has an abnormal strength; he is indifferent to the rough handling he receives; and he is obviously dissociated and dazed when the performance is over, unaware of what has passed. The manner in which the mask is borne depends on achieving trance. It does not fit over the head of the performer like the mask in *réyog* but is held at arm's-length between the rigid, flat palms of his hands, his head and back being covered by the cloth body of the mask. Once the performer is in trance (*dadi*) the mask is said to be fused to his body and cannot be wrenched free. Quite how he manages to eat the leaves put before him is something only the performer could know, though he claims to be conscious of nothing; but that he does so is 'proved' by the fact that he sometimes vomits the leaves up as he comes round. (Standing back from the welter of impressions, one notes again the paradox of a vegetarian tiger.)

In the eyes of spectators, the authenticity of the possession marks an important difference from trance-dances put on solely for entertainment, such as the *jaranan*, which are assumed to involve trickery as well as a half-believed meddling with spirits. As I was often told, outsiders disbelieve in the powers of Buyut at their peril. When the barong was hired for a wedding at Kenjo, a youth kicked the tiger head and fell into a fit ('possession') which lasted some hours. But as with unshared sightings of were-tigers, inconsistency or partial failure does not tend to provoke scepticism. A degree of scepticism is even assumed, but this is directed at specific instances rather than at the whole phenomenon. The usual attitude is that one must look at each case individually: some possessions are authentic, others may be half-willed or incomplete. Why? Perhaps the percussion was mistimed, or the spell incorrect; or perhaps daylight was breaking and Buyut would not come out.

Let me sum up. We have seen that the plot provides a narrative link between the melodrama of Lundoyo and the dawn spirit possession, but that this link is undermined, even denied, by the change of perspective participants bring to bear at the pivotal moment. In a sense, Lundoyo's *coup de théâtre* points up a characteristic of the whole show: its generic diversity. The ingenuity of its makers cannot disguise the fact that, unlike the Balinese barong, the combination of indigenous and non-local elements does not make for a harmonious synthesis within a unified dramatic framework. Like its eponymous hero, the barong show of Bayu remains a hybrid, a curious and outlandish creature pulling in opposite directions. Consequently, it makes little sense to ask what the show means as a whole, as if it had one author and belonged to a single tradition. And we must resist the urge to infer a general conception or intention from one section to another – to see Buyut Cili's appearence in the finale as little more than a circus turn, or, conversely, to regard the clowning as part of a sacred ritual simply because the show climaxes in collective effervescence.

Instead, I have highlighted the varying purposes of different sections and the changing relation of performance to reality, identifying a movement from fantasy through a representation of occult reality to an invocation and manifestation of the occult. I have also shown that this progression corresponds to a change in attention from mild engagement to captivation.

The appearance of the tiger is a vivid reminder to villagers of the power of the supernatural world epitomized in Buyut Cili: this is what they come back at the end to see, and this is the impression they retain as the new working day dawns and the comic routines of the night fade from memory. What seems to be missing, however, is a more clearly articulated relation to the workaday world which would give significance to the play and put the supernatural aspect into a meaningful social context. The ingenuities of plot serve only to mask this gap. The perennial themes are here in plenty – love and marriage, men and the gods, male versus female, civilization versus savagery – but they are rendered in caricature. It is not clear why this should be so, given that Javanese villagers, in general, have higher expectations of their popular arts. Our problem, then, is the negative one of explaining insignificance. Is it a consequence of the expressive limitations of a rough-hewn dramatic style or is there a deliberate evasion of meaning?

Meaning and legitimacy

In the last chapter we encountered many examples of the overdetermination of meaning, often based on the simplest of materials. Here the reverse seems to be the case. There is a general disavowal of meaning and a refusal to draw conclusions reflecting on the wider world.

Folk performances may, of course, be significant in a broad sense without containing an explicit message. But there is, in the barong, a studied irrelevance which is uncharacteristic of a regional culture devoted to symbolic meaning. In foregrounding the guardian spirit but refusing adequately to contextualize him the performance draws attention to the obscurity and secrecy that surrounds Buyut and to the contradiction between his ritual importance and his exile on the margins of village life. Unlike the spirit of neighbouring Cungking, whose veneration is open and whose exorcistic functions are explicit, Buyut cannot really be regarded as the object of a cult: the activities surrounding him are too dispersed and ideologically unfocused. Nothing of any significance is said to him at the shrine, and nothing is said about him in the barong – or in any other setting, for that matter. His powers are acknowledged but there is no acceptable language in which they can be discussed. The vacuity of the barong show is symptomatic of this predicament.

The contrast with Islam, the official faith, is instructive. Village Islam and the practices centred on Buyut have in common a taken-for-granted, unarticulated nature, but this is underpinned, in each case, by quite different conditions: an easy assumption of prerogative on the one hand, and a discreet cautiousness on the other. The unquestioned position of Islam is evident in the use of Arabic prayers in ordinary Javanese ritual (distinct from canonical Islamic ritual which is practised only by a minority). Almost no one – pious or otherwise – understands the prayers; they mean little (semantically) to the people who recite them; but their inclusion in slametans and other rituals such as those surrounding birth and childhood is obligatory. Nominal Muslims, even among themselves, would not think of omitting them. In contrast, one who disbelieved in the powers of the guardian spirit would be free to ignore him. Furthermore, whereas there is no *need* to justify or explain the saying of prayers or to elucidate their meaning, in the rival case there is no *possibility* of explication. To ask why ancestors and spirits are propitiated or to speculate about the powers of the guardian spirit would be to bring to light incongruities between antagonistic practices. Awkward questions might disturb the delicate consensus and force people to take positions, raising the spectre of contradiction and conflict.

This suggests a power differential, but the situation is complicated by the fact that the rival traditions are shared by the same set of people, though individuals have different stakes in them. Almost everyone acknowledges himself or herself as, in some sense, a Muslim; and almost everyone visits the shrine once in while. Nominal Muslims may control the shrine, but among the regular visitors are some of the most prominent pious Muslims. Their presence gives the shrine a certain respectability – doubters can reassure themselves with the thought that 'if the modin attends it must be all right'. Correspondingly, the modin is able to attend because everything to do with Buyut Cili – whether at the shrine or in the barong – is conveniently unarticulated, below the threshold of dogma or system, devalued, *vis-à-vis* religion, as mere *adat* (custom, tradition).[5]

Given this pattern of ecumenism and tolerance, one cannot speak of dominant groups or persons, only of dominant modes of religiosity. The source of Islam's privileged position is outside the local context, embodied in the state, not in a category of pious villagers. It is the state, in its educative and repressive functions, which authorizes Islam (and other approved religions) as the dominant form and which disqualifies certain practices as 'superstition' or mere 'beliefs'. For several reasons this bureaucratic authority does not translate into personal power at a lower level. In the first place, authority is exercised not by pious villagers but by agents of the state – the headman, the schoolmaster (who can compel his pupils to observe the Fast and punish their laxity), the district officer, and the police. These officials can prohibit 'heathen' practices, refuse permission for gatherings or performances which contradict their own principles, and they can harass villagers who express dissent on religious matters. However, with the exception of the headman, they generally have little to do with the daily lives of villagers and, in any case, they may have no interest in promoting Islam. Second, most nominal Muslims do not regard their minimal participation in Islam as a concession to the pious and do not feel in any way obliged to them. Almost all accept Islam as part of their heritage: what they differ about is its importance relative to other traditions. Third, in villages like Bayu where allegiance to Islam is not an exclusive identity, unequal factions based on religious orientation cannot easily form. It was partly for this reason that Bayu escaped the worst of the bloodshed in 1965 when political strife, based on older cultural antagonisms, led to the decimation of many nominally Islamic communities throughout Java.

The privileged position of Islam thus gives the pious very little leverage over the less committed. As a means to respectability and influence, piety counts for less than wealth, education, and political connexion. What Islam does achieve, however, is the effective censorship of ideas which may appear to threaten it. Indeed, it is doubtful whether a focused and explicit cult around a guardian spirit could withstand the hostility of institutional Islam. It would quickly become an identifiable and vulnerable target. Or else, like the cult in neighbouring Cungking (described in the next chapter), it would have to develop a degree of sophistication and accommodate to other sanctioned forms of religious knowledge – in that case, mysticism.

Buyut's is the cult that dare not speak its name. And the barong, as his showcase, cannot but reflect this predicament. If we want to understand the role of the guardian spirit in village life we must therefore look outside the narrative frame of the show, with its muted, undeveloped symbolism, to the ritual uses of the barong and to Buyut's function as exorcist. Only then, can we come back to the question of whose interests are served by the form of the show, by its persisting popularity, and by its claims to importance.

Ritual uses of the barong

There is no doubt among villagers as to which parts of the performance are important. The show begins and ends with the barong and thus with Buyut Cili, its keeper. The barong's appearance and the tiger-spirit possession are, in terms of village welfare, the only parts of the show that matter: the rest is entertainment. Apart from full-scale performances, the barong is also brought out on important occasions such as the annual *slametan desa*, when it is paraded through the village in a sort of mystical spring cleaning (analogous to the barong's exorcistic role in Bali). Lebaran, the feast after the fasting month, is similarly regarded as a time of renewal when people rid themselves of the year's accumulated resentment. Again, this event is not complete without a parade through the village accompanied by bird figures and the percussion orchestra. Failure to do so would result in plague or famine. A procession at weddings and circumcisions, with or without a full performance, is also thought to confer protection.

The barong and its counterpart, the tiger, keep epidemics at bay and protect the village from marauders, whether human or supernatural. Both are said to be Buyut's *rawatan*, his creatures or minions; but he is only incarnated in the tiger. One might say the two masks (cut from the same tree) personify Buyut's complementary aspects, the benevolent and protective versus the demonic and dangerous.

In Indian iconography similar attributes are combined in the figure of the *bhoma*, or Face of Glory, which Napier (1986: 144–5) sees as a prototype of the barong. These monstrous heads guarded thresholds and the entrances to Hindu-Javanese temples, as they still do today in Bali. The Bayu barong, with its massive head and outspread wings (analogous to the *bhoma*'s hands) is particularly reminiscent of this figure.

The materials of the barong suggest further connexions with the pre-Islamic past. In Indian cosmogony (known in Java through the wayang and mystical texts) the white sap from certain trees flowed into the ocean to become the elixir of immortality (Napier 1986: 160, 212). Barong masks – including that of Bayu – are traditionally made from the wood of the *pule* tree.

Pule is one of the sacred trees that, because of its milky sap, has extraordinary *rasa*; it possesses so much of this powerful life force that it may, as may other milky trees in both Bali and India, become the residence of a demonic spirit. *(210)*

We can now, perhaps, begin to see how the white-sapped *suko* tree came to be associated with Buyut Cili, were-tiger and barong owner; and why the resin burned at his slametans – and at no other – is derived from this sap. Indeed, since the tree no longer stands beside his shrine, the materialization of its resin is a magical manifestation of Buyut; it is his personal product. Every Thursday and Sunday night the caretaker burns the white resin beneath the barong mask to 'feed' it. The same action is also performed when, periodically, the barong and tiger masks are the object of meditation and ascetic practices (*tapa*) intended to strengthen and recharge them.[6]

If the masks are powerful, indeed dangerous, during performance, as vehicles of the spirit, at other times they remain potent reserves of *kasekten* (power). A sick person can be cured by drinking water which has been poured over the barong. The remedy is especially effective if someone has fallen ill during a performance. Only the shrine's principal caretakers are able to perform this service. They stress that neither of them has ever studied magic or learned special spells: their powers stem directly from their closeness to Buyut. The point of this disclaimer seems to be twofold. First they are not to be regarded as priests of a shadowy, unorthodox cult; second, they are not magicians manipulating spells and objects but innocent mediums for the benevolent power of Buyut.

Buyut himself is often asked, through mediums, the source and remedy of a particular ailment or run of bad luck. At one seance I attended in the shrine, a man was instructed to search his house for sorcerer's medicines which may have been planted there bringing bad luck. Buyut's voice – spoken in a stage-whisper by the medium – also warned the man to beware of a neighbour who had been his rival for a woman and who may have been practising sorcery against him. This kind of private consultation seems to be quite common, but despite the provocative nature of the disclosures such things rarely cause conflict unless they converge with wider disturbances in society. During the independence struggle and the period of lawlessness of the early years of the republic, and again during the upheavals of the 1960s, 'anti-social elements' – whether political agitators, criminals, or alleged sorcerers – were disposed of in a general 'cleansing'. Buyut, through his mediums, was a source of accusations against sorcerers and magicians. The fact that his victims were often prominent Muslims only serves to underline the point that the shrine and the prayer-house are not contrasted as, respectively, the homes of heathen magic and religion. To the contrary, magic is felt to be within the orbit of practical Islam (however it may offend against dogma), as it depends on a mastery of Arabic spells. In contrast, Buyut is 'pure' (*suci*) and cannot be employed either to cause harm or to obtain selfish ends.

His powers and those of his creatures are exercised benignly, even if their manifestations are sometimes terrifying and demonic.

Brief history of the barong – or how the tiger got his spots

Although associated in popular imagination with Bayu, in fact the barong show derives originally from Dandang Miring, an Osing quarter of Banyuwangi. Balinese settlements in town and elsewhere may have had their own *barong kèt*, but Dandang Miring had the only *Javanese* barong troupe in the area. Although the resemblance to the Balinese barong is close and influence seems plain enough, the troupe leader, Sukib, is said to have made the barong according to his own imagination – hence the unusual features such as wings.

In the late 1920s Sukib, then old and infirm, agreed to sell the barong and its orchestra to Salimah of east Bayu. Salimah was one of the caretakers of the village shrine and a spirit medium; and it was at Buyut Cili's request that he made the first approach. However, since some of the Dandang Miring troupe were unwilling to part with their barong, Sukib agreed to make a copy of the original (see photo in Brandts Buys and Brandts Buys-Van Zijp 1926). My neighbour, a carpenter, helped cut down the *pule* tree from which the barong head was made; what remained was used to fashion the other mask. Since no one had ever seen a real tiger the result was anatomically something between a tiger and a spotted leopard (the word *macan* covers both species). Before they could be used, both masks were fed incense and asked for a sign that their bearers would be acceptable to Buyut. After 'forty-four' days of fasting and veneration (*puja*), a sign was given – no one can remember what – and the equipment was pronounced ready.

It seems that Bayu had 'always' had some kind of barong pageant coupled with a tiger-possession – so, at least, the oldest villagers affirm. Salimah's contribution was to revive a moribund folk performance and turn it into a full-scale show which had both ritual and commercial uses. He was able to capitalize on existing skills in that the village had previously boasted a masked drama group. But he also drew on a wide network of regional arts, experimenting with scenarios from local and east Javanese sources (the Panji cycles, Damar Ulan) and scavenging props from other troupes. All this was done, it should be remembered, at the behest of the guardian spirit. For reasons no one questioned, Buyut Cili wanted a new show to replace the *seblang* trance-dance which he now ordered to be moved to neighbouring Olehsari.[7]

The double nature of the barong performance was thus established from the beginning: mediums became maskers and Buyut Cili was brought out of the shrine and put on the stage. As on a number of later occasions, villagers in a weak position were able to mobilize support and enhance their situation by appeal to the authority of a supernatural source to which they had privileged access. From the outset, both the barong and (less exclusively) the shrine have remained under the control of a group of related families in east Bayu. The semi-professional troupe of twenty-five are mostly kinsmen. Consistent with this dual role as performers and guardians of a tradition, most of the members are middle-aged men, not the juniors who usually take the roles in popular Javanese drama.

Why Buyut should have decided to revive the barong at this particular moment is something nobody could explain, so I can only speculate. Islam was not yet perceived as a threat to traditional practices; and politically, at village level at least, it was a relatively uneventful period. Economically, however, it was a testing time for the poorer villagers, who were mainly concentrated in east Bayu. The depressed economy and various contingent factors had led to many of them losing their land and becoming sharecroppers or wage labourers. But work was scarce and there was a need to supplement incomes from new sources. The new show was a tremendous commercial success and went on tours as far afield as Situbondo, a heavily Madurese area in the north. One of the veterans of those days told me he was so often away from home that his plough ox died for want of care.

But evidently some kind of legitimacy in the home village was needed as well – otherwise, one could rate the barong as no different from other folk arts which have come and gone in the recent history of the village. Whether this need was to offset a decline in status among the newly landless or to counter a growing indifference towards the shrine they controlled is difficult to ascertain. At any rate, it seems that Buyut Cili needed a more public stage to reinforce his following, and what better advertisement (and admonition to sceptics) than the climax of the barong show. Salimah, in whom all currents converged, seized the opportunity.

Some years after this auspicious launch Salimah was succeeded as group leader (*pengarep*) by his son, and the barong has remained within a related group of families ever since. The few who do not belong to this close-knit group are invited to join by Buyut Cili, either through dreams or visions or by the mediation of his spokesmen. A request may not be refused. One villager – now a popular ape-demon – was plagued with illness until he joined.

The format of the show, too, is protected by appeal to the authority of Buyut. Local cultural bureaucrats who wish to 'develop' folk arts for nation-building and tourist potential bemoan the fact that the Bayu barong is immune to improvement and unlikely ever to match the quality or appeal of the Balinese barong. The troupe's resistance to change is put down to peasant stubbornness and a conservative insistence on the sacredness of the barong itself. But there are other interests involved. For members of the troupe, who are among the poorest in the village, the barong forms a steady source of income; moreover, a source over which they have exclusive control. A full-scale performance costs 125,000 rupiah (about £45 in 1992); and each of the principal players receives 5,000 rupiah, which compares well with the 2,000 rupiah to 4,000 rupiah they earn in their regular work. (The *pengarep*, who oversees the mystical safety of the performance and controls the possessing spirits, receives only a nominal fee.) Any effort to 'improve' or 'modernize' the barong would involve ceding control – and income – to outsiders. The troupe has steadily resisted such interference and Buyut Cili has conveniently backed them in their struggles, showing his displeasure 'in ways that had better not be disbelieved'. But the situation is paradoxical: the poorest section of the village, uneducated and without a voice in village affairs (without even the right to vote in some cases) operates a show which is essential to the well-being and prosperity of all. The barong men, liminal figures all, have capitalized on 'the ritual powers of the weak' (Turner 1969: 88). It is through their mediation that the guardian spirit makes known his wishes, and through their co-operation and supplication at the shrine that everyone's weddings and feasts run smoothly. Politically and economically marginal, they remain at the heart of village and family ritual. Buyut Cili's shrine has proved to be their sanctuary.

Consider what happened in the aftermath of the political killings of 1965–6. During the late Sukarno era the barong troupe was subject to the same general politicization as most groups and associations in Javanese rural society.[8] Based in the impoverished eastern section of Bayu, the barong was run by men with left-wing sympathies. In contrast, the rest of the village – for the most part slightly better-off small farmers – was dominated by followers of the Indonesian Nationalist Party (PNI) led by a Christian schoolteacher. (There were no representatives of Muslim parties.) After the coup in which the present military regime took power, around three-quarters of a million communists and alleged sympathizers all over Java were rounded up and killed by army units and civilian groups backed by the army (see Cribb 1990). In Bayu, the barong leaders were arrested and interrogated but were judged innocent of plans to overthrow the state. 'Only those who could write, like the village secretary, got killed', as a barong man explained to me. Nevertheless, the barong was 'implicated', its reputation tarnished, and the troupe was disbanded in case it should again serve as a vehicle for political agitation.[9]

At this point Buyut Cili made a timely intervention. The bottom rung of military supervision in Java is occupied by a person bearing the acronym Babinsa who is theoretically responsible for law and order in two or three villages (Tanter 1990: 221). After the 1965 coup, such low-ranking, often undisciplined, soldiers were an influential presence on the local scene, some even becoming temporary village headmen where a communist had previously reigned. The Babinsa responsible for Bayu was known to attend Buyut's shrine, in quest of magical strength, on his visits to the village. When he fell ill he contacted the caretakers and they happily informed him that Buyut Cili was miffed by the turn of events and had decided to 'bother' him. Before long the suspension was lifted.

This was the first step in the rehabilitation of the eastern bloc. But there remained a problem of leadership. The previous *pengarep*, nominally the troupe leader, was not allowed to continue as he was now on probation. No other senior figure in the troupe was free of left-wing association, so a replacement had to be sought from elsewhere. The PNI leader, who was the real power in the village at the time and the man responsible for turning over alleged communists to the authorities, took charge and set about reorganizing a show suitable to the professed unifying, modernizing theme of the New Order. This pattern was repeated in other villages of Banyuwangi where drama troupes were 'implicated' (as the political jargon has it).

Resistance to these organizational changes seems to have been muted. Once again, the only dissenting voice was that of Buyut Cili. One of the new organizers, a PNI man who had participated in death-squads, introduced some changes into the show. A story with a faintly proletarian theme – a landlord gets his come-uppance and his daughter marries a sharecropper – was thrown out as subversive and replaced by a tale adapted from the *janger* drama. There was no way of opposing these innovations directly. But the barong's keeper became ill with a rash and Buyut Cili's disapproval was divined: the new story contained a queen and therefore insulted his own pre-eminence in the village (only the barong may wear a crown). The PNI man was forced to withdraw.

The PNI head, who had effectively ruled the village throughout this period, appointed as troupe *pengarep* Pak K, his wife's uncle. Although he was not one of the 'barong family', and, as a resident of central Bayu, had no regular ties with the troupe members, Pak K was nevertheless something of an insider. He is one of the shrine's caretakers and is a locally famous dhukun, thus adding to the prestige of the troupe. The other members seem content enough with his position: he is not regarded as a political stooge and would not act against their interests. An occasional dissatisfaction with his leadership, however, is evident in the fact that, at the end of the show, he often gets bitten by the tiger as he brings the performer out of trance. As ever, Buyut Cili has the last word.

To conclude an account of a folk deity with these reminders of a national tragedy is to recognize that – whatever the local rivalries and intricate compromises which animate cultural politics at village level – the decisive moments in the recent history of the village and in the lives of its people have been played out on a wider stage and shaped by factors beyond their ken. Yet there is an analogy, perhaps, between the misleading busyness of the barong drama and the Orwellian industry of New Order historiography, each enterprise masking an unspeakable truth. If the events of 1965, as the government portrays them, are the charter myth of the New Order, there is a grim, half-repressed folk memory which contradicts the official version – a collective trauma of unacknowledged guilt, suffering, and victimization that cannot be told (one might almost say: cannot be thought) but which explains much about contemporary Indonesia – the emptiness of legitimate politics, the substitution of slogans for arguments, and not least the peculiar unreality of much of its popular culture. Such is the depiction of those bloody events – as something set apart, mythologized, taboo – that to mention them in a chapter about a spirit cult must seem like a digression; yet it is the final piece of the jigsaw puzzle which makes the picture – or at least one corner of it – appreciably clearer.

The old feelings are difficult to recover, buried as they are by a generation of propaganda and a well-grounded fear of authority. Barong members whose relatives were killed or whose houses were burned down speak of 'gratitude' to the village strongmen for sparing them, and of their own folly in being led astray by communist lies. For their part, the strongmen, who were Sukarnoists loyal to the old regime and had very mixed feelings about the new military government, claim they were motivated by a desire to protect the ignorant and innocent. By turning over a few ring-leaders for execution – under duress, they say – they had saved a much greater disaster. Had they not stopped truckloads of Muslim youths from Delik from coming in to murder and vandalize in Bayu? In any case, they argue, the half-dozen deaths in Bayu compare favourably with the slaughter in some neighbouring villages where Ansor (the Muslim youth organization) was allowed to run riot.[10]

One factor which saved a lasting resentment was the way in which civilian executions were organized. Each village handed over its quota of suspects for 'processing' at Kalibaru, a plantation in the east of the district. There they were interrogated and allocated for execution, imprisonment, or probation. Many hundreds were taken by military truck up a mountain road and halfway between Kalibaru and Jember were thrown over a cliff. (I met the driver of one of these trucks who told me there were twenty loads a day during the high-point of the killings.) Others, in batches of four or five, were sent to villages different from their origin where they were hacked to death by thugs. Each village – if it wanted to – was thus able to avoid having the blood of its own people on its hands. In many villages which had pronounced religious-cum-political factions there was enthusiastic communal killing and the army occasionally had to step in to maintain discipline (see Anon. 1986). But Bayu, like several other Osing villages around Banyuwangi, was culturally and socially well integrated. The divisions were sharp but recent and did not go deep. Moreover, only two or three villagers were killed by their own people (the killers have subsequently died in peculiarly unpleasant ways, suggesting a moral to some). Hence, the assumption of responsibility for the barong by the PNI men and the general acquiescence in this is, perhaps, less surprising than one might expect.[11]

Conclusion

The practices described in this chapter – mediumship, the propitiation of spirits, possession – might be said to belong to the indigenous strand of Javanese syncretism: the elementary forms of religious life in Java. But their simplicity is deceptive, and those seeking a straightforward reflection of social processes in ritual life will be disappointed. The difficulty is that such indigenous practices no longer form a coherent, distinct tradition – if indeed they ever did. They could not survive as such. And the practitioners themselves – the shrine's supplicants and the barong's spectators – are not simply peasant animists; they are simultaneously Muslims, co-villagers, and modern citizens, subject to the constraints that go with these identities. However much they try, actors cannot entirely separate their various roles. Thus, when the modin visits Buyut

Cili he asks a Muslim question (the origin of the turban); and by his very presence he affects the status of the shrine and its acceptability within village life. The shrine's regulars, for their part, are conscious of their delicate position on the fringes of respectability, ever mindful of the prerogative of Islam (backed, as it is, by the state), and they adjust their language accordingly. The interest of this situation evidently lies less in the intrinsic meaning of particular elements than in their combination and in the shifting, multiple affiliations of actors – much as in the barong itself.

As we have seen, the shrine is controlled by a disadvantaged group on behalf of the whole community: it is their sanctuary. The barong, in turn, serves as a means of demonstrating the powers of the guardian spirit and compelling belief while signalling the ritual importance of its keepers. But the performance is something of a screen, obscuring rather than displaying its significance. It is not, like the Balinese cockfight, 'a metasocial commentary ... a story they tell themselves about themselves', as Geertz characterizes his exemplar of cultural performance (1973c: 448). Indeed, it is far from clear what is being told to whom and by whom. The social relevance of the barong is denied; there is no social commentary, *meta* or otherwise.

The barong – by implication Buyut Cili – is vital to the community's welfare. But the guardian spirit remains a shadowy figure outside the flow of village life. The devaluation of Buyut Cili *vis-à-vis* the dominant faith can be summed up in two contrasting images. Dewa Ayu, the Balinese barong, is kept in a temple, the beloved object of ritual care and devotions. His Javanese counterpart, between shows, hangs from the rafters of a dingy room in east Bayu, where (with wings beating faintly) he hovers like a nightmare over the bed of Mr and Mrs Sapiki. As for Buyut himself, he remains the perpetual fugitive, exiled to a lowly shrine on the village boundary. His eclipse by a more powerful deity could hardly be plainer.

4

A Javanese cult

No ideas but in things.

William Carlos Williams

If the guardian spirit of Bayu is a shadowy and paradoxical figure, the spirit of neighbouring Cungking, despite his greater publicity, remains a conundrum. Buyut Cungking, as he is called, has a biography of sorts and a legacy of cryptic teachings; but the cult which surrounds him centres on a mystery: there is nothing definite about him; consequently, nothing about him can be challenged.

His story was related to me by the caretaker of his shrine.

The sage

The man who became the first caretaker – Lumut was his name – was already old when the story begins. He was childless and lived in great poverty. In those days Cungking was still surrounded by forest and Lumut used to spend his days there foraging for berries and edible roots. One afternoon, when it was growing dark and no longer safe to be out (there were tigers), he sat down on a stump and sighed in despair. Suddenly, as if from nowhere, a little old man appeared and asked him what was the matter. Lumut explained that he had found nothing to eat that day. The gnome pointed to a spot and told him to dig. Lumut quickly unearthed a hoard of wild tubers, more than he could carry. Amazed at his good fortune, he questioned the old man but could find out nothing: his benefactor seemed to have no home or village, no discernible origin. He would not accompany Lumut back to the village, promising to come another day. But he never came and Lumut soon forgot about him. Then, one day, when Lumut was out scavenging in the woods again, he came across a child, a small boy. He was dressed in white and his head was shaved except for a lock of hair at the back where a pigtail might be. This was not the only strange thing about him. He had no name, parents, or origin; he was a 'waif blown by the wind'. The childless Lumut invited him home and took him in. Only later did he remember the mysterious gnome and wonder at the connexion. But how could an old man become a boy?

Other things about the boy astonished and even alarmed Lumut. He would climb up a palm to fetch betelnuts and then slither down headfirst like a lizard; or he would run along the strings attached to scarecrows, laughing and holding up a miniature windmill in the breeze. Put to watch the fields, he would let the birds devour the crop; but somehow, when the sheaves were brought home at harvest the ears of rice would be full. Sometimes he would be put in charge of cattle and would take them outside the village to graze. One day Lumut decided to follow him. It turned out that the boy used to go all the way to Baluran, a wilderness on the north-east coast. There he would amuse himself sliding down a hill or collecting medicinal herbs. It was a mystery how he could show up in Cungking the same day. And when Lumut wanted to cook *gondho* leaves the boy would fetch them from Bali in less time than it took to boil the water.

This foundling 'without origin or destination', swift as the wind, mischievous but benevolent, and with forelock (*kun-cung*) to the rear (*wing-king*) is remembered today as Buyut (= Old Man, Great Grand-father) Cungking. Ostensibly unpromising material for a cult, he is revered as a person of magical power (*wong sekti*) and for his teaching. His following spans the range of Banyuwangi society, from plantation workers and peasants to Chinese shopkeepers and petty officials. As with saint cults worldwide, Buyut's moral and magical aspects, though closely connected in the minds of followers, appeal in different degrees. Some people emphasize his exemplary nature, others are drawn by his magical powers and see him principally as a source of blessing. But Buyut's teaching, unremarkable in itself, is compelling to the more contemplative of his followers because of what he was; and, on the other hand, even the most simple and credulous adherent sees his powers as an aspect of his moral virtue.

Combining virtue and power, Buyut Cungking was not a teacher in the conventional sense. He left no legacy of writing or sayings but taught by example: he himself was an example. His relics – an inscribed bracelet, a zodiac beaker, a blurred inscription on copper – and symbolic inventions such as the windmill, sum up the person himself: mute but pregnant with meaning, embodying a language of simple verities.

Buyut Cungking is identified in local legend with Wangsakarya, the adviser and spiritual preceptor (*guru*) to Tawang Alun (d. 1691). (Tawang Alun founded the last Hindu kingdom in Java at Macan Putih, a few miles south-west of present-day Banyuwangi.) Some say the boy-waif grew up to be the powerful magician and court guru; others say he was an earlier incarnation of Wangsakarya. But whatever the connexion, they are contrasting figures: the one a man of words, an historical person, the other a dealer in symbols – indeed, a symbolic personage. The identification – which not everyone accepts – is based on the widely held view that Buyut's shrine in Cungking is the resting place of Wangsakarya. Confusingly, but perhaps lending some support to the theory, there is also an obscure hamlet called Cungkingan next to the village – no longer a kingdom – of Macan Putih. This hamlet, like Cungking proper, was settled by Wangsakarya's followers.

Our knowledge of the guru Wangsakarya is limited to a few popular stories about his magical feats and accounts given in the court chronicles of Tawang Alun and his dynasty (Pigeaud 1932). But while these chronicles, completed in the nineteenth century, are unknown in present-day Banyuwangi except to a handful of scholars, a simpler oral tradition survives. The best-known story concerns Tawang Alun's trip to Mataram in Central Java, then the dominant power. The context of this possibly fictional journey is important (Pigeaud 1932: 249–51). In the previous generation, the Mataram empire-builder, Sultan Agung (d. 1647), had subjugated and destroyed the westerly part of Blambangan. After his death, sovereignty over Blambangan passed back and forth between Mataram and Bali until a new local strongman emerged. Tawang Alun established his state at Macan Putih, in the ruins of the old realm, and in 1676 he was finally able to shake off the yoke of loyalty to the Muslim overlord (Lekkerkerker 1923: 1043). The chronicles tell how he journeyed to Mataram with his adviser seeking recognition of his independent status. But the sultan's own guru, Kadilangu (Gatilopo in oral tradition), sought to humiliate the visitors; he asked for Wangsakarya's dagger, dissolved it in water and then swallowed it. Wangsakarya, left holding the empty sheath, was not to be outdone. He summoned his dagger and it burst from the body of Kadilangu, killing him in the process.

Pigeaud suggests this story is best seen as a fanciful triumph over the former conqueror of Blambangan and as a demonstration of the superiority of 'heathen' science over Islam (1932: 251). Wangsakarya emerges from it as an emblem of the buda religion and champion of traditional Javanese knowledge against the rival faith. Three centuries after his triumph, with the conquest of Islam all but complete, something of this consciously non-Islamic stance persists in the contemporary cult of Buyut Cungking, although the tone of confrontation has been drastically muted. In this sense, too, the guru and the foundling are one.

But one is left wondering at the transformation of the man of words and heroic deeds, conqueror of Islam, into the harmless, dumb, and strangely neuter guardian spirit. To echo Lumut, the cult's first votary: how could the wise old man become the boy? An unwritten and probably unrecoverable cultural history lies behind the answer, but a few simple facts tell much. Cungking was one of the last villages in Java, outside of the Tengger region, to hold out against Islam. According to Stoppelaar (1927: 28), an administrator in Banyuwangi in the early 1920s, it was the last village in the area to have a prayer-house, and that was only 'a few decades ago'. Van der Tuuk (*Encyclopaedie van Nederlandsch–Indië*, s.v. Balambangan) reported that Cungking was 'still entirely Sivaitic' in 1840, an astonishing 350 years after the defeat of Majapahit by Muslim forces. One can only speculate about what had become of the Hindu-Buddhist tradition by then. It is impossible to imagine the panoply of Sivaite priests and temple ceremonies surviving long under Dutch rule (since the Dutch installed Muslim regents) or public worship persisting in the face of a growing influx of Muslim immigrants which was transforming the whole character of the region. If Cungking was still buda in 1840, it cannot have been buda in the way Wangsakarya knew. One can imagine a preference for private forms of worship and esoteric symbolism, a stress on interior states rather than public piety – forms of compromise which characterize Javanism today. But the historical record is a blank; similarly, between 1840 and the present there is a gap which folk memory cannot fill. All one can say with certainty is that the historical reality of buda tradition has been lost entirely from view and with it any real sense of continuity. A religion – a way of life – was fragmented and absorbed into syncretic Javanist tradition and reformulated in much narrower terms. The epithet buda, which a few adherents use controversially of the Cungking cult, has come to stand for something else. Its meaning is contrastive, denoting the non-Islamic rather than the pre-Islamic (since no one knows any longer what that was). And this contrast with Islam is undoubtedly part of the cult's appeal.

Material symbols

Since there is nothing in the way of doctrine or explicit teaching in the Cungking cult, great emphasis is laid on the materials, the buildings and relics themselves, which have to speak for their originator. A good example is the treetop windmill (*giling*). One of the most familiar scenes in the Banyuwangi countryside is a vista of rice fields dominated by a row of windmills, their long slender blades turning on the tops of the tallest palms. These giant toys, which have no practical function, are human symbols, their constituent parts comprising a symbolic, if grotesque, anatomy. The curious, ungainly contraption which supports the blade has a 'fringe' of sugar-palm fibre, a bristling 'moustache' and, like its inventor, a 'forelock' at the rear – part of a counterbalance which trails in the wind like some outsize pigtail. The two halves of the blade are different: the 'male' half is thicker and slightly crooked (it is the bend which produces the vibration), the 'female' half is slighter and straighter, therefore silent, and is twisted at an opposite angle to the male. I asked the headman of Bayu to explain.

Men are superior in strength and capacity, they support the woman; so you carry the blade by shouldering the female section.

His wife corrected him:

It is women who are honest and 'straight' and have to put up with men in silence; men are devious and unfaithful.

The headman then conceded: 'The blade wouldn't turn without the female end.'

But it is the sound which is all-important. The bass note of a big giling – a deep throbbing whirr, vaguely menacing like some distant helicopter invasion – is a joy to enthusiasts. People planting in the fields look up from their work and 'forget their tiredness' as the whirring begins. Experts compare the tone and volume of their giling, reminisce about fine specimens, and miss no opportunity for installing them if a good steady wind is expected. (The best examples are too valuable to be left in place.) A windmill maker in Bayu checks the television weather forecast every night hoping for gales. Once, when the main news was a hurricane in Florida – scenes of flattened houses and swirling debris – he observed that 'We Osing would be up there fastening our windmills!'

Whether or not Buyut actually invented the giling, the symbolism of its parts is said to be his inspiration. One of my neighbours, Pak Surya, explained:

The windmill's movement depends on the wind, just as our life is breath. As it rotates it disperses heat, just as our bodies need and produce heat. It is self-correcting, adjusting its direction to the wind; just so, we must correct ourselves by introspection, watch our orientation (*mawas kiblat*). By *kiblat* I don't mean 'turn to Mecca', the Muslim's *kiblat* – one should orient oneself to what is important, whether it is north, south, east or west. A fixed windmill without a free axis would break, shattered by a gale from another direction. It means, also, that one should know how to place oneself relative to others. You are not just Andrew, you are the son of your father, the father of your child, the pupil of your teacher, and so on, and you behave accordingly. This is knowing one's place in both senses. The *doni* [fringe] means *aja wani-wani*, 'don't be overbold'; the *manggar* means *aja mlanggar*, 'don't transgress'; the *ginci* [a metal pin] means *pandai mrinci*, one must be 'clever at discriminating', distinguishing the important ethical principles. And so on.

The virtues expressed here – of self-correction, *politesse*, hierarchy, obedience, restraint, and adjustment to superior force – are typically Javanese. The emphasis on ego-centred relativism, which in a sense undermines, or at least *relativizes*, the other values is both Javanese and, especially, Osing, as is the faintly ironic adaptation of a Muslim concept, *kiblat* (Mecca as the sacred point of orientation). Strong winds blow from that direction, but one turns with them, and one is clever in discriminating!

For those who understand such things, Pak Surya pointed out, the giling represents the cycle of reincarnation (*cakra manggilingan*) and also the wheel of fortune.

I am on a downward path. My ancestor was a nobleman, an exile like Buyut Cungking, who founded Tamansari [a neighbouring village]; but since then we've lost ground and prestige. I myself was only a headman. And take my wife: I'm not saying I made a mistake in marrying her, but she's on the same steep descent; her family have been losing land for generations. If you marry someone who is going up, like Pak Sumo did, it can correct your own descent. But I sense our decline is bottoming out. Neither of my children works hard but they are doing well. Perhaps it's the spirit of my ancestor coming back.

And so the turning of the windmill, while distracting the weary peasant in his fields, is a reminder of life's vicissitudes, thrumming out the message: do not be complacent or hope for too much, but do not despair either. The function is epitomized in a rhyme-definition: *giling – kang lali bisa iling*, 'windmill: [so that] the thoughtless may become aware'.

Why should Buyut Cungking have chosen such an odd and amusing method of educating his followers? Pak Surya gave me an explanation which I often heard in connexion with problems of interpretation, whether of mystical symbols, the lyrics of the gandrung, or the meaning of a drama. When the Dutch began to assert control over the Javanese courts they feared the magical and ethical power of traditional knowledge and exiled or killed its exponents. Those who survived went underground, disguised as wandering hermits, traders, or beggars, biding their time for some later self-revelation. Others, exiled to remote areas like Banyuwangi, continued to spread their knowledge; but they did so in symbolic forms inaccessible to the colonial masters. These sages were called *pendéta* or *wali pendéta*. The terms call for exegesis. *Wali (yullah)*, 'apostle of God', rhymes with *polah*, 'doing', and is therefore said to mean 'teaching by example'. *Pendéta* (from Old Jav. *pandita*) is explicated as *pendidikan-kang-nyata*, 'tangible education', the science of the concrete or, as my epigraph has it: 'No ideas but in things.'[1]

The definitions are apt, but the history is dubious. Javanism, as found in Banyuwangi, seems to have lacked any hint of political resistance and cannot have been perceived as a threat to Dutch authority, so it is unlikely that the Cungking cult and other Javanist practices took their present form in response to Dutch oppression. The proto-nationalist account is belied by the continuing inhibition of Javanism – its failure to come out of the shadows in the post-Independence period. The abjuring of explicit doctrine and the corresponding recourse to symbolism are better understood as a response to Islam, which cannot have been similarly indifferent to Javanism. Popular history projects this compromise conveniently onto the past and thereby avoids identifying a more intimate and persistent adversary. But the true source of influence – a resurgent, institutionally powerful Islam – is everywhere felt.

Local traditions have made their compact with the dominant faith in different ways. As we saw in the last chapter, the price of survival in the case of Buyut Cili and the barong was to *mean nothing*, to abjure meaningful social comment; in the case of Buyut Cungking, it is to *say nothing* – everything in the cult being a matter of inference and interpretation.

However, this restraint – a form of self-censorship which characterizes most 'legitimate mysticism' in Java today (Stange 1986) – does not, in the case of Cungking, imply a definite withdrawal from society. The cult is not a quietist sect. To the contrary, its followers remain active members of the community – headmen, minor officials, as well as ordinary farmers and tradesmen; and the rituals of the cult form a central part of village life. Nothing emphasizes this fact more than the position of the cult house and the shrine in village space.

Buildings of the cult

Cungking lies on the edge of Banyuwangi, bordered on its west and south by rice paddies and on its east and north by the urban district of Mojopanggung, to which it now belongs. The town has expanded to meet the outlying settlements, and the green fields which once separated villages have mostly been lost to haphazard development. Though it is now a semi-urban kampung rather than an agricultural *desa*, Cungking retains the appearance and much of the character of a typical Osing village. The form of the settlement, with its narrow streets of closely packed houses, is Osing rather than urban: the crowding is (or was originally) a matter of custom rather than demographic necessity. The dwellings, too, are the houses of villagers – narrow and trim, with red-tiled roofs and whitewashed walls of split bamboo, dirt floors, cleanswept front yards, and fences overgrown with hibiscus and festooned with washing. Away from the din of traffic on the main road, the noise is that of a village – chickens fussing in yards, bicycle bells, songbirds in ornate cages. People still go to the river to wash and gossip. One has a sense of life lived outdoors, in yards and between houses.

The buildings of the cult – unspectacular, even drab – blend unobtrusively into this village scene. Only if one remembers that two miles away is the town centre, with its bustling market, raucous bus station, and government offices, is one forced to recognize incongruity and anachronism. For the buildings hark back to an earlier period. Their materials and design are not simply conservative but archaic: thatched roofs instead of tiles, an obsolete three-ply bamboo weave for the walls, rattan ties instead of nails or screws.

The two foci of the cult are the shrine (*kandhapan*) which dominates the village cemetery and a meeting house (*bale tajug*) which forms part of a complex of buildings in the heart of the village. Most rituals oscillate between the two centres. The shrine is also referred to as a *pasaréan*, 'resting place', a euphemism which usually means tomb. Nevertheless, many people say that, like similar holy figures, Buyut Cungking vanished or dematerialized leaving no remains.

Like the windmill, the buildings are a sort of condensed ethical guide: edifices for edification. Their messages are conveyed through visual analogy and puns. Just as the medieval Javanese pavilion (*bale*) was inscribed with poetic graffiti for the pleasure and enlightenment of way-farers (Zoetmulder 1974: 138), the buildings of the cult comprise a text-cum-sanctuary. As adherents themselves put it, to contemplate the shrine is to 'read' its signs. The difference from the pre-Islamic pavilion – and it is a difference which epitomizes a history – is that the message is only to be inferred: Buyut Cungking dealt solely in symbols (*perlambang*).[2]

The methods of interpretation are familiar from slametan exegesis. Half-rhymes and wordplay suggest that the *bale tajug* (pavilion with pyramidal roof) is the cynosure or destination (*jujugan*) of many; and the shrine itself (*kandhapan*) reminds one of the need to *andhap asor*, act with humility. Both structures have thatched roofs, *atep lalang*, showing the virtue of *tetep* ('to remain, endure') and *langgeng* (that which is 'eternal'). Devotees know how to read every part of the structures, even down to such details as the fibre which fastens the bamboo panels and which signifies mystical austerities.

The messages seem uncontroversial, even platitudinous, and hardly require a disguise; but they direct one to a wider contemplative world which lies outside mainstream religious orthodoxy – a zone of 'inward-ness' disclosed by signs and symbols – and they exemplify a way of thinking which contrasts with the literal-mindedness of the dominant faith. Just how far practice departs from orthodoxy will become apparent from a description of the rituals themselves.

Ritual in Cungking

The slametan

Before considering the main event of the Cungking year, the cleaning of the relics, I will first describe a *slametan Buyut*, a ritual meal analogous to those already described in previous chapters but with important differences. The general sequence of a slametan – the invocation over incense, the formal address by a delegate over symbolic foods before witness-guests, the closing Arabic prayer – is by now familiar. So how is it done in Cungking?

Preparations

A few days before the slametan one goes to the caretaker (*juru kunci*, 'keyholder'), who lives behind the *bale*, to give formal notice of one's intention. On the day of the meal – Thursday or Sunday, as with any ordinary slametan, reckoned as the 'eve of Friday' and 'eve of Monday' – one brings the ingredients: a chicken, two kilos of uncooked rice, a newly fallen coconut, spices, banana leaves, and firewood.

In all the preparations there is a greater emphasis than usual on purity. The chicken is washed by the caretaker or his deputy no less than three times – before and after killing it, then again after it has been plucked. It must be a 'flawless white' male, with pale beak and claws, and it should not yet have been mated. Buyut himself was clad in white, had white blood, and 'never kissed a woman'. The correspondence is not meant to suggest a sacrificial substitution; rather, 'what is pure must be approached by means of what is pure'. For the same reason, the cooking must be done by a woman past menopause who is deemed to be free of sexual urges. Usually it is the caretaker's sister who performs this office, for which she is paid 2,000 rupiah. While cooking she may not taste or even smell the food, as it must be offered intact (*utuh*). Likewise, the flowers which the sponsor brings for the slametan may not even be sniffed – nothing may detract from their wholeness – and any damaged ones are discarded.

Purity is associated with physical integrity and freedom from blemish. This is why a person with a running sore may not attend a slametan, nor may a woman during her period. (Indeed, some people thought that it was inappropriate for fertile, sexually active people to attend at all.) But supplicants stress that outward purity must correspond to an inner purity and singleness of motive: one would not attend if troubled by bad feelings towards someone or straight after a quarrel. As we have seen, these conditions apply loosely to the ordinary slametan, but usually they are justified by appeal to the social virtues of mutuality and whole-heartedness rather than purity.

Compared with the standard slametan, there is a greater stress on rules. Even the treatment of firewood involves strict stipulations. The wood may not be stepped over, and it must be carried from home to the *bale* kitchen with its ends pointing the same way; that is, the root ends must not be placed alongside the upper ends, which would be to confuse the direction of growth and life (an observance common in housebuilding elsewhere in Indonesia; see Beatty 1992: 22). I was told, but did not myself observe, that the fire over which the meat is roasted is composed of four pieces of wood with the root ends pointing inwards to form a cross, making a four-five symbol.

Curiously, there are no vegetables, except during the month of Besar when a *tumpeng serakat*, 'mound of misfortune', is included. Given that Buyut Cungking was a vegetarian and shunned the stimulating properties of meat this seems odd, but as the caretaker said to me, 'We are the ones who will eat it, not him. What matters is the purity of our intentions.'

Slametan Buyut

Once the food is ready, around late afternoon, the sponsor – one cannot speak of a 'host' in the usual way since the slametan is not held at home –

sits with the caretaker and his assistants drinking coffee in a shelter next to the *bale*, waiting until there is a quorum of about half a dozen. These people need not belong to the sponsor's party; they may have their own requests to make at the shrine. Usually there are women as well as men present, unlike the usual all-male gathering; indeed the sponsor may be a woman.

The sponsor can personally attend the shrine ceremony or can ask to be represented by someone else, in which case, while still seated in the shelter, the delegate (*wakil*) tells the caretaker of the sponsor's intention in organizing the meal. The speech takes the form of a short formulaic address ('May she be prosperous and slamet, may her harvest be good', etc.), much like the address of an ordinary slametan but spoken, as it were, in preview. The speaker's role here, as later in the shrine, is formally to 'represent' (*mwakil*) her – not in relation to Buyut Cungking himself, but to the caretaker who presides over the ceremony and who mediates personally with the spirit. This conception of ritual representation closely parallels that of the Hindu Tenggerese (Hefner 1985: 111).

The procession from the *bale* to the shrine is in a prescribed order. The caretaker leads the way, carrying a small clay brazier (called *prapèn*, as in Tengger and Bali, rather than the usual term, *pengaspan*). His deputy comes next, carrying leaf packets of flowers, followed by the others bearing the rice mound, two dishes of water, a flask, a brass betel set, and a rolled-up mat. The line of supplicants files quietly through the village, down a slope to the cemetery. Within the perimeter wall is an enclosure containing the shrine, a large, sturdy, rectangular hut overshadowed by a huge tentacular banyan tree (a species associated with guardian spirits in both Java and Bali).

A series of thresholds is crossed with increasing solemnity: first the entrance to the cemetery, then the gate of the shrine's compound, which the caretaker unlocks after performing an obeisance, then the opening of the shrine itself; finally the interior wall of the inner chamber is lifted out and propped up, revealing a pair of headstones set in a smooth concrete base and oriented east–west like the whole building. The bamboo walls of this inner chamber and the headstones themselves are draped with white shrouds. Every year these shrouds are taken down and washed at a sacred spot in the river north-west of Cungking.

The supplicants sit around the mat in the outer chamber in a relaxed but quietly serious manner. The usual careful attention to posture and dress is lacking and some men forgo the otherwise obligatory black hat; neither is there a separation of the sexes. These small differences emphasize the non-Islamic nature of the ceremony. The caretaker himself sits next to the stone step which marks the threshold to the inner sanctuary and beside which are placed the ritual paraphernalia. Before beginning, the wakil hands him a leaf parcel containing flowers, betel ingredients, and face powder, which the caretaker opens and places on a wooden dish next to the near headstone. When everything is ready, the caretaker and the wakil sit down facing each other and then – remarkably, in the context of a slametan – commence a formal dialogue. The caretaker asks what is being sought and the wakil begins a list of requests. Each part of the petition is answered, repeated almost word for word by the caretaker. For example, the wakil says: 'Mbok Sri requests health-and-safety as she has been ill; may illness be driven off and welfare restored.' To which the caretaker responds, 'May Mbok Sri obtain health-and-safety, may her illness be driven off and her welfare restored', adding, 'and may this be requested of Eyang who is resting here'. Each section of the petition – concerning Mbok Sri's health, that of her family, her crops, her children's success at school – is uttered by the wakil and then repeated by the caretaker, back and forth until the list is exhausted.

As mentioned, apart from the slametan sponsor there may be other petitioners or their delegates present. At the end of the requests for a particular person the caretaker draws from the rim of his hat a small leaf packet containing a pair of dried *sari kurung* buds to be burned as incense.[3] Like the spirit of Bayu, Buyut Cungking has his own special incense; ordinary benzoin may not be used. The caretaker puts the incense beads on the brazier after the dialogue has finished and everyone watches intently as the smoke begins to rise. When the last wisp has disappeared and the incense has been entirely consumed he says *Sampun!* (done), confident that the request has been received. The caretaker now enters the chamber and moves the tray of flowers and betel to the far headstone. Then he returns to his place ready for the next petition. The next set of flowers is put beside the near headstone and another dialogue begins.

Sometimes there are two or three wakils, each representing a number of petitioners, besides the slametan sponsor herself. On one occasion when I was present the caretaker's deputy submitted requests for ten individuals. Although, in theory, an offering of flowers is made for each petitioner and incense is burned after each complete petition, since there were so many to get through, only five offerings were made and incense was burned five times (thus one ritual sequence for each pair of petitioners). All the requests, however, were spoken in full, section by section. One person was sick, another about to make a journey, a fisherman wanted his new boat blessed, and so on. The ten petitioners were from all over the district – as far afield as the hill plantation of Kalibendo and the port of Ketapang, nine miles north of Banyuwangi. They had approached the deputy at home or at the *bale* in the previous days and asked him to 'offer flowers' (*ngaturi sekar* or *nyekar*) on their behalf. (*Nyekar* is the word commonly used for grave-visiting – one of a number of usages which suggest, somewhat misleadingly, that the shrine is thought of as a grave.)

To 'offer flowers' is to make a presentation to Buyut analogous to, though on a lesser scale than, 'offering food' (*ngaturi dahar*) in a full slametan. The same event thus brings together people with varying degrees of investment: the caretaker, the wakil, and petitioners of various kinds – whether absent or present, offering food or merely flowers – along with their respective parties. This complex division of ritual labour is quite unlike the slametans we have seen in previous chapters.

When all the petitions have been heard, ending with personal requests from the wakils themselves, the wakil of the slametan sponsor uncovers the rice mound and speaks a formal address (*ngabulaken*) in the familiar slametan idiom, repeating the main points of his client's petition. The caretaker responds in like manner. This concludes the spoken part of the ceremony, which may already have lasted an hour if many people were represented. The ritual paraphernalia and the rice mounds are then put aside so that each person can come forward to make an obeisance to Buyut Cungking, beginning with the caretaker. Sitting cross-legged before the threshold to the inner chamber, he bends forward slowly until his head touches a wooden platter (called *rembagan*, 'consultation' – another verbal object). He performs this action three times, while murmuring a prayer. Then the others shuffle forward, one by one, in no strict order (a roughly anticlockwise sequence seems to be common), to 'ask Buyut's forgiveness' or to 'ask for his prayer (*donga*)'. Some follow the caretaker's example; others place hands together before the face, recite a silent spell or request for blessing, then pass the hands over the face in a washing gesture, as people often do at the end of slametan prayers. The caretaker performs his obeisance for a second time and thus concludes the ceremony.

The party then ambles back to the meeting-house where the food is served. The men sit on a large platform like a four-poster bed, while the women eat in the adjoining building. Unlike a conventional slametan, the formality of the preceding ritual does not carry over into the meal; there are no further prayers or speeches. The meal and the ritual are clearly separated by their distinct locations.

Later that same night some of the participants, and whoever else wishes to attend, may meditate in the shrine. Customarily, 'in the buda way', those present wear only the minimum necessary for modesty. The session begins after midnight and goes on until the small hours when the contemplatives emerge to compare notes on 'what they experienced' or 'what Buyut granted them to see'.

Comparison with standard slametans

Many of the basic elements of the ceremony are common to ordinary slametans – the ritual paraphernalia, the formulaic requests, the act of witnessing and, not least, the designation slametan. However, the way these elements are put together, the different foci of attention, the organization of personnel and, most important of all, the object of veneration, suggest something quite dissimilar. What these differences amount to is a controversial, politically delicate question which it would be invidious and, I believe, misleading to answer in unequivocal terms – misleading, because equivocality or ambiguity is a fundamental characteristic of the slametan Buyut, as of the ordinary slametan. Before considering further aspects of this question, however, I want to look more closely at three areas of difference in the performance and organization of the slametan: its speech forms, its division of labour, and its constituency.

Speech in the slametan

Formal speech in the shrine differs from that of the ordinary slametan in several respects:

1. There is a dialogue instead of the usual monologue before witnesses.
2. The petition goes beyond the usual general requests for welfare to list particular problems, often in some detail.
3. Although the expressions of desired welfare are in the jargon of the typical slametan, for which High Javanese is preferred, there are no rhetorical flourishes or archaisms: the dialogue is a simple exchange rather than an address or quasi-prayer. In cases where there is no wakil, when the petitioner presents his or her own requests, the dialogue is even closer to ordinary speech, albeit

hedged with respectful polite forms, and often takes place in a murmur inaudible to witnesses.

4. There is no symbolic exegesis or mention of other spiritual beings such as the Muslim saints, God, or the four spiritual guardians.

5. The request is made directly to Buyut Cungking, who is referred to throughout as 'Eyang, who is at rest here' (*Eyang kang sumaré wonten ngriki*). *Eyang* is a kinship term for the generation senior to a *buyut*, i.e. great-great-grandparent, but its use here is honorific. It is cognate with Old Javanese *hyang*, deity, and retains a sense of divinized forefather. The directness of the appeal is another unusual feature. In the ordinary slametan address there is an indirectness and ambiguity deriving partly from the use of verb forms which blur the identity of the blessing agency and partly from an avoidance of names (cf. Hefner 1985: 110).

6. There is no Arabic greeting or Arabic prayer. If a prayer or mantra is spoken – and this is not obligatory – it is done silently at a later stage in the ceremony.

The combined effect of these differences is to emphasize the personal and individual at the expense of the public and social. The dialogue has little significance for the witnesses; it does not refer to the shared world of signs and symbols or to the spiritual beings that feature in other slametans. They are not required to give their assent to a set of propositions about the world and their function as witnesses is greatly diminished. They, too, make their communication individually with Buyut.

Representation

The wakil's presentation of the sponsor's petition is analogous to that of the delegate in an ordinary slametan, a role which is not usually named. However, in this case, the function of delegate is shared between two people, the wakil and the caretaker. Both are conceived as mediators (*lantaran*) between the petitioner and Buyut Cungking, but only the caretaker has direct access to the spirit – at least, during the slametan. In this limited sense he is a priest. It is not simply that he is 'keeper of the keys' (*juru kunci*) to the shrine, like similar caretakers all over Java; he has a hereditary personal relation with Buyut Cungking and can act as his spokesman. Thus, in the daily affairs of managing the cult buildings, he is guided by dreams and portents which, by his own interpretation, contain messages or indications of Buyut's wishes. These messages – for example, the wish to repair the fence or replace the thatch – are incontrovertible.

Hefner (1985: 108–9) sees the *juru kunci* as a case of 'cultural compromise between Islamic religion and an earlier tradition', perhaps recalling a time when knowledge of Islam was confined to specialists. Such ritual specialists are usually masters of Arabic spells and prayers learned from divination manuals as well as of Javanist lore. The caretaker in Cungking, however, is, or was, master of a pre-Islamic tradition and none of his activities has any reference to Islam. As such, his office may perhaps be said to lie halfway between that of the typical shrine caretaker of lowland Java and the explicitly non-Islamic priesthood of the Tengger highlands. In assessing the comparative significance of his role, it is also important to note that the Cungking caretaker is not regarded as a dhukun, a magician or healer. His priestly function is not based on personal powers or charisma, and he is free of the suspicions of black magic and trafficking with spirits that often attach to a dhukun. Nor is there any hint of venality in his behaviour. He cultivates simplicity and receives no remuneration for the office.

The present caretaker, Pak Rasno, is a man of about sixty-five who recently took over from his elder brother. The job is hereditary, but the present incumbent can trace his line of succession back only three generations. A woman, Pak Rasno's grandmother, once held office, though it seems that her position was honorary and it was her younger brother who officiated at the shrine.

Pak Rasno has a deputy, a man from Wonosari who has assumed his position by assiduous attendance at the shrine. He often deputizes in the less sacred functions of the job but is not regarded as qualified to conduct slametans; his usual role is assistant and wakil to petitioners. About eight or nine men from other villages are regular visitors and are often asked by their co-villagers and kin to represent them at the shrine. Regulars from Cungking itself include a former headman, a mechanic, and lesser village officials. There is no discernible pattern in the background of these people – they belong to no single occupational or economic class and are not distinguished by level of education from other inhabitants. The same can be said of the much larger number of people who occasionally visit the shrine or attend the annual cleaning of the relics. At most one can point to the predictable fact that followers are not usually santri, conventionally pious Muslims, and that kinship and neighbourhood play a part in influencing who attends among an otherwise amorphous category of people.

The qualification for representing others at the shrine seems to be familiarity with the procedures and the fact of 'being known to Buyut', rather than superior knowledge. However, a minimum requirement is the possession of certain sacred formulas or *japa mantra*. There are very few of these and their obscurity seems only to add to their value as emblems of old Java. Some formulas are secret and can only be divulged by the caretaker after ascetic preparation. (They are powerful and therefore dangerous to the uninitiated.) Others may be divulged to someone with a serious interest. The following is an example:

Awakku sang cendana putih	My body/self is white sandalwood
Atapa ing sa'luhur ing wenang	Perform austerities in the utmost power
Papanku muji gampang	May my place be made easy
Teka wenang	Let the power come [said thrice]
Saking Allah	From God [optional]

The meaning of this prayer (called a *pewenang*) is obscure, and the translation is conjectural. But it is not necessary to understand a prayer in order to use it effectively. What is important is to obtain it under the right conditions so that one can employ it safely; and, of course, one must know when to use it. The former caretaker who gave me this *pewenang* told me he uses it before eating rice (recite once before three mouthfuls); another follower uses it at the annual cleaning before examining each relic.

Without the intercession of knowledgeable representatives, one who lacks the requisite spells and prayers would not benefit much from participation in the rituals of the cult; but many people know a little – sometimes a fragment of a prayer or an appropriate phrase. A number of senior men in Bayu have mastered the handful of Cungking spells – learned from the old caretaker – and incorporated them in their repertoire of Javanese mystical knowledge. The diverse sources of *kawruh* are overlapping and complementary, mutually illuminating to adepts.

To sum up, in the ordinary slametan, as we have seen, no special qualification is required in order to preside, other than an ability to speak the formal address. In the slametan at the Cungking shrine, in contrast, the concept of representation is paramount and gives rise to a specialized occupation.

The constituency of the slametan

The shrine has a number of overlapping congregations or constituencies, from the smallest group – the real devotees who sit up all night meditating and for whom Buyut is the touchstone of sanctity – through the regulars, who form the cult's rank and file, to the occasional visitors seeking solace or blessing. The big slametan at the annual cleaning attracts a much larger crowd. Attendance at the shrine does not, in itself, show much about one's purpose or degree of commitment or whether one regards Buyut Cungking as a sage, a repository of magical power, or perhaps even a divine incarnation.

Despite this diversity of opinion, several characteristics of the cult place it beyond controversy and allow it not merely to be tolerated in the heart of a Muslim community but to be accepted as integral to its life:

1. The lack of a collective identity and shared ideology among the shrine's visitors – in attending one need not be associated with anyone or anything in particular.
2. The preference for symbolism over explicit doctrine. This might be said of the ordinary slametan, but at the Cungking shrine even prayers are recited silently, unlike the public, collective recitations described in previous chapters.
3. The notion of representation: someone who needs to obtain Buyut's blessing for a project or celebration (whether because this is expected or because he genuinely desires it), but who does not want personally to perform an obeisance (for the sake of appearances or out of scruple) can have this done on his behalf.
4. The fact that the shrine is used for various purposes, some of which fall within the scope of traditional Javanese Islam.

Concerning the last point: in its broader social function, the shrine differs little from other village shrines. Its rituals, despite their peculiarities, fit into the wider pattern of calendrical and household slametans around which village life revolves. As in Bayu, a slametan at the village shrine is a prerequisite for a major celebration. Buyut Cungking fulfils the duties of an ordinary guardian spirit, warding off crime and black magic, counteracting agricultural pests, and watching over community and household celebrations. He is often asked to protect festive stores of rice and crockery from petty pilfering. As a guardian spirit, Buyut Cungking's congregation is the whole village. Indeed, his tutelary sway extends beyond Cungking to Bakungan, where he also has a *bale*, and to Bayu, whose founders derived from Cungking. An inhabitant of Bayu who is about to hold an important celebration may attend his own village shrine or that of Buyut Cungking. (The reverse does not apply: the Cungking caretaker has never visited Buyut Cili.)

This coincidence of village and congregation is made clear in the *slametan desa*, the annual village feast which takes place during the pilgrimage month.[4] In the afternoon before the evening's communal feasting, which constitutes the *slametan desa* proper, a smaller event is held at the shrine, attended by village officials and others. On the occasion when I was present, the headman's delegate begged Buyut Cungking to 'make the people obedient' so that the government's programmes could be carried out and so that the forthcoming general election would proceed smoothly with the return of the government party (any change signifying chaos). He also requested blessing on the crops of farmers and the work of artisans, harmony between bosses and labourers, clarity of mind for schoolchildren, and a general blessing for villagers.

The caretaker and the headman are symbolically *besan* to each other, that is, they stand in the relation of (respectively) a bride's parents to a groom's parents. On the day of the village feast, in token of this quasi-affinal role, each pays a formal 'pre-wedding visit' (*nglamar*) to the other. There is in this arrangement a suggestion of diarchy, or 'complementary governance' among temporal and mystical powers (Needham 1980a), reflecting an emphasis on the complementarity of male and female and a dualism characteristic of Javanese culture.[5]

Evidently, Buyut's following – at whatever level of inclusiveness – cannot be defined as a sect in any accepted sense of the term (O'Dea 1968; Wilson 1968). Devotions are not guided by a distinct sectarian ideology; there are no criteria of association or membership; and followers adopt no consistent ideological position *vis-à-vis* the world, neither rejecting society nor attempting to reform it (see Wilson 1969). It seems more appropriate to speak of a *cult*, a less all-embracing concept than religion, and one which lacks the group implications of *sect*. The term *cult* has the further advantage of drawing attention to the act of devotion or religious expression, which is – for devotees, opponents, and observers alike – the most interesting and problematic aspect of the whole phenomenon.

In pursuing this theme, the slametan can take us only so far. It remains primarily a personal communication tailored to individual needs. The interpretative density and social complexity of the Cungking cult can best be seen in the annual cleaning ceremony – to which I now turn –

serving as it does individual needs, the welfare of the village, and the spiritual integrity of the whole region.

The Cleaning of the Relics

Nothing better displays the curious combination of intense, concentrated interest and opaque, muted symbolism – the stifled quest for significance which characterizes the whole cult – than the Cleaning of the Relics (*resik kagungan*). Analogous ceremonies are performed all over Java, from the great court rituals in Yogya and Solo, when the palace regalia are paraded before the masses, down to rustic slametans at which heirlooms are bathed and reverently fingered in a brief revitalizing contact with a legendary past. Nearly all of these ceremonies, great and small, involve compromises of one kind or another with the fact of Muslim domination. As Javanese themselves put it: if the precious and powerful 'content' of tradition has its source in pre-Islamic times, the protective receptacle or vessel (*wadhah*) is necessarily Muslim. Hence the recourse to Arabic prayers and readings, invocations of the Javanese missionary-saints, processions to the mosque, and the supervision of santri. Since the inner and spiritual is superior to the outer and material (*wadag*), the compromise concedes less than is apparent while satisfying the demands of 'normative piety' (to use Woodward's apt phrase) – or so Javanists would claim.

Whether the metaphor of vessel and content is adequate to depict the complex interrelation of the Islamic with the Javanese is a separate question; but it is obvious that the case of Cungking does not readily lend itself to such a conception. Here compromise has taken a different course. There is no protective Islamic shell or vessel into which tradition has been poured. Consequently there is no official, public level of meaning which conceals a profounder esoteric truth, no bright surface covering hidden depths. Yet, as we have seen in previous chapters, Javanese interpretation depends on there being such a dual reality. Without it, exegesis must falter. In the Cleaning of the Relics this habitual symbolic quest is not abandoned but, if anything, pursued with greater zeal. Much of the ritual is concerned with extracting meaning even where little is forthcoming.

Let us begin, then, with externals – the prescribed sequence of actions which make up the ritual – and follow participants in their efforts at interpretation. The description which follows concerns the ceremony held in 1993.

Description of the ceremony

14 Rejeb, the seventh month of the Javanese year. People began to gather in the *bale* complex around eight in the morning (see figure 1). Pak Rasno and his wife – chief cook for the day – received contributions of food in the kitchen, while their son, now being groomed as a future caretaker, was serving coffee in the shelter outside. The smell of clove cigarettes was everywhere and there were the usual relaxed pleasantries and composed chatter of a Javanese gathering. By nine o'clock about sixty men and thirty to forty women had assembled. They came from all over the district (including fifteen from Bayu). As the day wore on others arrived and, towards the end, garrulous crowds of Cungking women packed the complex to ask for consecrated water.

The front wall of the *bale* was lifted out to reveal the *planca*, the four-poster platform on which the most important ritual would take place. At 9.30 a.m. a dozen men were seated on the platform for an introductory slametan, five of them from Bayu – an indication of the continuing link between Cungking and its offshoot village. Also present were the Cungking headman and senior figures from other villages. The caretaker's deputy gave a brief address. The purpose of the slametan, he said, was twofold: to open proceedings and to ask forgiveness of Buyut, as the special food, the 'porridge of forgiveness', was meant to symbolize.

There was no burning of incense, unlike slametans in the shrine, and no prayer. After the speech, plates of the white gruel were handed round, each man taking a scoop with a leaf spoon, then the plates were passed to others seated in the shelter.

The caretaker himself then supervised the removal of the relics (*kagungan*, possessions) from a rack in an adjacent building called the *bale wadon*, female hall, and took his place at the head of the platform in the *bale tajug* (which is also known as the 'male' hall). Each item, swaddled in white, was passed gingerly from hand to hand then unwrapped and placed on a pillow next to the caretaker. The relics

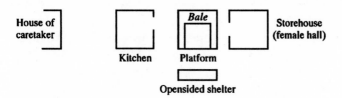

Figure 1 The *bale* complex

testified to Buyut's travels and adventures: a spear with a detachable dagger-head which many associate with the magical weapon used by Wangsakarya against the guru of Mataram; a pair of silver bracelets; a copper inscription; a white 'heavenly stone'; three pebbles obtained on a flight to Mecca; a grey stone egg (a 'world symbol') excreted by a buffalo in Baluran; a decorated beaker; a piece of fin from a shark which Buyut defeated at Lampon; and part of his costume which Rara Kidul, the spirit-queen of the southern ocean, had brazenly tweaked when she tried to seduce him.

The caretaker removed the spearhead from its sheath, brushed off a coating of powder and held it up. 'How many bends does it have?' he asked. All agreed it had five bends.[6] Each relic was displayed in turn to the crowd, then laid down with exaggerated care as if it might at any moment dissolve into dust.

Food was served. We ate in shifts on the platform, dining in the powerful effulgence shed by the relics, and then settled down to the serious business of the cleaning. The women, who ate separately, did not take an active part in the ritual.

It began with the wavy-bladed spear head. With an air of great solemnity, the caretaker held the ancient weapon in his left hand and rubbed a split lime along its length three times, turned it over and painstakingly repeated the action, then sprinkled rice husks over the wetted metal and scoured it with bamboo shavings. The man on his right then performed the same operation. (The blade itself must be turned over to the right – anticlockwise – and one who consciously errs will die.) When the spearhead had completed a circuit, the caretaker inspected it minutely and cleaned it again, as if underlining the ritual nature of the purification. The men on the platform then vacated their seats for others and the cleaning began again until all the men present had participated, a process which took about two hours. Remarkably, there was no diminution in the care taken – each man began as if anew, rubbing and scraping diligently, helped along by advice from the crowd at his shoulder. Finally, somewhat thinner but undoubtedly cleaner, the spearhead was powdered and put back in its sheath.

The other items were then passed round for inspection and handling. Each man would hold the relic against his forehead or close to his bowed head while murmuring a silent prayer. With the last relic, Buyut's cloth, each pressed it to his face and inhaled to imbibe its protective powers; after which the relic left the circuit and was passed into the crowd where women jostled each other to 'ask for its blessing'.

Two of the relics bore some kind of writing and therefore merited special interest. The silver bracelets have an inscribed design which, some say, resembles Javanese script. But its meaning 'depends on where you begin reading' or what you are inspired to see in it: 'the words come and go'. Similarly, the *layang* ('letter'), consisting of tiny copper tablets whose inscriptions are so worn as to be indecipherable, conveys its message symbolically or evocatively. It is not everyone who is 'granted' a glimpse of its meaning; some could stare forever without seeing anything. (Indeed, many looked as though they would do just that.) The message this year was granted to the village deputy, and interpreted in group discussion. It was thought to refer to the need for repairs to the shrine fence.

One of the relics stands out from the rest and has a special significance for followers of the cult. The *sangku*, a bronze beaker with relief carvings of zodiac figures, is the symbol and instrument of Buyut's white magic. Each of the twelve figures is said to represent one of the Lords of Illness who collectively are known as *pangiwa*. This term, also known in Bali, means literally 'figures of the left', and refers to witches or demons.[7] As a schoolteacher explained to me, with striking sociological insight, 'Nowa-

Plate 6 Relic cleaning ceremony at Cungking

days we say the "extreme Left"' (demonized in New Order Indonesia). Appropriately, then, this relic makes its circuit in the opposite direction to the rest, travelling clockwise, 'to the left'. Each man holds the beaker on his left palm and carefully revolves it, fixing the Lords of Illness in turn and silently reciting their names. Only people initiated by the old caretaker, Pak Untung, 'possess' this litany and many in attendance could not have known what they were supposed to be doing. The recitation is at once a talisman, protecting one against the diseases borne by the Lords, and a commemoration of their defeat by Buyut as he roamed the area.

Accompanied by two mystics from Bayu who had been initiated many years before, I was invited by Pak Untung to a midnight session at which he revealed the names of the *pangiwa*, their locations and associated spells. I was not permitted to write anything down and had to learn the beaker-litany by repetition. However, once informed I was later able to check the lists with cult veterans. The locations are well-known haunted spots – forests, inlets, crags – listed in a sequence describing a clockwise circuit around the region: a tour of the sacred geography. The names of the Lords (which need not be cited here) are garbled and run together, though informants' recitations are surprisingly consistent. One can distinguish Javanese and Balinese titles from the pre-colonial and early colonial periods, but I have not been able to identify any of the names in myth or local history. Neither is there a clear sense of which diseases correspond to which Lords. Nevertheless, this litany or spell (*rapal*) is regarded as very potent, the most treasured piece of knowledge bequeathed by Buyut Cungking. It can be used to ward off evil or disease, and may even serve as a talisman at the epidemic preceding the coming of the righteous prince. (Messianic allusions are otherwise rare and uncharacteristic of the cult.)

The sangku is a human symbol capable of diverse interpretations. It is made of bronze, an alloy: and what is a human being if not a superior alloy, a fusion of male, female, and divine elements? The very name sangku evokes the mystical concept of *sangkan paraning dumadi*, the 'origin and destination of being.' Indeed, once one enters the hermeneutic circle, interpretations multiply with a compelling aptness and inevitability. At the Cleaning of the Relics in 1996 I discovered that the base of the sangku has an image of a four-leafed flower depressed into its centre. No one could remember having observed this, probably because no one had ever looked inside it (and there were some who thought I had been 'granted' the image by Buyut). Nevertheless, interpretations were quickly offered. One man thought that the four petals represented the four spiritual siblings or faculties, with *rasa sejati* (pure feeling/the godhead) in the centre. The self, thus figured, is surrounded by – and repels – the evil influences represented on the circumference. When I added that each petal was bifurcated, he connected this spontaneously with a theory of perception underlying much of Javanese mystical discourse. If the spiritual siblings are the faculties (sight, hearing, etc.), each faculty has a double aspect in that it unites the perceiver with the perceived, the seer with the seen. So the sangku is not just a human symbol; on this view, it represents humanity in its coexistence with Creation, in its necessary relation to the world. Another follower, a practising Muslim, took the more orthodox view that the flower represented a *tulak balak*, a spell to ward off evil emanating from the four quarters. Yet another was reminded of man's four passions which give rise to the many forms of evil in the world.

No one to whom I spoke recognized the sangku as a zodiac beaker of the kind used in pre-Islamic Java, and no one was aware of its analogues in contemporary Hindu ritual. In fact, buda priests of the Tengger highlands still use these ancient vessels (which they call *prasèn*) for sprinkling consecrated water (Hefner 1985: 27; Kohlbrugge 1896).[8] And metal water beakers figure in the temple ceremonies of Balinese and Hindu converts in Java to this day.

Whatever its historical provenance, in Cungking tradition the sangku (like the windmill) is the personal invention of Buyut Cungking, not the instrument of a buda priest. The link with the past, despite the tangible evidence, is lost. No amount of handling and painstaking scrutiny can make the beaker yield up its secrets. Indeed, each 'reading', each tracing of fingers over figures, further erases the original outline and blurs the meaning, widening the scope for ambiguity – an apt metaphor of Javanism's predicament, one might say. Like the copper inscriptions which tell of an earlier, forgotten era, and whose words are now illegible (replaced by contemporary fancy), the sangku is a vessel for a different kind of Javanist knowledge, diffident and accommodating, in a world no longer Hindu. In this ideologically mixed and politically sensitive setting, the important thing is not the clarity and permanence of a message – characteristics one might expect of a copper inscription – but its transience ('the words come and go') and bland relativism ('it depends where you begin reading'). Nothing definite can be said and no one is required to make a stand: everything is off the record. Consequently, there is no possibility of taking offence. The relics are inscribed with writing, then, but it is a curious form of writing whose meaning depends on the reader. In this, it resembles the material symbols of the shrine and the windmill: no ideas but in things.

It hardly needs saying that this symbolist and relativist conception of meaning contrasts absolutely with that of the dominant faith. The Koran – the paradigmatic holy scripture – is regarded by the devout as fixed, eternal, universal, self-fulfilling, and complete. To most Javanese, it is also quite meaningless, in that they understand no Arabic, though many learn to recite without comprehension. In the face of this inscrutability, there is no need for the uncomprehending 'reader' to supply a meaning; his or her interpretation is irrelevant and superfluous. The Javanist, by contrast, discovers meaning by 'reading his own Koran', that is, by introspection. The messages contained therein are said to be 'written without a board/place': a notion which captures both the symbology and the cultural predicament of Cungking. Interpretation is not, however, regarded as a purely subjective act, a projected fantasy, but an illumination deriving from an inner reality which transcends material forms. One is granted glimpses of the inner reality either in contemplation or through the grace of an enlightened spiritual being such as Buyut Cungking.

In handling the relics with such care and concentration, it was evident that devotees were intent both on absorbing their powers and extracting their hidden meanings. What was poignant, for the outsider, was the intensity of this need and the relatively small return for such effort. I watched, with fifty others, as the caretaker immersed the copper tablets in one of the bowls of water and counted the bubbles that streamed upwards, first quickly, then slower and slower, until it seemed minutes would pass between each bubble. Inevitably, one was drawn into the miniature drama happening at the bottom of the bowl, as a tiny bubble emerged trembling on the thread linking the copper tablets; and one shared in the collective relief when it finally broke free and floated – or was willed – upwards. When the bubbles had ceased, the caretaker drained the tablets and lowered them into the second bowl of water. Again heads craned forward in rapt concentration. It took about ten minutes for forty-seven bubbles to emerge. But what did the number signify? As with the 'five' bends in the spear head, it was anybody's guess. Somebody suggested to me that, by means of a numerical formula, one could derive from it an omen; or the numbers four and seven could themselves be construed as symbols. But perhaps the intensity of regard was in inverse proportion to the meaning – the less there is to 'read', the harder one looks for a meaning. The previous year, as some recalled, no one had thought to count.

The relics, newly washed, were wrapped again and put away for another year. One bowl of water was put aside to be used as holy water in slametans at the shrine. The other was poured into barrels of ordinary water, thus consecrating it, if diluting its potency. Participants joined the huge throng of local people who had recently arrived and eagerly drank from the barrels, filling bottles to take home and share with their families. After the solemnity and decorum of the ceremony there was much friendly pushing and shoving, gulping and splashing – a profligacy with the sacred liquid which had been so carefully created. This throwing off of normal restraint enacted, perhaps, the abundance and prosperity expected from the ceremony, and reflected a more pragmatic, less mystical, side to popular participation in the cult. The limes and cleaning materials used on the spear, too, were the object of jostling and grabbing. These ceremonial leftovers are placed in the uppermost rice terrace as a means of warding off pests.

There was no formal leavetaking and the participants dispersed.

Conclusion

The cleaning ceremony and the shrine slametan offer many clues about the continuing appeal of the cult and – despite certain unique features – an insight into the attraction of similar shrines, places of worship, and pilgrimage found all over Java. In contrast to Islam, the cult is emphatically local. It acknowledges a sacred landscape familiar from legend, folk history, and personal experience; and it provides a sense of continuity (however weakly substantiated) with the past which reminds followers of their regional identity, as heirs of Blambangan, and of their sense of themselves as Javanese.

This self-conscious Javanism is neither opposed to local identity nor to a broader, more universalist perspective: it is a concept which has little to do with nation or ethnicity, denoting, rather, enlightened civility, the personal incorporation of culture, and awareness of one's place in the cosmos. From a Javanist perspective, one attains to universal truths not by acquiring external, foreign-derived knowledge, but by looking inwards, matching outer symbol to inner reality, and thus acquiring that mental equipoise and awareness which is called 'knowing one's Javaneseness' (*wruh jawane*). From this perspective, the world religions are, paradoxically, revealed as local and historically bounded, therefore of limited value, whereas the truly local – Java, Blambangan, Cungking, oneself 'at the still point of the turning world' – connects one to what is universal.

Whatever the philosophical appeal of the cult and its connexions to a wider set of Javanist ideas, there is, too, an appeal at a more immediate and simpler level which cannot easily be matched by official religion. As we have seen, despite an obvious cultural conservatism, ritual is closely tailored to contemporary needs (success at school, the general elections, harvests, festivities). And it harmonizes with patterns of sociality prevailing in daily life. Unlike Islam, it does not radically segregate the sexes or impose on women a subordinate and silent role which they would not accept in ordinary life.

As a mode of religious experience, the cult is personalistic, devotional, and undogmatic. It allows for the expression and satisfaction of particular, mostly worldly, needs in a simple and vernacular idiom, as well as indicating a path to self-knowledge and enlightenment. Above all, it is something adherents choose for themselves, not something they are obliged to perform either because of social or political pressures. Its piety is voluntarist rather than normative. This voluntarism is a prominent theme of Javanism in general, and is similarly stressed by Javanese converts to Hinduism. It gains a special significance in a context where affiliation to an official religion is obligatory, and where Islam, the dominant religion, is typically characterized as a set of obligatory practices.

Whether the Cungking cult is buda, syncretist Islam, or something else is a matter of opinion. It resists categorization by potentially hostile parties, and it is expressly open to anyone. As the caretaker insists, there are adherents of every religious persuasion – Muslims, Christians, even Taoists. And one is free to use prayers from any tradition, though the proper Cungking mantra are pre-Islamic. Most of the regulars could be called nominally Muslim, though pious Muslims are among those who attend the cleaning ceremony.

The former caretaker, with the candour and licence that comes with great age, is willing to declare himself buda. (I feel no concern in reporting this.) But what he means by buda is a vague loyalty to a dimly remembered pre-Islamic past and a principled abstention from Islam, as well as, more positively, adherence to Javanist mystical traditions owing more to Islam than he admits. Were he to be confronted with Bali's pantheon and its elaborate temple rituals – which bear some resemblance to those of Old Java – he would probably find them as alien as he professes to find Islam. As he admits, when in the company of ordinary

Muslims at ordinary household slametans, he is comfortable enough 'using the *bismillah*' (the invocation of Allah). Nevertheless, despite this easy ecumenism, the contrastive aspect of the cult as non-Islamic (not anti-Islamic) remains important to many of its followers.

To end this account and to counterbalance what may strike readers as an overemphasis on the intellectual appeal of the cult, I will close with two rather different, but in their own ways typical, testimonies. Bu Dewi is an elderly farmer and a lifelong devotee of Buyut. She claims never to have performed Islamic worship or 'spoken the *bismillah*', though, like many Javanists, on occasion she fasts. It is clear that her conception of divinity has nothing to do with Islam. For her Buyut is simply the Lord, *pengeran*. 'His place is in the sun', she said, using a local old-fashioned term for sun, *panutan*, which also means religious exemplar, guiding star. 'His congregation [umat] is everything that lives, even the grass and the trees. That's why you strew flowers in the *wangan* [top rice terrace] after a slametan. Buyut likes the smell. He was a farmer too.'

On the morning of Idul Fitri, the highpoint of the Muslim year, when most villagers were receiving guests, Bu Dewi was at the shrine performing a slametan. She goes there every week to ask for slamet. Anyone can go, she explained, Buyut doesn't discriminate. She 'replaces' her parents who used to go; her husband replaces his father; and when she is dead she hopes her daughter will replace her. 'That's what we mean by an afterlife: there is nothing else.'

I asked whether, after going to the shrine, she felt slamet. Did she feel looked after by Buyut? Yes, she replied, beaming.

Bu Suwana is one of a number of women from Bayu who go every Thursday morning to sweep out the shrine. A former gandrung, now in early middle age, she is married to a ward head who once stood for headman and was a PNI activist during the turbulent 1960s. She began to attend regularly after her husband had a stroke and nearly died. She had made a vow that if he recovered she would 'present food' to Buyut; and, partly in gratitude, she has continued to visit. But she also obtains tranquillity by attending the shrine.

You cannot go if you are not calm in mind, if you've been quarrelling with your husband or having bad thoughts. If your heart is not white, you'll come away with nothing. If you have had sex you must wash properly before leaving home. There are all sorts of stipulations. On the way there – you can only go on foot – you may not drop in on anyone; that means you can't deviate in your purpose. If you do succumb and drop in you have to cancel the trip. But those who 'understand' won't call you if they know you're going 'to sweep'. No one can invite or persuade you to go; it has to come from your own desire or it's worthless. Usually there are about a dozen people there, men and women. We go down with Pak Rasno to the shrine; he prays at the gate before opening it, then we sweep it out. Afterwards we drink holy water from the flask. This helps to give you clear, tranquil thoughts. When you pray at the shrine you pass your hands over your face and hair, like this, and say: May my grandchildren be well, give me good fortune, brighten my heart.

Two shrines, one home to a were-tiger, the other home to a saint. Ostensibly similar in function but answering different purposes, the shrines of Bayu and Cungking represent alternative forms of compromise with Islam and the modern state. Buyut Cili, though essential to village welfare, lurks on the fringes of respectability, uncomfortably close to the amoral otherworld of sprites and demons, 'figures of the left', and tainted with political controversy. Buyut Cungking, no less essential to his community, remains central, unambiguously benevolent as champion of white magic, politically neutral, but in other respects ambiguous and enigmatic, retreating behind a screen of symbols. Both shrines are tolerated by the authorities because they are represented as being outside religion as it is officially defined. They do not pose a threat to the official faiths. But their survival has been at the cost of expressive significance. As fewer and fewer people delve into Javanese tradition, the symbolic forms of the Cungking cult risk becoming empty of content. Without the exegesis that draws adherents deeper into the complex world of mystical knowledge, the signs and symbols can retain only a magical significance or serve as reminders of harmless platitudes. Younger people, brought up with the din of religious and political propaganda in their ears, are deaf to the subtleties of Javanism and they see no advantage in taking it seriously. One day I was talking about the shrine with the old caretaker, struggling with his old-fashioned vocabulary and often baffled by his toothless pronunciation. His grandson, a youth of about sixteen, came to my aid and repeated the difficult phrases. Then he translated them in a way that showed he did not understand. I could see that he was new to the ideas and he frequently laughed in surprise and embarrassment. It was all *kolot*, old-fashioned, he said, something for the older generation. Now we were more 'progressive'. Suddenly the blare of the mosque loudspeaker drowned our conversation; it was the call to prayer. He picked up his prayer mat and Koran – he was going to stay on afterwards to practise 'reading' – and, with what seemed like a mixture of pride and relief, made his exit.

5

Practical Islam

In a field usually characterized by its extremes, the middle ground of Javanese religious belief and practice is often overlooked. Studies of normative Islam in Java (e.g. Nakamura 1983, Peacock 1978a and b) have generally concentrated on urban and modernist Muslims or the traditional Islamic schools as representatives of orthodoxy, to the neglect of Islam as it is practised in ordinary villages. The typical informants in these accounts are knowledgeable and highly articulate with clearly formulated ideological positions. They are also, usually, members of fairly discrete communities and their contacts with non-santri are often limited to the workplace or market. The separation of santri religion from that of non-santri implied by this selective focus is further empha-sized by recourse to typologies which exclude intermediate cases. For example, in Geertz's (1960) presentation, one gains the impression that practitioners of the three religious variants inhabit separate worlds and each is consistent in his or her separate identity.[1] However, as we know, much of rural Java is populated by heterogeneous communities, and many individuals in these communities are neither clearly santri nor abangan but something in between.

It is this middle ground, of santri living intermingled with abangan, that I wish to explore here: a zone of compromise, inconsistency, and ambivalence which cannot be captured by a categorical opposition of santri versus abangan. My interest lies less in the delineation of types and subtypes (as within a static field) than in tracing the fluctuating inter-relations between people of differing orientation – the compromises, role switches, and half-measures that make up daily life in a mixed commun-ity. As we saw in chapter 2, concerning the slametan, common ground is not simply neutral territory unclaimed by rival camps; it is a carefully constructed area of compromise: the crucible of syncretism. A typological or synoptic approach, which most authors on Java have taken, cannot register this kind of complexity.

Koentjaraningrat, for example, though critical of Geertz's terminology, tends to follow his either/or model:

A description of the religion of the Javanese should, therefore, as Clifford Geertz has done in his book *The Religion of Java*, make a clear distinction between two very distinct manifestations of Javanese Islam, that is, the *Agami Jawi* and the *Agami Islam Santri*.   (1985: 317)

Both authors minimize the common ground between the two variants. Whereas earlier sources (e.g. Mayer and Moll 1909) report a full range of feasts among rural santri, Geertz locates the slametan within abangan religion and gives only the briefest mention to santri slametans (1960: 154). Koentjaraningrat, likewise, gives the impression that slametans play a very small role in santri ritual life (1985: 364, 390, 394–5). But is this true of rural santri or only of urbanites and modernists?

Among both native Osing and immigrant Javanese in the Banyuwangi area, there is no great difference between santri and others in attachment to the slametan – at least in the mixed communities. In fact, many graduates of *pondhok-pesantren*, the traditional Islamic boarding schools, learned their slametan prayers at the feet of a *kiyai* (traditional Muslim leader), the fount of rural orthodoxy. It is only in a minority of communities which have made a deliberate break with tradition, such as Tamansuruh (the village next to Bayu), or where the modernist organization Muhammadiyah has penetrated, such as Banjar in the same district, that a distance opens up between santri and the rest.

Perhaps, then, a simple dichotomy (or trichotomy, if we include the priyayi) is too crude an analytic framework. Ricklefs (1979), among others, has suggested revisions of the standard categories, finding multiple shades of grey between the polar types. But the complexity of Javanese civilization resides not just in plurality but in interrelation, in the dynamics of religious adaptation and change. A multiplication of categories obscures this fact rather than illuminates it. Interrelation can only be understood in terms of local conditions, not in terms of ideal types or categories which, by definition, are one or two steps removed from the compromises of social reality. A pious Muslim living next door to a Javanist mystic is influenced by the fact and does not act in the manner of one who inhabits a mosque quarter. But the significance of this only becomes apparent if we examine the nature of the predicament and its solutions; sorting into types will not help much. Geertz himself is aware of this grey area (though he does not explore it), pointing out that, in terms of worldview, the conservative santri often has more in common with abangan than with modernist Muslims (1960: 160):

the conservative tries to work out a halfway covenant with the reigning (abangan) tradition which will both make his own transition [to a fully assimilated Islam] easier and lessen the tension between himself and his neighbours who do not agree with him.   (1960: 161)

It is the nature of the covenant that I wish to explore in this chapter.

Once one recognizes the ideological diversity within a Javanese village, the conditions of that diversity demand explanation. It is not enough simply to note that *'Agami Jawi* and *Santri* are present in all Javanese communities' (Koentjaraningrat 1985: 318) and leave it that. We need to ask what intra-village diversity implies about the nature of the community as a whole and individual arrangements within it? On the face of it, one would expect either conflict leading to segregation (as often happened during the 1960s) or a working arrangement of compromise and situational flexibility. The very existence of relatively stable, mixed communities implies a spectrum of variation rather than a stark contrast, a softening of distinctions and criss-crossing of boundaries.[2]

But these are suppositions, unexplored implications of what has always been known. What of the reality in Banyuwangi? The brief sketch which follows will serve as an introduction to a discussion of local Muslim practices.

Pak Saleh: faith as ritual

Pak Saleh, a middle-aged farmer with two sons educated at a local *pondhok*, would be counted as one of the more solid and representative Muslims in Bayu. He comes from a respectable, God-fearing family and, like his brothers, rarely misses daily prayers or Friday worship in the mosque. 'Religion is in the blood', was how he put it to me. (Bayu's pious, it should be noted, are not newly Islamized abangan.) He shares a birthday with Muhammad – 12th Mulud – and celebrates the day with a slametan of red and white porridge. 'People born in Mulud are rather stubborn', he said, 'and if they like religion they tend to be firm.'

Like many of the pious in Bayu, Pak Saleh is as conscientious in observing tradition as he is in practising his faith. And it was a matter of tradition, rather than Islam, which had brought me to his house. I had gone there in the dead of night to attend a rite in honour of his baby grandson whose navel scab had lately dropped off. At an Empty Slametan (*slametan suwung*) – one of several such humorous rites in the life-cycle – guests sit down to a spread of empty plates and dishes. 'Nothing to see, really', said Pak Saleh wryly. He went on to explain that the rite 'symbolizes that woman is empty until filled by man's seed, making a child'. Hence, after the guests' pantomime of surprise, the empty rice baskets are replaced by brimming bowls and the slametan is repeated.[3]

A bizarre custom, and a typically Javanist explanation; yet there could be no question of my host's Muslim credentials, as a glance round the room confirmed. In an otherwise ordinary interior, with its marble-topped coffee table encircled by rickety chairs, display cabinets of crockery and family photos, it was the tokens of piety that stood out – a well-thumbed Koran resting conspicuously on the antiquated television; a calendar with an aerial view of Mecca crowded with pilgrims; a framed tin frieze with *burak*, the Prophet's winged steeds, etched in relief; little wooden shields with Koranic mottoes hanging on the walls; and hovering above, on the lintel, the ubiquitous double portrait of President and Vice-President, placed either side of the Pancasila state ideology: the final, authenticating detail. These pious touches are common enough, even among the uncommitted, but their number and combined effect is noted by visitors.

As with all such appointments, the 3 a.m. start was approximate. While we waited for the other guests, Pak Saleh, normally taciturn and quizzical, spoke about the Fast which was due to begin in a few days. He looked forward to it every year as a challenge and as a time to take stock. He had always fasted during Puasa, he said, not like some who had only lately caught on to the idea. But he admitted he was outdone by his neighbours, Sahran and Sukib, who fast every month for two or three days. People fast for different reasons: some for health, some for tradition's sake. It doesn't matter, as long as you fulfil the obligation and do so with a pure heart. Whatever your motive, you are rewarded with good fortune and slamet.

I supposed he was thinking of salvation but he corrected me:

Slamet is when you go to bed at night, get up in the morning and you are still there; nothing has happened. Slamet is not being bothered by demons.

It was the same with the five-times-daily prayers (salāt): they bring you peace and slamet. But this only lasts a short while, so you have to be regular and diligent.

Was there no more to worship than the quest for slamet, then? With a sigh, my host explained: God made men and spirits for no other purpose than worship (*ibadah*). Performance of salāt is the only repayment He expects. In worship we give thanks that we have arms and legs, that we can feed ourselves, that we exist.

These were explanations offered to a non-Muslim; what Pak Saleh thought I could make sense of. What he did not elaborate upon, but nevertheless effectively conveyed in our subsequent conversation, was that worship was a direct encounter with God, a submission before God's Majesty, and an affirmation of His existence and Oneness; and that to pray was to identify oneself as a Muslim. Nor did he dwell upon the spiritual satisfactions and quiet dignity that attend Islamic worship in Bayu as everywhere else in the Muslim world: this was perhaps too obvious to deserve comment. Indeed, I had seen it for myself.

Instead, he went on to name all the regular worshippers in the block and listed those who usually fasted, pointing out who had dropped out the previous year.

'Pak Narto lasted the whole month (his wife never fasts); Man Uri said he had
   toothache after three days; Sucipto fasts, so does Oso.'
'What about Pak Sumi [the diviner next door]?'
'Oh! I don't know about him!' he said, making an ironic face.

Each keeps a close eye on his neighbour; but sinful or otherwise, laxity in religion is one's own business. The point about fasting, he continued, is that only you yourself can benefit from the rewards, but if you learn to control your anger by self-discipline it makes for a better world.

As he presented it, the rewards of fulfilling scriptural obligations were mainly in this world. (Had I pressed him on doctrine, he would, perhaps, have given equal weight to the hereafter.) Even when we came to discuss grave-visiting, it was earthly blessings that came to mind.

Ninggal dunya [die] has a double meaning. It means 'departing the world', but it also means 'leaving wealth behind', that is, leaving your worldly goods and rice fields. So when you visit the grave of your parents you think with gratitude of what you owe to them and send them your prayers, even ask them for things.

Whether they heard or not, he couldn't say. 'Who knows. After all, the dead are bones in the grave!' Then, as if to cover his tracks, he quickly added: 'I don't understand these things. I just do them. It's for others to explain.'

When we turned to the matter of prayer postures and repetitions, again he began to explain and then retreated. 'Two cycles (*raka'at*) signifies male and female; three signifies "the three-in-one."' But he could not expand on this mysterious trinity (probably picked up from conversations with the mystics) and referred me to his pondhok-educated son.

Ritualism versus dogmatism

Pak Saleh's observance of the ritual prayers and prescribed practices of Islam is consistent with his fondness for the intricacies of Javanese ritual. But his ritualism is not simply an aesthetic preference for elaborate concrete forms over the abstractions of dogma – a kind of Javanese rococo; it is grounded in a sense of cultural and religious forms as rule-governed and in a deep respect for the authority of tradition, whether Islamic or ancestral. His emphasis on techniques goes with a certain unreflective modesty and willingness to defer ultimate responsibility.

To modernist Muslims, who point to the need for discrimination and awareness of basic principles, this is mere conformism coupled with an inability to see the wood for the trees. But a fairer characterization would be conservatism tempered with a certain ecumenical tolerance. One conforms because a particular usage is or feels right, and it feels right because it has always been done in a particular way. Whereas a modernist would be forced to select and exclude, traditionally minded Muslims like Saleh stress the complementarity of religion and custom. Indeed, the distinction between the two is somewhat blurred. The Fast is seen as both obligatory and customary. Like the prescribed prayers, it yields Javanese (rather than specifically Islamic) benefits, such as tranquillity, security, and self-mastery. These benefits are sufficient justification for ritual observance: there is no need to delve deeper into the nature of scriptural authority.

Pragmatic ritualism of this kind is open to criticism from another quarter. In the eyes of some of the more reflective mystics, such philosophical timidity makes the celebration of ritual, whether Islamic or Javanese, a hollow sham, much like the Empty Slametan. An emphasis on rules and techniques at the expense of meaning leaves ritual pointless, even ineffectual. The mystics describe this action-level of behaviour – the how-to of cultural performance – as *saré'at* (from Ar. *shariah*, Islamic law), as distinct from *hakékat*, the inner truth or esoteric meaning.[4] Since outward form is regarded as inferior to inner meaning, the implication is that pious Muslims like Pak Saleh never rise above blind rule-following. This view, again, is unfair since it totally ignores faith, which, for many, is at the heart of ritual observance.

If these comments suggest that the ordinary pious Muslim is squeezed between reformists, who would root out un-Islamic custom, and mystics, who would transcend ritual altogether (or at least invest it with special significance), this is not really the case. Muslims in Bayu with modernist sympathies are a small minority, and they seldom express their opinions in public. And the mystics, for their part, have long ago established a *modus vivendi* with the pious which sets limits to mutual criticism. I mention the rival viewpoints here to underscore the point that normative Islam in Bayu is generally seen as preoccupied with practice and is almost devoid of doctrinal concerns. For the pious – those who pray five times a day, perform the Fast assiduously, and spend hours at a time chanting in the prayer-house – Islam is a system of ritual prescriptions rather than a coherent and explicit system of beliefs, an ethical code, or a cosmology. Among the few who are willing to discuss doctrine, one quickly comes to a bedrock of unquestionable axioms and idiosyncratic speculation. After such unnerving detours into the unknown they return with relief to the details of practice.

Words as things

A second characteristic of village Islam, complementing the disposition to ritualism, is a certain naive realism. By this I mean a tendency to accept the package of ideas handed down by tradition as a factual description of reality, without symbolic nuance, and to regard Islamic and customary usages as acting on this reality in a direct, almost mechanical, fashion. This naive realism contrasts with the indifference and vague scepticism of many nominal Muslims concerning Islam and the opposite tendency of the mystics to see symbols in everything. We have observed this literal-mindedness already in santri interpretations of the slametan. But it also permeates more explicitly Islamic activities. Pious Muslims gather on Thursday and Sunday evenings to chant litanies called tahlilan, one purpose of which is to win merit (*pahala*). The chants are dedicated to the deceased, either the unspecified dead or named beneficiaries. Merit is conceived as 'provisions' (*sangu*) which the dead soul carries on the journey to heaven: the more repetitions the more provisions. (Chanting is not done for a deceased infant since the burden of provisions would be 'too heavy' and might slow its progress.) People do not trouble themselves about how the system works, and indeed many believe the chanters themselves benefit, either by winning personal merit or by pleasing the ancestors. What is clear, however, is that chanting yields merit.

It is a short step from this simple causal nexus to a quantification of results. A retired mosque official told me that on the 21st of the fasting month, the Night of Power, God 'lowered down profit and loss' (note the realist turn of phrase) and that the consequences of good or bad conduct on this day are hugely magnified. 'The rewards of a single day are equal to those of a thousand months.' Similarly, if you extend the Fast for a further six days (after a week's break) the rewards are equal to those won by a whole year of fasting. It sounds like a proven method; but questions about when benefits are reaped, whether they are transferable or how they are calculated, trespass on doctrine and are usually met with a defensive rebuff. The unfolding of eschatology and fate are accepted as mysteries beyond the comprehension of men. As with requests to the ancestors, one hopes and assumes that litanies and good deeds are 'received'; but one 'feels' the results at best indirectly – in better harvests, improved health, and confidence in one's ultimate salvation.

In this spiritual exchange, prayers and devotions are conceived almost as material missives rather than meaningful communications. At a commemorative sedhekah for the ancestors, one 'sends prayers' and incantations as bundles of words directed upwards on a stream of incense. The words themselves are not understood, but this does not matter; they are inherently powerful, and their effects are multiplied by repetition. As Bowen (1989: 611) notes of Koranic verses recited in salāt, for non-Arabic speakers, 'the semantic meaning of these verses may be of secondary ritual importance to their sacred quality as the words of God'.

A similar notion of verbal efficacy attaches to scriptural recitation outside worship. One month before departing on the pilgrimage to Mecca, the candidate hosts a feast at which the Koran is recited in its entirety. Thirty men each take one of the thirty divisions (*jus*) and read it aloud *at the same time*. Again, unmistakably, the medium is the message, and it is quantity, ritual completeness, which brings results. A substantial offering entails a substantial reward; and the prospective pilgrim, his spiritual bags bulging with merit, can depart in safety.

As this example shows, understanding is not of primary importance. Even accomplished performers rarely understand anything of the content: all the effort is on the skilled crafting of externals – tone, rhythm, correct pronunciation. Since the Koran is the literal word of God, it is imperative – and meritorious – to reproduce it correctly; but merit is won by performing the ritual action not by attending to its message. This subordination of meaning to performance (or their dissociation) is not confined to uneducated rural Muslims. In a survey of Koranic training in leading pondhok-pesantren, F. Denny (1988: 293) records:

Teachers often confessed to me that most students learn only the sounds of Arabic, and few comprehend what they recite ... Many Muslims believe that God's grace falls on anyone who recites the Qur'an excellently, with or without understanding.

Denny then quotes an Indonesian author who, recalling his Islamic education, admitted: 'God never said anything I was able to understand'. Put baldly, Islamic ritual in Java is conducted in a language understood by hardly any of its practitioners. Its meaning must therefore be located not in the words themselves but at a meta-linguistic level, thus outside the sphere of scripturally encoded orthodoxy.[5]

A religious life conducted in an uncomprehended tongue: this is a striking fact, but one which is not, I think, given sufficient prominence (with a few exceptions) either by ethnographers or Islamicists. The tendency is to pass over the fact, or to note it and then ignore it in formulating one's conclusions. W. Graham (1985: 28), for example, emphasizes the Koran as a 'living, active, immediate reality in people's lives rather than merely a completed, transmitted piece of writing'. But in the case of most conservative Javanese Muslims (and, presumably, traditionalists elsewhere who lack Arabic and who are averse to translations), the contrary holds: the Koran is a sacred object but, as far as the details of its message are concerned, a closed book.[6]

It is symptomatic of this conception of scripture as powerful and manipulable but inscrutable that, in Banyuwangi, there is a popular association (rarely, of course, attested in fact) between magical powers, even sorcery, and expertise in Arabic. Two modins of the past generation in Bayu were reputed to be sorcerers and were blamed for causing numerous deaths. Modin S was eventually killed by a mob; modin P fled and turned into a were-tiger who haunts Alas Purwo, the eastern forest. Several descendants of these 'sorcerers' were forbidden to learn Koranic recitation by their parents as it would later open them to accusations of sorcery. Abstinence from normative piety can thus, in special cases, be justified on respectable grounds.

To sum up, the pious conception of Arabic, the language of Islamic worship, as an opaque but powerful medium, is part and parcel of an action-orientation, a disposition to ritual as opposed to doctrine, which contrasts with other orientations, notably the contemplative, symbolist perspective of the Javanists. A tendency among the pious to treat words as things, objects for ritual manipulation, contrasts with the Javanists' passion for seeing things as words (a world grasped through puns, the body as a script, etc.).

This characterization is at odds with the typical depiction of santri as 'people of the book', 'scripturalists', men of ideas and dogma as opposed to ritualists.

abangans are fairly indifferent to doctrine but fascinated with ritual detail, while among the santris the concern with doctrine almost entirely overshadows the already attenuated ritualistic aspects of Islam.   (Geertz 1960: 127)

But perhaps an overemphasis on modernist views, and expert views at that, has led Java's ethnographers to undervalue the 'fundamentally *ritualist* orientation' of Islam (Graham, cited in Bowen 1993: 22), as exemplified in rural conservative Muslims. It is undeniable that ordinary, faithful practitioners indifferent to dogma – Muslims like Pak Saleh – are unfamiliar figures in the ethnography, victims of the typologist's law of excluded middle. It is the louder, better educated voices which have always prevailed.

Conditions favouring ritualism
The strikingly undogmatic, inarticulate character of normative Islam in Bayu can be accounted for by a set of closely related conditions: the mixed nature of the community demands a situational flexibility in orientation (which is linked to a characteristic moral and perceptual relativism); and this flexibility is facilitated by a preference for ritual action over speech.

Thus, while dogma dominates the lives of santri in strict and relatively segregated communities such as Tamansuruh and Pesucen, in mixed villages like Bayu, which make up well over half of the district, its role remains minimal. This is not just because the santri of Bayu are 'less Islamic', as Tamansuruh would have it, but because in a mixed community dogma is dangerous and is therefore to be avoided. As the ethnography testifies, throughout Muslim Indonesia doctrinal dissension is almost always accompanied by social fission and the creation of factions. A densely populated community – and Osing settlements are unusually dense, even by Javanese standards – cannot withstand serious disagreement. As Jay (1969: 235) has written: 'A neighbourhood [is] an arena within which maximum pressures are exerted on individuals toward conformity with the values of rural society.' Such pressures are most visible in gatherings like slametans and prayer-house activities which constitute the neighbourhood as a social entity. One who opts out, or who disputes the form of the ritual, places himself outside its social boundary. In villages like Tamansuruh, it is precisely on questions such as the permissibility of the slametan and the efficacy of langgar chanting that Islamic debate is focused.

Bayu's hyper-cautious, but practical, solution to the problem of religious diversity is an old and reliable one – nobody remembers a time (except during the aberrant 1960s) when life was any different – but it has been reinforced under the New Order. Tight governmental control of religious debate is part of a general restriction on the exchange of ideas. Western-style democratic party politics and free expression concerning any important matter are seen as inevitably leading to strife, and propaganda ceaselessly drives home the message that difference equals conflict. The 'proof', constantly invoked, is the bloodbath of 1965. But from time to time the message has been reinforced by communal violence, some of it 'opportune', some of it organized by elements within the government and armed forces. Indeed, this blending of government admonition and exemplary chaotic violence has characterized the handling of Suharto's exit from power as much as it has his 32-year rule.

It would be misleading, however, to overemphasize external factors in what is, for the most part, a local and traditional arrangement. The ecumenism which characterizes religious life in the village is not seen as an imposition from above but a response to a shared interest in social harmony. Events on the national scene may have sharpened that interest, but Bayu could have gone the way of Tamansuruh and broken the consensus had enough villagers wanted change.

The peculiar character of Islam in this setting – undogmatic, unarticulated, embedded in local custom – presents the anthropologist with a quandary. To record the comments of a few fluent spokesmen would be misleading – partly because such figures are unrepresentative, partly because commentary itself is unusual. An approach through 'discourse', in the manner of Bowen's admirable study of Sumatran Muslims (1993), would be impossible since there is very little discourse to register: no coffee-shop schisms over doctrine, no impromptu debates in which points of theology are brandished and positions refined, and little in the way of indoctrination. As the Sumatran case shows (or, closer to Bayu, the villages of Tamansuruh and Banjar), such doctrinal contention within the Indonesian umat arises in response to the challenge of reformism and its assaults on syncretist tradition.[7]

The questions which divide Bayu's Muslims go much deeper than the controversies over canonical ritual which divide modernists from traditionalists in Indonesia. At issue are fundamentals like the status of Islam as a revealed religion, the transcendence of God, and the nature of meaning. But these questions are far too delicate to be spoken about, let alone debated, in public. There is, moreover, a difference of approach, which I have highlighted, between the ritualism of the devout and the intellectualism of the Javanists, which makes any such debate difficult to conceive. The religion of men like Pak Saleh, who form the backbone of Islam in Bayu, is a thing 'done' not said (this is how he himself puts it): a matter of practice, display, and moral action rather than doctrine. As such, its significance is best discerned in the interplay with other religious and cultural forms and in the positioning of the faithful within village society. Following a brief definition of terms, it is therefore to the immediate society of Islam that we now turn: the Muslim congregation, prayer-houses, the influences of school and neighbourhood, and the lives of santri among non-santri.

Elements of the umat

Whether Muslims like Pak Saleh count as santri or not is a moot question, but not a very important one. The puritans of nearby Taman-suruh would class most of Bayu's pious as rank syncretists. But it is enough for the present discussion that there are genuine and consistent contrasts between villagers over and above the usual idiosyncratic variations. While it is not all that surprising if a town mosque official, an unschooled peasant, and a blue-blooded bureaucrat hold different views on most subjects, including religion, the range of opinion and practice within a small-scale, fairly uniform rural population is quite remarkable, whatever labels one uses, and calls for explanation.

Individual quibbles aside, I use the term santri here, following Geertz and others (Snouck Hurgronje 1906: 340; Pigeaud 1983: 78; Koentjar-aningrat 1985: 196–7), as shorthand for pious Muslim. The people of Banyuwangi themselves speak of santri in the double sense that Geertz noted (1960: 178): in reference to a student of Islam and with a broader meaning denoting those who take the orthodox tenets of Islam seriously. Diagnostics vary, but in this region as in Modjokuto in the 1950s, 'it is fidelity in performing the prayers which, ultimately, defines a santri' (Geertz 1960: 215).

The contrasting term which Geertz applies to nominal Muslims, abangan, is rarely used in Banyuwangi. Instead there is a more tenden-tious distinction between *wong Islam*, Muslims, and *wong Jawa*, the Javanese, implying either the foreignness of Islam, if one is a Javanist, or the impiety of other Javanese (usually a neighbour), if one is a santri. But the terms are not always used oppositionally. The distinction may refer to the same person's identity in different contexts, and in a broad sense almost everyone is both Muslim and Javanese.

A rough breakdown of the umat (the community of faithful) in Bayu gives the following figures: four *haji*s (men and women who have performed the pilgrimage to Mecca), with a further two poised for departure; one modin (mosque official) plus two retired modins; six owners or leaders of prayer-houses, three of whom serve as unpaid Koranic teachers (*guru ngaji*); one religious instructor in the primary school (*guru agama*); and some thirty graduates of pondhok-pesantren, traditional Islamic boarding schools. Besides these, there are as many pious Muslims who have had no formal training in Islam but who carry out the obligatory 'pillars of the faith', notably the five-times-daily prayers (salāt). Pak Saleh would be a typical example. Friday worship at the mosque brings in a still larger number of self-consciously 'good Muslims'. On an average Friday I once counted some ninety worshippers, including about twenty-five women. As *wong Islam*, though certainly not all santri, almost all villagers are involved in celebrating Muslim feasts such as Muludan, the commemoration of the Prophet's birthday, and Lebaran (Idul Fitri), the end of the Fast.

Whereas there would be rough agreement about who are to count as santri – those diligent in worship – the broader category of the umat has no consistent range. Indeed, the concept of a community of faithful is rarely invoked and in many conversations I had with prominent santri the word umat was hardly ever used. This caution, again, is probably a function of the social setting. To refer to one set of people (say, Friday mosque attenders) as the umat would be to draw a boundary invidiously excluding a large proportion of the village. Yet to include the many lax or indifferent Muslims within the boundary and exclude only the odd Christian or heretic would be pointless. The contrast with Geertz's portrait of Modjokuto Muslims in the 1950s is instructive. He found that 'for the santri, the sense of community – of *ummat* – is primary' (1960: 128); and this characteristic, combined with 'a tremendous interest in doctrine', defined 'two distinguishing features of the santri religious pattern' (129–30). Geertz was of course writing of a semi-urban, relatively solidary grouping at a time of intense factional politics: a situation exactly the opposite to the one I am describing here.

One further distinction within the umat must be mentioned, that of gender. Women play only an ancillary role in the organization of village Islam. They have their own chanting sessions in the prayer-house and may attend Friday prayers in the mosque (segregated behind a curtain);

but no woman enjoys prestige as a leading Muslim independent of her husband. The wife of a haji is expected to be a model of piety and is addressed as Mother Haji, even if she did not accompany her husband to Mecca; but many santri wives do not share their husbands' religiosity.

Plate 7 A young woman reads the Koran at her wedding

Some are indifferent; others say they are 'too busy' to take an interest. The relentless duties of home and family ensure that women have less free time than men, and there is no female equivalent to the cohort of young idle men or pious elders who make up a large part of the langgar congregation.

Educational differences also contribute to the male domination of village Islam, though this situation is now changing. Whereas many middle-aged women, including the wives of many santri, never learned to recite Arabic or master the few prayers necessary for minimal participation in Islam, all village girls today are expected to attend Koranic classes and to acquire basic competence in the liturgy. Education at state school includes a heavy religious component and piety is a prominent aspect of an emerging national youth culture. In the village context, it is still too early to see whether the changes of recent years will mean that women in general become more active in Islam, as youthful piety persists into maturity, or whether piety will simply become associated with girlhood. In any case, a girl's Islamic education ceases upon marriage. Her official completion of the Koran (*khataman*) is often incorporated into the wedding festivities with a ceremonial reading before guests, and afterwards she withdraws from public participation in Islam. A young mother, according to custom, may not attend the langgar or mosque. (There is a banal 'reason' for this exclusion. Young mothers or carers carry babies on the hip and their clothes are frequently wet with the child's urine, disqualifying them from worship.)

Young men, on the other hand, continue to play an important role in the organization of Islam. They staff committees to collect the annual *jakat pitrah* (alms), organize visiting speakers and calendrical celebrations at the mosque, and they are active in promoting a more vigorous role for Islam in village life.

Socio-economic categories

No particular social or economic category of villagers has a monopoly of piety. Among leading santri are the richest landowner (a haji), an ex-modin who carries bricks for a living, a factory artisan who commutes to town by bicycle, a harvest broker, and various small farmers. Devout Muslims are scattered throughout the village, with slight clusterings around the mosque, the central area, which is called Talun, and Sukosari, near the village shrine. These clusterings have come about not through a gathering of like-minded souls but simply as a result of neighbourly influence and kinship. New households tend to be established in or near the parental home and tend to reflect parental orientation. The santri of Talun and its offshoot Sukosari are descendants of two elders who attended pondhok-pesantren during the 1930s.

The mainly landless peasants and wage-labourers of east Bayu have tended to be less active in religious matters, and it was this section of the village which had links with the communist party in the 1960s. Nevertheless, it has a prayer-house, rebuilt in 1965 just after the coup which launched the annihilation of the Left in Indonesia. Some survivors of this repression are among the regular Friday worshippers and their weekly walk in prayer-garb up to the mosque is a public demonstration of their position. Whether their compliance marks a change of heart, a claim to respectability, or merely an insurance against future repression is debatable. All that is required, in any case, is outward conformity. A new force for orthodoxy within the same neighbourhood is the young primary school religious teacher who sees himself as a missionary among the heathen. He occupies, rent-free, a house owned by one of the leaders of the barong troupe. This erstwhile leftist sympathizer is now being 'taught to pray' by his zealous tenant, a man half his age. Such humiliations, suffered with a certain grudging humour, illustrate the predicament of non-santri who lack prestige or education.

In other parts of the village the non-santri have less to fear. Indeed, wherever Javanists (i.e. Sangkan Paran mystics and unaffiliated kejawèn types) outnumber santri it is the latter who have adopted a tight-lipped, defensive posture, grimly sticking to their prayers and chants despite murmurings of 'exhibitionism'. The greater self-confidence of Javanists outside east Bayu can be put down to two factors. First, they were not tainted by leftist affiliation, being for the most part middling peasant farmers who supported the PNI during the Sukarno era. Secondly, as adherents of a complex mystical philosophy, they are unimpressed by santri criticism. As with the santri, affiliation has tended to reflect kinship ties and most mystics can be located on a handful of genealogies. This, again, has led to small clusterings of two or three similar households; but nothing large enough to count as a block.

In and among the clusters of santri and mystics can be found villagers of every persuasion, with a slight preponderance of indifferent, moderately poor peasants and artisans, unconstrained by a dark past and uncommitted to any philosophy. Diversity, then, is the norm and a separation of neighbourhoods along religious lines would be unfeasible. The culturally and socially significant grouping is the (overlapping) slametan guest-list of up to a dozen neighbouring households; and almost every such grouping in the village would include people of differing orientation.

This dense intermingling is one reason why affiliation to mass Muslim organizations is at present very low: anything which smacks of political exclusivism – of 'standing out' – will, it is feared, lead to factionalism. So, at any rate, it has proved in the past when Islamic parties were briefly active. (The mystical sect, in contrast, keeps a low profile in village affairs and does not attempt to recruit members.) A reluctance to engage in organized Islamic politics reflects a general desire not to upset the political status quo rather than a lack of interest among santri in the promotion of Islam. This, of course, may change as the political profile of Indonesian Islam changes or if a common interest in the social consensus diminishes (see chapter 9). In other, less compact, villages in the region, the traditionalist Muslim organization, Nahdlatul Ulama (NU), is well represented, both among Osing and migrant Javanese groups.

Despite a substantial santri presence in Bayu, the level of knowledge of Islam is low. There are no scholars (*ulama*) or clerics and Bayu has never produced a kiyai. The graduates of pesantren for the most part attended for just a few years, though one of the modins spent twelve years in various establishments. Nobody in the village has been associated with Islamic mystical brotherhoods such as the Shattariyya or Naqshbandiyya, otherwise well known in the world of East Javanese santri (Bruinessen 1992: 167–74); and nobody I met claimed to know about orthodox mysticism, although *tasawwuf* is one of the subjects taught in pesantren. Other core subjects include the study of hadīth, traditions concerning the Prophet and his companions which form part of the *sunna*, and *fiqh*, jurisprudence (Dhofier 1980). Again, apart from a few well-known hadīth, village santri tend to regard such knowledge as the speciality of experts. This is not the case, however, in neighbouring Tamansuruh, and a brief description here will illustrate many differences in the cultural situation.

Tamansuruh

Less than two miles from Bayu, the village of Tamansuruh displays a polarization of the kind familiar from earlier ethnographies (notably Jay 1963) but now (at least in this area) relatively uncommon – a strictly orthodox hamlet focused on the mosque with miscellaneous settlements scattered to the periphery. The santri of the central hamlet call themselves *ahlus sunnah wal jama'ah*, traditionalist orthodox Muslims, as

opposed to modernists.[8] Criteria vary, but traditionalists generally
preserve certain usages which modernists regard as deviations or illegitimate innovations.[9] In Tamansuruh, for example, worshippers use the
kunut prayer at dawn worship; they speak the *niya* (intention) aloud
before performing salāt; they recite the *talkin* address at a funeral
(though, 'for the benefit of the living, not the dead soul'); and they recite
litanies (tahlilan) for the express purpose of winning religious merit.

There are no Muhammadiyah members in the hamlet, though many of
the reforms recently carried out are in tune with Muhammadiyah
thinking. The village secretary told me most people are adherents of
Nahdlatul Ulama, which has a mass following in East Java. Since NU is
now officially neutral in regard to party politics, many people choose to
vote for the government rather than for the umbrella Muslim party (the
PPP) in general elections. This is a matter of expediency, not preference.
If a village is found to have a majority vote against the government the
headman can be replaced and other sanctions applied.

The Islamic revival in Tamansuruh was spearheaded by Pak Ja'i, now
a white-haired patriarch, who returned to his village in 1945 after years
of study in Pondhok Cemorong, a rural pesantren to the south-west of
Banyuwangi. His life's work, continued by his family and followers, has
been to purify the faith of the accretions of custom: the sole guide for
Muslims should be the scriptures and law books. As his son told me,
ancestral traditions are to be 'wiped out' if they disagree with Islam.
Even customs which are not actually prohibited should be discarded as
'having no use'. For example, the elaborate wedding rituals common in
other villages are drastically simplified – only the joining of thumbs and
the Islamic *nikah* ceremony are necessary. There is no procession or
retinue and no all-night sitting of the bride and groom: 'one who is
enthroned cannot worship'. Likewise, the usual tambourine drumming
which accompanies the joining of thumbs is banned as it would disturb
sunset prayers.

Slametans have not been entirely eradicated, but the symbolic offerings
and incense have been eliminated as 'smelling of Buddhism'. Naturally,
the long symbolic explication is omitted: there is nothing to explicate.
One just states one's purpose and recites a prayer. Lacking even the red
and white porridge and the flower-water, these prayer-meals have so little
of Java in them they are better regarded as belonging to Malay Muslim
culture. In fact, the term most often used in Tamansuruh is the Malay
word *kenduri* rather than slametan.

The scriptural and doctrinal basis of these reforms has been fully

assimilated. After inveighing against the polytheism of traditional slametans, the village secretary quoted to me, in Arabic and then in Javanese,
the hadīth which justifies the retention of sedhekah, commemorative
feasts.[10] Any deviations from strict monotheism, however, are condemned as *syrik*, the sin of idolatry. If one intends to hold a feast to
safeguard the rice crop, one should pray only to God, he said, not to
some non-existent place spirit; and at funeral sedhekah one may ask God
to reward the deceased, to relieve their tortures in the afterlife and so on,
but the dead themselves are beyond communication and it would be
futile to address them. The calendrical slametans added on to the Muslim
holy days in Bayu and elsewhere have mostly been dropped as 'unnecessary'. For example, concerning the feasts held on the eve of the Fast,
called *Nampa Puasa* (lit. 'welcome the fasting month'), the secretary
scoffed in derision: 'What is the point of "welcoming" the Fast, especially
if, as in Bayu, you only fast for three days? Any excuse for a slametan!'

Anxious to salvage something for tradition and the reputation of my
host village, I replied:

'Surely such feasts do a lot for solidarity and harmony in the neighbourhood.'
'But we are harmonious without them, so they are obviously unnecessary.'

Besides this uncompromising attitude towards tradition – a sweeping
aside of shibboleths, the comforts of habit, and even Muslim entertainments such as chanting with tambourines ('it is a sin to strike something
while pronouncing God's name') – there is a positive effort to apply
Islamic law and to breathe an Islamic spirit into everyday life. As well as
regular Koran-readings, there are monthly gatherings in the mosque for
intensive indoctrination. On the appointed day, beginning at dawn, there
is a recital of the entire Koran, performed in shifts by readers nominated
by the mosque committee. After *isa'* prayers (around 7 p.m.) there is
group chanting and then committee-style speeches on government projects, matters arising, etc. Then, after a further scriptural reading, there is
a discussion panel. The leading santri give prepared answers to questions
submitted to them beforehand. They apply the law books to such
everyday matters as 'whether a woman may take a pill to end her period
if it has lasted more than five days'. Indeed, the law books are a familiar
sight in Tamansuruh. In several of the houses I visited I found the
densely written tomes lying around on coffee tables.

Behind this fierce dogmatism lies a perfectly reasonable argument, put
to me many times, that if one claims to be a Muslim one had better
behave like one. Tamansuruh's santri see little room for interpretation in

this matter: the rules are set out in black and white for all time. Since almost everyone is a Muslim, any deviations from scriptural obligations can only be regarded as backsliding, deserving of scorn and disapprobation. As we shall see, Bayu's uncommitted are rarely faced with such stark judgments; when they are, there is little they can say in reply and they take the offence deeply. Only the accomplished mystics can handle the challenge with aplomb and turn it back on the santri. Instead of justifying their laxity they question the santri's narrow definition of Islam. But in Tamansuruh there is no room for such latitude.

'Isn't the important thing to believe in God, as everyone does, even the mystics?' I said.
'Mystics! Even the devil believed in God. There's no merit in that. Belief without worship is worthless.'

After this chastening insight into Muslim practice in a strict santri community we can return to Islam in Bayu better aware of its diverse and often equivocal character – inclusive and ecumenical where the other is puritan and uncompromising, indifferent to dogma where the other is bookish and prescriptive.

The rise of a langgar

Normative Islam in Bayu is based in the langgar (prayer-house). In its catchment, the langgar is to the neighbourhood what the mosque is to the village; but since the neighbourhood is the principal arena of social life and the sphere in which moral action is moulded and judged, the langgar is of greater practical importance. A village can survive without a mosque; indeed, Bayu had no mosque until 1953. Before then, santri had to walk to the next village to attend Friday prayers. Without the mainstay of a langgar, however, piety in effect ceases to be normative: scriptural obligations remain obligations, but santri solidarity and community pressure fade away.

There are six langgars in Bayu in a suggestive variety of architectural styles. The hamlet of Sukosari has a tiny bamboo shelter erected on stilts, said to resemble the buda sanctuaries (sanggar) of former times. During the day, boys and old men sit in its shade, watching rice dry on mats in the yard. But it is too small for communal worship and only the oldest inhabitants use it for prayers. The rest perform their salāt either in the mosque or in a dilapidated prayer-house in the ravine below. Sukosari is the most solidly devout hamlet in the whole village and only two out of its nine families abstain from prayer.

Three larger langgars and the mosque itself are certified, or in the long process of being certified, as *wakaf* (Ar. *wakf*), Islamic foundations recognized by the state (Djatnika 1985). The langgar of east Bayu was built in 1965, just after the coup, with donations from a neighbourhood eager to prove its faith. The old modin, who owned the plot, transferred it to representatives of the neighbourhood in 1967. In the west, the current modin runs a large langgar next-door to his house, built with donations in 1980 and certified as *wakaf* in 1991. The plot originally belonged to his grandfather. Two other langgars in central Bayu, whose varying fortunes I shall discuss, are built on privately owned land. A brief description will give some idea of the physical setting and typical activities of village Islam.

Ali's langgar, which he calls Nur Jannah (Light of Paradise), was built ten years ago with contributions solicited mainly from the immediate neighbourhood. With its mossy tiled roof, whitewashed bamboo walls, and creaking wooden floor worn shiny by worshippers' knees, it looks much older. Perched unsteadily on piles, it has a faintly ramshackle air as if about to slide at any moment into the gully below. The only incongruous note is a pair of electronic megaphones which

Plate 8 Old-style prayer-house

project from the roof. These are now used to call the faithful to prayer instead of the traditional buffalo-hide drum which still hangs from the eaves.

The langgar is a scene of fluctuating activity and is rarely empty. Like the *meunasah* of rural Aceh (Snouck Hurgronje 1906: I, 62), at quiet moments it doubles as a kind of men's house – a cool and shady retreat for old men and youths at a loose end. Then, at the set periods prescribed by Muslim law (dawn, noon, afternoon, sunset, and late evening) it fills up with worshippers: three or four at noon, as many as twenty in the evening. Male worshippers stand on the left, facing Mecca, females stand on the right, screened off by a white curtain.

The langgar is as much a place of study as worship. One wall has a row of pictures showing prayer postures and a chart displaying the evening's educational activities: Monday 'learning the Arabic letters', Tuesday Koranic recitation, Wednesday 'building of faith and religion', Thursday salāt practice, Friday *Barzanji* (a devotional chant) and recitation of Sura Yasin (used in funeral feasts), Saturday lawbooks, Sunday hadīth (traditions of the Prophet). These sessions for adults are poorly attended, whereas the Koranic classes held every afternoon attract almost all neighbourhood children of school age, even those of parents indifferent to Islam. Ali receives no payment for his work and supports himself entirely by farming.

In contrast to Ali's traditional prayer-house, Slamet's langgar is an extension of his home, a modern town-style building next to the road. Slamet is pondhok-trained and has close ties with the modin, but he has no vocation to teach and he built the langgar as an act of personal piety. As a harvest broker often away from home, he is content to leave its direction to others. At various times during my stay it was the scene of neighbourhood feasts, hellfire sermons, electioneering speeches and all-night chanting.

The character of a langgar is apt to fluctuate and its fortunes can change quite rapidly. A donation or grant can revive enthusiasm and give a sudden boost to membership; a defecting leader can take his followers with him and thus deplete a congregation. Given the uneven appeal of Islam in any neighbourhood, much depends on the character and zeal of key persons and the tone as well as the import of their message. There is a fine line between the encouragement of backsliders and the giving of offence. A misplaced word can quickly empty a langgar or isolate it from the sustenance of the neighbourhood.

The two rival prayer-houses may serve as an example. When I arrived at the end of 1991, Slamet's langgar seemed moribund. He had been at the centre of a scandal in another village and his wife had turned him out of the house. While the neighbourhood was enjoying these antics and had all but lapsed into paganism, the langgar suffered a loss of prestige and for several months lay empty.

Meanwhile, Ali's langgar some fifty yards away was flourishing. Apart from the regular evening classes, on Thursdays and Sundays about a dozen men and boys gather for devotional chanting (tahlilan). (Women have separate sessions.) A good loud noise testifies to the vitality of a langgar better than anything else – at least that is the general opinion. So for an hour or two the loudspeakers blare and chanters wrestle for control of the microphone. During the intervals, or when voices tire, a cassette is broadcast at maximum volume, drowning the competition from other langgars.

During the fasting month religious activity reaches a peak. Ali's langgar was packed every night for the (highly meritorious) supplementary prayers. The regular congregation more than doubled to about thirty. Afterwards, half a dozen young people took turns chanting the Koran, completing three full readings in the space of a month. Mornings began at 3 a.m. with the deafening cry of *sahur! sahur!*, the signal to prepare breakfast. During the hour before *imsa'*, the warning to stop eating, sermons blasted across the neighbourhood. Slamet's langgar, meanwhile, was silent.

But then things began to change. The holy month climaxes in Lebaran, a week of feasting and visiting; after this, dullness and routine returns to village life and Religion is put away for another year. At least, that is how many would prefer it. Having stacked up merit with the nightly chanting and discharged the year's accumulated sins by fasting, many feel they have earned the right to sleep. But Pak Sidik, the *imam* (prayer-leader) had other ideas and continued his apocalyptic pre-dawn broadcasts. More irritating still, his rendition of the *tamba ati* ('balm for the heart'), a Javanese exhortation to piety, began to depart from the usual lyric, alleging that backsliders 'become ghosts'. Some felt insulted. My neighbour – a man who has never prayed – objected: 'Sinners go to hell; they don't become ghosts' (apparently a worse fate). He then sang the correct lines:

Wong aras-arasan iku digandoli syétan
Wong sungkan sembahyang bakal getun ring mburian
(The apathetic – after them Satan flies,
Those reluctant to pray are in for a big surprise.)

Pak Sidik was eventually silenced by a hail of stones lobbed onto the roof of the langgar. The culprits, two respectable middle-aged men, told me they did not want to complain as they would have been open to taunts of *kafir*, unbeliever; nor did they want to break relations with their pious neighbours. The protest was all the more effective for being indirect. A seemingly aggressive act, far from provoking a reaction, provided an escape from personal confrontation. Ali understood the objections and asked Sidik to leave; but the reputation of his langgar was tarnished and it had lost its most zealous member.

At about the same time a new figure appeared on the scene, a young paramedic from Surabaya. Although he wasted little time in affronting people with his brusque manner and town ways, Basuki was conspicuously devout and better educated in Islam than anyone else in the neighbourhood. When he and Sidik joined Slamet's langgar its fortunes began to revive. Within weeks he had organized funding for new and powerful loudspeakers (which Sidik tested to destruction) and suddenly a congregation materialized. He insisted that the family with whom he boarded attend prayers and chanting, and he applied similar pressure to other waverers in the block. People were impressed by the fact that he made Sidik give up the microphone and take turns with him. 'Harder than tearing a baby from its bottle', as one man said. There were several defectors from Ali's langgar along with Sidik and, together with the new recruits, a respectable congregation of eight or nine was assembled for evening prayers.

Further innovations followed. Every Thursday night after chanting there was a sermon followed by a meal. Each week one of the congregation acted as host and brought the food. The sermon, given by one of the prayer-leaders or other santri in the block, was on familiar themes of living up to one's obligations as a Muslim (praying five times a day, fasting, etc.) and topical matters such as development and conduct during the elections. The tone was admonitory and patronizing. Parents were told of the importance of loving their children and of setting a good example. Several sermons emphasized the role of education in creating pious and law-abiding citizens. Indonesian – the language of school and officialdom – rather than Javanese was used for these addresses, even though some of the congregation could not understand.

Apart from these regular gatherings there was an effort to incorporate traditional Muslim feasts into congregational life. Thus, the whole neighbourhood was assembled to 'welcome the Fast', filling the langgar and overflowing onto the nearby verandah. The aim of the organizers

was evidently pragmatic. They stressed the advantage of pooling resources; and nobody objected that men and women sat together on the
verandah, something as unusual as it was unorthodox. Traditionally
most such feasts have been celebrated in the home by a group of
neighbouring households. But by making the event a langgar affair the
organizers were able to identify the concept of congregation with that of
neighbourhood, showing that 'we are all good Muslims here'.

The cumulative effect of these innovations was widely noted. In a
previously dormant neighbourhood there was an appreciable quickening
of the faith and a number of nominal Muslims had come into the fold.
The early gains were consolidated over the following months and during
the next Puasa, in contrast to the previous year, there was a high turn-
out for supplementary prayers and a much wider observance of the Fast.
But perhaps most significantly, a number of active younger santri who
had hitherto lacked a spiritual home suddenly found themselves at the
centre of a newly defined neighbourhood umat.

The motivations of the younger santri and the tenor of their piety are
quite different from those of the older Muslims. They have come to Islam
via a different route. Indonesian villages are full of young people who
have completed high school or further education and acquired a knowledge of the modern world which sets them apart from their parents but
which offers them no prospect of employment or prosperity. They are
fluent in Indonesian, conversant with urban ways, and mostly sceptical
of parental 'superstitions'. This vast, underemployed reserve of energy is
increasingly directed, and directing itself, towards Islam. The constant
linking of religion with development and nation-building in official
pronouncements and educational programmes has established Islamic
piety, in recent years, as a respectable way of being 'progressive' (*maju*)
and in tune with national goals.[11] Becoming a good Muslim, which is the
self-conscious aim of the young pious, means joining this great onward
march. It offers respectability and a sense of participating in a greater
good, where other avenues to status and power are blocked. Accustomed
to languishing on the sidelines, pious youths are now presented with an
immediate challenge and sphere of influence in the shape of the neighbourhood.

The changing position of this younger generation within the community will largely determine the future course and character of Islam in
Bayu. Leadership is still in the hands of an older generation of conservative, pondhok-trained Muslims who are proficient in the liturgy but
unequipped to deal with modern realities. The two imams of Slamet's

langgar, Sidik and Tasim, are representative: middle-aged, old-fashioned santri, deeply devout but with little ambition to propagate the faith or extend its influence beyond customary limits. Traditionally, Bayu's santri have thought that setting an example was the best way to bring others to the 'straight path'. Among the young, however, a true missionary spirit is gaining ground. The new champions of the faith reflect the emphasis of government-backed pietism: inclusive, pragmatic, conscientious, and non-political. They also tend to be reform-minded but gradualist, which suggests that they will probably be able to carry the rank-and-file with them as they slowly replace the old guard.

A langgar activist
One of the leading lights of the langgar, and of Islam in the village as a whole, is a man of thirty-five named Purnomo. His predicament as a reform-minded santri in a mixed, conservative village illustrates some of the compromises forced on evangelists and exemplifies how Islamizing Java often turns out to mean Javanizing Islam.[12]

Purnomo was marked out for piety from birth, being one of those rare individuals, like the Prophet himself, born 'already circumcised'. (This was said of several pious men in the area and is traditionally attributed to certain prophets (Wensinck 1953b: 255).) Although his father is an old-fashioned pondhok santri, Purnomo attended technical school, eventually becoming a lathe operator in a Chinese factory. He never learned to *ngaji* (recite) properly, but he sees his secular education as a positive advantage, allowing him to break out of his father's narrow ways and to think for himself about Islam. He speaks Indonesian and reads the Koran and hadīth in translation, whereas his father recites the Arabic texts beautifully but without comprehension. Purnomo sees this attitude to textual authority as typifying the generational difference.

The older santri cannot discuss Islam; they simply read out their Friday sermons in the mosque from printed texts. Ask them a question and they cannot reply unless it is on a point of procedure. They cannot develop an idea or relate the scriptures to daily life. And they are repetitive. Young people find all that boring.

In the drive for Islamization, men like Purnomo are the counterparts of the Tamansuruh puritans – lacking their Islamic expertise, to be sure, but matching them in zeal and in many ways better equipped to harmonize village Islam with the state ideology. Unencumbered by medieval law books, Purnomo is able to present Islam almost as a government programme, a contribution to development and progress. With his emphasis on the civic virtues of duty and obedience to authority, he lacks the divided loyalties so common among Muslim activists. If Islamic piety enhances loyal, forward-looking citizenship, this is because everything – modern education, scriptural Islam, government policy – appears to point in the same direction. Traditional practices, such as burning incense or asking the dead for their blessing, are both unIslamic and irrational from a scientific point of view; slametans are both superstitious and wasteful in the Era of Development. In contrast, the doctrines of Islam and science are complementary, and officially so. School science books begin with the divine creation; technocratic ministers become hajis.

The language and tone of Purnomo's piety – earnest, censorious, modern-sounding – obviously have little to do with traditional Islam. Purnomo and Saleh, sponsor of the Empty Slametan, would seem to be poles apart. Even Ali, a contemporary of Purnomo, seems to belong to a different era, positively disposed towards adat and tolerant, if not wholly sympathetic, towards unorthodox practices. Whereas Purnomo regards the Buyut Cili cult as a haven of superstition, a theatre of illusions, Ali merely avoids its wilder expressions, preferring to leave the barong show before the spirit arrives at dawn. Moreover, as a *guru ngaji*, Ali is committed to the reproduction of an older form of village Islam with its rote-learning and devotion to an uncomprehended scripture.

However, at the level of *practice*, there is little difference between the new men and the old, and it would be a distortion to represent them as modernists against traditionalists. Village life blurs such distinctions. Mindful of his circumstances, Purnomo voices his opinions rarely and with great caution. One evening we were sitting in the house of the langgar prayer-leader, Tasim. I had just returned from a trip to Alas Purwo, a forest notorious for its haunted spots, and there was talk of were-tigers and spirits. Purnomo quietly doubted that there could be anything in a forest but trees, but Tasim knew people who had encountered the spirit of Sukarno, revered first President of Indonesia, in one of the forest caves. 'And such things may not be disbelieved', he added with finality. Around us heads nodded and Purnomo was silent. We had just participated in a slametan for Tasim's cow. A Javanist neighbour had invoked the aid of Suleiman and the blessings of the ancestors, and we 'bore witness' to the offerings of sticky rice. Purnomo, would-be reformer and opponent of slametans, led the prayers.

On another occasion Purnomo sponsored a circumcision feast. On the eve of the operation, which is often said to mark induction into the adult faith, the candidates were *dikalani*, rid of supernatural dangers (*kala*) by undergoing a symbolic circumcision.[13] While Purnomo looked on impassively, his two small sons, faces daubed yellow (the colour of transition), were smoked with incense and fortified with mantra. The modin, who always wears a trilby for such unmodinlike occasions, then performed a bizarre and amusing sequence of actions before a crowd. He snipped a lock from each boy's head and anointed the 'wound' with coconut oil; then, after fanning the patients, he spilled cock's blood, turmeric fluid,

Plate 9 The *modin* exorcises boys about to be circumcised

and fragrant water over each boy's head-penis in a sequence of red, yellow, and white.

What was interesting about this ritual – more interesting than its symbolism, which need not be explored here – was the fact that the sponsor and the performer are both leading santri, moreover santri sympathetic towards modernist Islam. They had chosen the moment when a child is confirmed as a Muslim to endorse – apparently – a different kind of religion, a different conception of man's relation to the supernatural world. Only the modin's levity showed that it was not really intended to be an endorsement. For him it was a concession to tradition; for the crowd, however, an ambiguity remained. The mismatch between Islamic prescription and Javanese symbolism was unresolved and therefore mildly subversive as well as funny.

When I tackled Purnomo on this public deviation from principle and the polytheistic slametan that followed, he merely shrugged and said that people would be upset if he did not follow custom. A circumcision is one of a few occasions when a householder is expected to host a major feast. A good proportion of the village attends, including all those who have ever received a contribution from the host at *their* feasts. Records of payments and debts are strictly kept. The obligation to participate, that is, to repay and to receive repayments as well as to play the lavish host, is binding. Failure means loss of prestige, even disgrace. Purnomo, having been a guest for many years but never a host had little alternative but to hold a big feast embellished with a crowd-pleasing ritual.

Would-be reformers are thus faced with a dilemma which involves more than cultural compromise. To purify the faith means reneging on traditional obligations, thus breaking ties with family and neighbours and forfeiting prestige in the village as a whole. Only if reformers are able to carry their supporters with them, in other words to create a substantial faction willing to opt out of tradition or remodel it on different terms, do they stand a chance of success. Not surprisingly, the modernist organization Muhammadiyah arose in an urban setting and remains popular mainly among city-dwellers who are able to cut their ties and choose their associates in a way difficult in a village. In those few rural communities of Banyuwangi where it has a following there is strife. Sympathizers in Bayu, a few of whom send their children to Muhammadiyah schools, are therefore cautious of expressing support and so far nobody has joined. Purnomo, among others, told me that Muhammadiyah members practise 'genuine Islam' (*Islam temenan*) – genuine, because based solely on the Koran and hadīth. But he is unwilling, indeed unable, to commit himself further, enmeshed as he is in the festive cycle. In a village of over two thousand, only two men do not hold slametans and they are both outsiders: a Catholic headmaster from Cungking and a reform-minded Muslim from Mojokerto. Yet even they are unable to refuse every invitation and they have to find other ways to reciprocate.

Purnomo's struggle with tradition illustrates the difficulties and frustrations faced by the would-be reformer. Any advance in the progress of the faith, whether through recruitment drives or the appeal of personal example, seems to entail a retreat on principle. The recent popularity of the pilgrimage, often presented as proof of Bayu's Islamic revival, further emphasizes this point.

The haj: religious merit and worldly prestige

According to figures compiled in 1887, Besuki (which then included Banyuwangi) was one of only four out of twenty-two Residencies in Java and Madura in which religious teachers outnumbered hajis (Kartodirdjo 1966: 332). Banten, a fervently Islamic region at the opposite end of Java, had seven times as many hajis proportional to its population. By the 1920s, however, the trip to Arabia had become much easier, thanks to a relaxation of government restrictions (Koentjaraningrat 1985: 392), and Banyuwangi was catching up with the rest of Java. The colonial officer, J. W. de Stoppelaar, was surprised to find hajis among the 'road coolies and oxcart conveyers' as well as among the 'rich and notable' (1927: 8). But the popularity of the *haj* brought a decline in its religious prestige (Geertz 1960: 205). The sheer volume of traffic – around 80,000 to 100,000 pilgrims go annually from Indonesia – means that what once entailed a great personal sacrifice and commitment, marked by a title connoting religious distinction, has become almost a matter of routine. Pilgrims have little contact with Muslims from other nations or with their Arab hosts, and little opportunity to meet Islamic teachers and broaden their understanding of Islam. The stories they bring home and are politely asked to repeat are not of religious awakening or spiritual brotherhood (though this must form part of their experience) but of cultural oddities glimpsed from a crowded bus or passed on second-hand by other pilgrims.

The government monopoly on organization of the pilgrimage ensures a uniformity of experience packaged in the familiar ideology of Pancasila. Prospective pilgrims pay the 6-million rupiah fee (roughly £2,000) to government agencies, attend preparatory classes, and upon arrival are shepherded about by Indonesian officials. The whole event is a highly profitable appropriation by the state of personal religious endeavour. As the pilgrimage has become popular among a previously indifferent leadership, its once-sensitive political implications have evaporated. Following the President's own example in 1992 there has been a well-publicized scramble of top ministers and army chiefs to become hajis, and a similar effort at provincial level. (The governor of East Java and the regent of Banyuwangi performed the haj during my stay.) These developments nationally are noted by villagers, as they are meant to be, and would-be hajis can be confident that their piety – often newfound – will not be misinterpreted as a vote against the government or as a sign of Islamic radicalism.

Given this dilution of its religious and spiritual significance, there is a greater effort at making sense of the pilgrimage in local terms. In so far as the religious nature of the rite is emphasized, it is turned into a locally conceived, albeit Islamic, rite of passage.[14] The pilgrim is given a send-off which has elements of the funeral sedhekah. As it was put to me: 'we mourn her before her death'. She (or he) takes a winding sheet with her; and while she is away, on the third and seventh days, sedhekah are held in her honour. As after a funeral, there are nightly recitations of the Koran in her house by family and friends, with Sura Yasin being particularly favoured for its mortuary associations. About a month after her departure, a slametan with red and white porridge (symbols of life and reproduction) is performed to ensure her safe return. She flies home, reborn, after forty days. Her winding sheet is rolled out for her to walk over; then she is bathed in fragrant water by her relatives and regaled with a feast. Returned pilgrims are supposed to remain at home, or at least refrain from work, for the next forty or so days during which period they have a constant stream of guests. The hajis to whom I spoke compared this confinement to that of a newborn child or a bride and groom. It ends with a slametan called a *selapan*, analogous to the *selapan* given forty-four days after a child is born and with similar foods (*kupat-lepet*). As one haji pointed out to me, underlining the anthropological point, this renewal period of forty-four days is to be distinguished from the forty days of a commemorative funeral sedhekah.

Although there are obvious Islamic elements in this ritual sequence (as well as pan-Indonesian ones), and the numbers themselves (3, 7, 40, 44) can be given Islamic glosses (Snouck Hurgronje 1906: 264, 364), there is no doubt that the symbolic parallels between the different stages of life are conceived and ritually embodied in Javanese terms (death-in-life as an image of mystical withdrawal, red-and-white symbolism, rebirth). The hajis' insights, which suggest they have studied Van Gennep as well as the Koran, stem from a Javanese concern with universals in a cosmos with man firmly at the centre.

In moral terms, the haj offers the pilgrim the chance to wipe the slate clean, to repent of former vices and restore damaged relations with people whom he or she has offended. In fact, the pilgrim is not supposed to set off unless all debts and quarrels have first been settled. Unresolved problems or unexpiated sins will bring an appropriate fate in Mecca, for example at the hands of the much-feared 'Bedui' (Bedouin). Having departed from the world of the living (one's kin and fellow villagers) one faces Judgement – if not Last Judgement – in Mecca. A soldier from Olehsari who recently made the pilgrimage was expected to suffer violent death as a reward for his previous conduct in the village. I was told that people had even laid substantial bets on his not returning. Thus, the notion of moral purification is given social as well as religious emphasis. As with the annual moral 'spring cleaning' at Lebaran (Idul Fitri), past sins are absolved and the air is cleared of ill will; indeed, one cannot be sinless and remain the object of resentment.

The pilgrimage, by definition, is non-local and outside the ken of non-participants, but they reclaim it on their own terms. The performance of a religious duty is recast in Javanese terms of moral regeneration through withdrawal/social death and reintegration into village society. Since the haji belongs in Banyuwangi not Mecca, and wants to be admired at home, whereas in Mecca he was one among 2 million anonymous pilgrims, he readily accedes to this interpretation of his religious distinction; indeed, he is partly motivated by it.

But this localizing strategy is only half the story. Spiritual rebirth is the ideal face of the pilgrimage, the way the haji himself tells it. But nobody seriously imagines that a pilgrim returns in a state of enlightenment, cured of his vices. (Haji M quickly recovered his passion for cock-fighting and gambling, and nobody thought any worse of him.) The transformation wrought by the rite of passage is as much social as spiritual. Through the feasts which frame it, the pilgrimage is incorporated into the wider ritual economy and thus into the socio-political framework of rural society. To see how this works we must look briefly at the pattern of festive exchange in which the haji is enmeshed and which he exploits for his own purposes. (I speak of males here since it is men who are best able to convert their religious prestige into influence.)

Large feasts of the kind held at weddings and circumcisions show a complex balance sheet of income and expenditure. All male guests bring a cash contribution to the feast. At the time of my stay this was fixed at 1,500 rupiah (about $1 US). Their wives bring 2 kg of uncooked rice. Additionally, relatives contribute provisions, and dozens of women help with preparations. At the end of a feast, to which a thousand people may have come, the host may be left with a surplus of up to a million rupiah. This is not profit, since every rupiah and every coconut has to be repaid at the future feasts of his guests. But the system allows someone to hold a lavish feast without initial capital.

The haji makes use of this feasting complex but breaks the rules of reciprocity: he refuses contributions. A prospective pilgrim is expected, indeed required, to feed the whole village at his sole expense. The women help but bring no rice, and there is no donation from the men. The host is therefore a net provider and his guests are permanently indebted to him. Given the enormous importance of reciprocity and even-handed participation in the festive cycle this exception has great significance. I say guests are 'permanently indebted', but the fact is that the guests are not materially indebted at all; they owe nothing. But to receive without prospect of return creates a certain anxiety, as does the very notion of a 'free meal'. The poorest peasant will sell his last chicken so that he can make a respectable contribution at a feast. Since the pilgrim's guests cannot repay in kind, their debt takes a different form: it becomes a moral debt that compels respect.[15]

In 1993 there were two candidates for the haj and I was able to observe the build-up to their departure. Sanuri, who lived opposite me, makes a good living buying and selling motorbikes using the capital of a Chinese partner in town. He is also one of the largest landowners in Bayu with eleven hectares of paddyfields. His wife, Misti, keeps a shop. Prior to my arrival he had never attended the langgar and had shown no inclination to piety – or so I was told. He was much like our other neighbours in what was, until recently, a notably lax part of the village. His knowledge of Islam had hitherto been of the amulets-and-spells variety and he had never learned to recite prayers or chant the Koran. (Once, during a slametan held to improve the fortunes of the shop, he broke off half way through a prayer with a sigh: *lali wis*, 'I've forgotten!' Nobody knew how to continue and there was much shuffling and stifled laughter. Satmari, from next-door, offered to recite a prayer for a cow – the only one he knew. In the event, we settled for a loud and conclusive *Amin* and with embarrassed grins got down to eating.)

But ignorance is not an obstacle to piety, and during the next year

Sanuri became a stalwart of the revived langgar, as did his wife and young son; and he never missed Friday prayers at the mosque, driving up each week on a different motorbike. The shop, once open all hours, was now closed whenever the loudspeakers called. Before his departure on the haj (alone: his wife remained behind to look after business) Sanuri hosted a vast feast to which the whole village was invited. A hired kiyai gave a lecture and guests stayed up all night carousing. From being ordinary, if wealthy, villagers, Sanuri and Misti were staking a claim to superior status. During Lebaran week they made a great many visits outside the village, cultivating networks of the pious and influential. Afterwards they continued to wear the expensive Lebaran clothes normally put away until next year's visiting. There were corresponding changes in the behaviour of villagers. A new deference appeared among customers. My landlady, not someone to stand on ceremony, began to address Misti as Mother Haji, when hitherto she had called her by name.

The other candidate, an older man, hosted a more modest feast. But he too was allowing himself to be called Pak Haji before departure and he began to affect High Javanese, or at least the rustic Osing version reserved for formal encounters with in-laws and hajis.

As these examples show, as far as villagers and the pilgrims themselves are concerned, one is already effectively a haji *before* the event. The claim to status is made on the basis of prior feasting and display at home, and the actual pilgrimage merely sets the seal on the achievement. People are unimpressed by the haj as an act of piety; indeed it is often disparaged cynically as a way of 'buying a name'. One pays 6 million rupiah, sees the sights, and comes back a haji. But to win respect, to be able to *act* like a haji, one must fulfil – or, rather, exceed – the requirements of custom.

Feasting continues after the haji returns and he is expected to keep up a flow of good works (donations to the mosque, a sacrificial goat at Idul Adha, etc.) for the rest of his life. As a mark of respect he is given pride of place at feasts, seated at a table with visiting dignitaries at special events, and he claims a position in the front row at Friday prayers. A haji who cannot live up to his name in this way very quickly loses esteem. One of two pilgrims the previous year has not been able to sustain such losses and is now treated like anyone else.

The successful haji therefore combines worldly prestige with piety; that is, his piety serves as a legitimate, recognized means of attaining prestige. He has fed the village and compelled its respect, and his continuing good works are a form of public patronage. Other rich men do not have this opportunity for advancing their status. Given the strict norms of reciprocity and the exact reckoning of accounts, the rich man cannot exceed his customary obligations. In fact, the rich of Bayu live at a similar level to the average villager – they eat the same kind of food, wear old clothes, and live in ordinary houses.

I was not the only person to be intrigued by this self-imposed modesty. An agricultural extension worker from Mojokerto who had lived for some years in the area asked his wife to keep a check on neighbours' purchases for a month. She found that a neighbour who owned over twenty hectares of land spent only about 1,000 rupiah a day on regular food purchases (apart from rice). This was similar to households with one hectare. The landowner in question told me that it would be impossible for him to enjoy a higher standard of living without offending his neighbours. He cannot even make pleasure trips to town without a sense of embarrassment. As a Javanist mystic, he has no interest in performing the haj, so he spends all of his considerable income on acquiring more land. However, both his brother and his twenty-year-old son and heir are planning to do the pilgrimage.

Differences in wealth which have hitherto been concealed by an egalitarian ethos and customary rules limiting status competition may thus begin to acquire the cultural characteristics of a social class. Whereas the merely rich man wants to appear the same as everyone else, the rich-man-turned-haji wants to be recognized as different. So far this difference has not extended to daily consumption patterns, but piety, good works, title, festive credit, ceremonial precedence, links with hajis and kiyais in other villages, language, and not least a white cap, all set him apart from ordinary villagers.

Why should the wealthy suddenly seek this distinction? It seems likely that Bayu's recent haji boom (from one to six in three years) is linked to changes in the structure of the rural economy and the market position or 'class situation' (Weber 1948: 182) of the wealthy. In the absence of a traditional village hierarchy, Islam provides a means of legitimizing increasing economic inequality and the emergence of a relatively distinct landowning class (this was noted as early as the beginning of the century elsewhere in Java; see Vredenbregt 1962). The men who have made, or who are about to make, the pilgrimage are among the handful of big landowners in the village. And the proportion of the total resources they control is increasing as they buy up any land that comes onto the market. Traditional norms limiting consumption paradoxically promote this change by encouraging accumulation.

So far the political (in a narrow sense) aspect of these developments is insignificant and it is clear that the desire to become a haji is not consciously part of any political strategy or power manoeuvre. It is remarkable that none of the hajis has any special qualities or merits which would mark him out for a leading role in either the secular or religious affairs of the village. The hajis are not men of influence, formers of opinion, or wise sources of counsel, but simply wealthy and respected villagers.

How far other villagers are willing to assent to their status claim is arguable. A haji's privileges are not very substantial – he cannot exact tribute, labour, or make demands on people over and above what custom allows anyone in similar economic circumstances. And most people do not take his pretensions very seriously. But if it costs nothing to indulge a haji's dignity, there is growing concern about the economic realities that underlie his distinction as land steadily passes from the many to the few.

Counterblasts

The 'struggle of Islam' (as it is usually phrased) in a mixed village such as Bayu faces a number of obstacles, some of which I have outlined. There is the problem of backsliding and the constant effort needed to keep new recruits in line; the everpresent risk of compromising principles in the drive for 'converts'; and the sheer inertia of conservative tradition. There are also ideas and values which run counter to normative Islam, undermining its claim to universality and even questioning its status as a revealed religion.

Resistance is, by definition, reactive and is strongest where the pressure is greatest. A heavy-handed campaign to impose Islamic conformity on villages in the south of Banyuwangi in the wake of the 1965 coup prompted mass conversions to Hinduism. Throughout the region, the steady growth of Islam since Independence has been accompanied by a rise in affiliation to Javanist mystical associations. These two movements away from mainstream Islam are examined in chapters 7 and 8. Here we are concerned with the ordinary unaligned villagers and their response to the religion of their santri neighbours.

Scepticism

One of the negative forms of this response is scepticism – the most under-reported aspect of Javanese religion and perhaps of popular religion anywhere. Anthropologists, who mostly come from societies in which religious freedom includes the freedom not to practise a religion, tend to assume that participation implies faith, and that people who join together in a certain ritual more or less share a common commitment to its value and similar ideas about its meaning. We have already seen how the semantic content of slametan symbolism varies widely between participants. Mystics and santri do not mean the same thing by 'Allah', 'Muhammad', 'Adam', and so on. But a more general scepticism forms a significant background to religious thought and practice. This scepticism, which runs from the indifferent shrug to the most reasoned argument, plays a key role in the complex of tolerance, relativism, contextual change, and even conversion.

At its simplest, scepticism finds expression in doubts about basic dogmas of Islam: concepts of sin, salvation, and damnation; the divine creation of all things; the divine authorship of the Koran; the value of the 'pillars' of the faith, and so on. Ordinary villagers sometimes express doubts about such matters without going deeper into speculation about the nature of the deity: their quibbles do not amount to a reasoned or concerted attack on the faith. It must be said that many of the quibbles are based on ignorance of the scriptures and a travesty of Islamic teaching. But some objectors are quite well informed and, in any case, some of the objections could not be countered by superior knowledge since they strike at axioms of the faith.

Among those nominal Muslims classed by santri as *Islam KTP*, 'identity-card Muslims', there is a fairly widespread view that the sanctions of heaven and hell are imaginary.

'Everything is in the visible world', said Pak Sumi, the diviner. 'In the town square look west and you see the mosque; north is the palace of the Lord [*kanjeng*: title of a regent and the Prophet]; south is the market and pleasure – heaven if you like; east is hell, the police station.'
'So we don't need to worry about the Day of Judgment?'
'No! There's no afterlife (*akérat*). They say it's in the invisible [dark] world; but what that means is that if your deeds are bad you are already living in darkness and hell. If you are good and people say nice things about you, that's heaven. It may be otherwise: I'll let you know if I return from the grave.'

A less ingenious view is that of the ploughman Satmari: 'Hell is just something to scare you', he said. 'We are always hearing about it but where is it?' The sanctions of institutional religion are felt to be remote and somewhat unreal, whereas those of spirit beliefs – crop blight, illness, infertility – are immediate. Hence, the dawn broadcasts promising hell to the impious raise hackles rather than stir fears. Kresno, whose house trembles beneath the langgar megaphones, said of his tormentor:

A lot of people hate Sidik. He reproaches me because I don't pray and tells me I will go to hell. But then people don't hate me so I must be better than him. It's my own affair when it comes to the Last Judgement ... though you can be sure that if Sidik was doing the judging I'd be on my knees five times a day.

Behind this denunciation, spoken in fragments between salvoes from the langgar, lies more than a personal antagonism. The concept of sin, *dosa*, in its theological sense of disobeying divine command, seems to be absent from Kresno's thinking. Whereas, to the more orthodox Sidik, failure to perform obligatory worship is sinful (as its performance is meritorious), to Kresno it cannot be sinful since it does not impinge on what he takes to be the sphere of moral action.

Are those who have acted honestly not going to be received by the Almighty? Do you think only those who pray will be accepted while those who have acted well and spoken truthfully will be damned? It doesn't make sense.

Acting rightly means acting properly towards one's fellow men and nothing more. I heard various arguments supporting this contention, but they all seemed to entail a similar logic: What counts as correct conduct is self-evident; an action is intrinsically right or wrong and its value does not depend on an external divine arbiter; ritual prescriptions, whose only justification is their divine origin, are therefore outside the sphere of moral conduct.[16] Clearly this view is compatible with various conceptions of the deity as well as with agnosticism. A more sophisticated version was given me by Kresno's uncle:

God is in man (*manusa kedunungan Gusti Allah*), so a wrong against man is, indeed, as santri would have it, a sin (*dosa*) against God. But, conversely, it must also be true that if one has not wronged (*nyalahi*) men one has not sinned against God. To omit prayers therefore cannot be sinful, for whom has one wronged? That's why we Javanese prefer to use the word *salah* [wrong, at fault] instead of *dosa*, which we can well do without.

A broadly humanist understanding of ethics is, in fact, shared implicitly by many santri. At the Welcoming of the Fast event held in the langgar, Pak Tasim, who spoke the prayers and the formal address, appealed for the forgiveness of sins accumulated during the year; but these turned out to be 'faults (*kaluputan*) in word and deed towards one's fellows, left and right; faults and omissions towards the ancestors'. No mention of transgressions against Islamic law. Sins, in this light, appear to be breaches of social decorum or good neighbourliness (virtues exemplified in a langgar ritual) and violations of ancestral tradition. Given this tendency to conceive morality in Javanese, humanistic terms, many santri are reluctant to condemn laxity in Islamic duties or to pronounce their fellow sinners 'sinners':

[The speaker is a devout Muslim, son of a Javanist mystic] If others don't pray or fast that's their business. It may be sinful, I suppose, but that doesn't necessarily mean they will go to hell. How can a good man be condemned? We cannot say what we do not know. All we can say is that his prayers will be among the first things to be counted. But it is not for us humans to judge: each must do what is right for himself.

Not all santri are so tolerant or so finely balanced between competing ethical positions – some hold firmly to an orthodox line; but a substantial number are, and this makes a great difference to the mutual relations with non-santri.

A second area of scepticism, about which there can be no compromise with santri, is over the status of the Koran. A common misconception is that the Koran, like the other holy books, is supposed to have dropped from the sky. Probably this confusion stems from the wording of Sura 97: 1: 'Verily we have caused it [the Koran] to descend on the Lailat al-kadr (the Night of Power).' 'How can this be? Books are manmade', said a village official. When someone present reminded him that the Koran was dictated to Muhammad by the angel Gabriel, there came the sceptical retort: 'Have you seen an angel?' On another occasion a group of men were discussing the dawn broadcasts. One of them, irritated by the taunts of damnation, began: '*Akérat! When* is the *akérat* [the hereafter]? And where is the proof?' I said that the santri were not claiming personal knowledge of the afterlife but merely following the Koran, what the Book itself says.

'Ah! What it *says* (*jare*). But that's still only hearsay (*magih jare*). Their proof, then, is only paper and writing, that's all. And who wrote it if not men?'

What these comments amount to is a rejection of Islam as a revealed religion. Yet most of the doubters identify themselves as Muslims and all of them take part in rituals involving prayers, such as sedhekah, and in Islamic wedding ceremonies and funerals. There are very few who would answer my question as bluntly as the old Javanist, Pak Sarko.

'Have you ever prayed?'
'Prayed to what?'

As the tone of the comments I have quoted indicates, scepticism is formulated and expressed mainly in response to pressure from the pious. But this pressure is not constant and an airing of differences is uncommon. Many people have arrived at an accommodation with their santri neighbours which acknowledges the importance of Islam and the respectability of the pious but which allows the uncommitted to opt out of normative ritual. A typical example would be Pak Kardi. He stated his minimalist position as follows:

God told Muhammad that it was desirable to pray, but if you couldn't do the 'five times' at least attend congregational Friday worship, and if you couldn't do this at least acknowledge His name and you would be recognized (*diaku*).[17]

Like other non-santri, Kardi is anxious to avoid the tag of *kafir*, infidel, a word associated in Java with communism and the massacres of the 1960s. He makes up for his abstention from prayer by supporting his neighbourhood langgar, the Nur Jannah, in other ways; for example, he is active in raising funds and organizing events. As what might be called a prominent 'lay member' and a man respected for his decency, he retains an influence over langgar activities and is able to defend the dignity of non-participants. He was instrumental in the removal of Sidik.

The sort of moderating counter-pressures non-santri can bring to bear are illustrated in the handling of visiting speakers at Muludan, the celebrations of the Prophet's birth. Each langgar aims to boost its popularity and prestige by engaging a kiyai to give a lecture at the feast. In what is still largely an oral culture, there is an intelligent appreciation of oratory and almost everyone in the neighbourhood is keen to attend. Santri, especially young activists, learn the techniques of holding an audience; others enjoy the blend of moralism and gentle humour as the kiyai pokes fun at the indifferent and the pious alike. The kiyai, knowing that he is addressing a mixed audience, leavens the message with Javanist references, irreverent jokes, and winning touches of self-mockery. There is an air of the headmaster's speech on the last day of term. (When Kiyai Hasnan spoke in the mosque at Lebaran, the modin, whom I sat next to, giggled and gasped continuously for an hour and the audience clapped at the end.) No doubt somewhere, in somebody's statistical logbook, such visits count as an instance of *dakwah*, to be cited in surveys as an index of Islamization. But statistics take no account of how the message is received.

The choice of speaker depends on availability and access to networks beyond the village. The year before I arrived, my landlady's son, a man-about-town who happens to be a Christian, arranged a female speaker from Banyuwangi for Ali's Muludan. He informed her of what people wanted to hear – a bit about faith and the life of Muhammad, something on women's activities and health. She duly complied and the visit was rated a success. In 1992 the new paramedic, not knowing what was required but eager to make his mark, assumed personal control of the event. The speaker, an untried evangelist, instead of entertaining the audience harangued it for two hours. Nobody escaped his censure: the old for their backwardness, the young for imitating the West (e.g. girls wearing trousers), the whole village for its addiction to slametans. Ali and his father, deeply embarrassed, were seen shaking their heads throughout, and half of the audience drifted out – something that had never before happened. Next day there was a post-mortem, with apologies and excuses from Ali, vilification of the paramedic, and a general wagging of fingers. For many it was a rare moment to savour, an opportunity to enjoy the santri's prerogative of moral outrage. Pak Uri, a carpenter who claims never to have prayed, said the speaker should have stuck to the life of Muhammad. A bit of exhortation was acceptable, but not so much as to wound feelings: the preacher had to recognize that villages like Bayu were full of all sorts, or else stay put in his pondhok. Pak Kardi complained that the speaker hadn't endorsed the other four principles of Pancasila, as if religion were the only thing that mattered. The outrage was infectious and strengthened the position of non-santri at a time in the Islamic year when they most needed it.

Conclusion

One evening, when the modin was patiently outlining for me the basics of traditional santri religion – the purpose of ritual ablutions, grave visiting, what prayers to use at which events, and so on – I was struck, not for the first time, by the difference between his fluent, matter-of-fact pronouncements, which suggested the routine of blackboard and pointer ('Man consists of body, breath, and soul ... There are four realms: those of the spirits, the world, the grave, and the afterlife') and what ordinary Muslims in the village had told me. Unlike the modin, most people had no clear idea why they held a sedhekah forty days after a funeral ('At forty days the soul is enshrined in the realm of the grave'); why dawn prayers consist of two cycles ('God divided day from night, making two'), or why slametans are held on Thursday and Sunday evenings.

It was tempting to see the local expert as a spokesman clarifying the views of the many, or their views as muddled versions of his. One could then conveniently ignore the inconsistencies of popular belief or regard them as deviations from a standard. But what undermined such an approach was the fact that the modin himself, a man of many talents, sometimes stepped outside his orthodox role to tell ribald folktales or perform weird semi-pagan rituals which evoked a very different set of ideas. During the same conversation, after charting the progress of the Muslim soul, we turned to the subject of reincarnation. He thought reincarnation was unlikely, but said that if you tied a thread to a new-born's placenta before burying it, it was sure to reappear on the placenta of the next child, and so on up to the fifth child, proving that it was the *same* placenta. This assertion of spiritual unity in a set of five siblings owed nothing to Islam. But neither did it devalue the orthodox position which he had confidently presented. For the modin these were separate matters to be thought of in different ways. For the anthropologist, however, struggling to place ideas within a social context, the coexistence of these contradictory thought-worlds remains a problem, and one which grows ever more tangled when one comes to consider the less systematic views of the ordinary Muslim.

Resisting the urge to simplify and systematize, I have therefore chosen to present Islam in Banyuwangi as I found it – in and among the rival langgars, frustrated evangelists, young zealots, crusty conservatives, hajis, and sceptics. Despite wide variations in practice and belief, there is no organized schism, such as between traditionalist and modernist camps. To the contrary, among different kinds of santri, and between santri and others, much effort goes into finding a common language for diverse aspirations. The unifying factor is a willingness to make conces-sions in order to maintain social harmony in the neighbourhood. The fuzzy pattern that emerges is therefore not one of classes or blocs affiliated to distinct religious positions, but of interchange, dialogue, and compromise: a blurring of boundaries. On the santri side, as we have seen, unorthodox traditions are tolerated, even indulged, without imply-ing wholesale acceptance. Significantly, it is not just the borderline, middling santri such as Saleh who yield to tradition (indeed they are less aware that concessions are being made), but the leading santri, including the would-be reformers.

On the non-santri side there are matching concessions. Almost all Javanists, including some quite dismissive of organized religion, send their children to Koranic classes – 'to harmonize' (*kanggo ngrukuni*), as one mystic put it. And non-fasters do not discourage their children from fasting, even though this means someone has to get up at 3 a.m. to prepare a meal. As we have seen, non-santri often take a supportive role in langgar activities. Participation in Arabic prayers at slametans is universal, even when no santri are present. (Word might get around if the prayers were omitted and there would be 'misunderstanding'.) Again, it is striking that active compromise characterizes not only the middle range of opinion but the extremes as well: some of the leading mystics are among the most accomplished performers of Arabic prayers and litanies, and they are quite willing to 'help out' with chanting at funeral feasts while privately questioning the worth of such practices.

This willingness to give the appearance of adopting the other's position (something more radical than meeting another halfway), occasionally spans different faiths. My landlady hosted a thousandth-day sedhekah for her husband and invited fifteen elders, including prominent santri, to perform the Arabic litany. She is a Christian, as was her deceased husband. Good neighbourliness and reputation demanded a proper send-off and nobody worried too much about theology. This is an extreme case, but it shows how deeply compromise is ingrained in daily routines and ways of thinking.

In the interest of social harmony and inner calm one adjusts one's own behaviour to others, smoothing over differences, turning a blind eye when necessary; and one makes room for the other's practices within one's own scheme rather than simply reject them. Santri relativize supernaturalism as adat, custom, and thereby avoid confronting it as a challenge to formal religion; mystics relativize normative piety as a first step in knowledge, and they treat supernaturalism as a symbolic language referring to inner realities. Diversity is embraced as a fact of social life.

In the next chapter we shall see just how far such moral and conceptual relativism can be taken.

6

Javanism

He makes His secret knowable through symbols

Serat Centhini (Zoetmulder 1995: 246)

To move from traditionalist village Islam, as portrayed in the last chapter, to Javanist mysticism is, seemingly, to enter a different world with its own language and distinctive styles of thinking, a world at once complex and subtle, yet, despite occasional mystifications and a tendency to paradox, more clearly articulated and realized in everyday life than are the routines of practical Islam. Where Islam promises heaven through ritual compliance and devotion to the Koran, Javanism (kejawèn) takes the everyday world as its key text and the body as its holy book.

The contrast, however, is a matter of divergent orientations rather than exclusive and opposed cultural identities. All Bayu's Javanists are also Muslims in the straightforward sense that they take part in the activities which constitute village Islam: the celebration of Islamic holidays and feasts, Islamic rites of passage, chanting at funeral sedhekah, and grave visiting.

Javanists can be defined simply as those people who tend to stress the Javanese part of their cultural inheritance and who regard their Muslim affiliation as secondary. As with Islam, there are the relatively purer types (the kejawèn equivalent of santri) as well as the less articulate and loosely committed individuals who look to such people for their opinions. (There is also, as noted in chapter 5, a broad middle zone of the ambivalent and indifferent.) Javanists do not form a distinct class or group within rural society but, rather, a rough, unbounded constituency. Significantly, there is no collective noun corresponding to the term kejawèn.

In this chapter I outline some characteristics of Javanism in its

158

philosophical and mystical aspects: ways of thinking about meaning, approaches to learning, ethics, and various notions of man's relation to God. I hope to convey something of the texture of Javanist thinking on these subjects – to show how people arrive at a certain view, rather than to present their views as settled convictions. Only thus can one appreciate the force and reasonableness of the ideas to those who hold them. This is important because Javanist ideas are not learned like dogmas – their value has to be recognized and experienced before they can be assimilated. It is not enough to report the mystical equation, familiar from the literature, of God with 'I'. We need to ask what process leads to this realization. We know that, for Javanists, man is the microcosm, but what exactly is understood by this concept? Only by looking at how people grapple with the ultimate questions using the homely ideas and imagery at their disposal can one begin to make an answer. Given this approach, the organizing concepts and rhetorical styles of Javanist thinking merit as much attention as its content.

Although I shall try to highlight continuities with the diverse strands of Javanese literary mystical tradition, there are bound to be differences. Javanist learning at village level is an unco-ordinated, magpie enterprise, an unfinished business: bits and pieces are borrowed from different sources, trimmed and fitted to one's scheme; alternative views are maintained alongside each other; rarely is anything rejected outright. This eclecticism frustrates any scholarly attempt at unravelling sources and should direct our attention to a later stage in the shaping of knowledge. From this standpoint, the most important forum of ideas and source of knowledge is that composed by the villagers themselves – in after-hours *lontar*-reading sessions, late-night brainstormings, and casual discussion after slametans. The ideas which I present in this chapter and the next, where possible in villagers' own words, are therefore not to be seen as garbled versions of a philosophy better understood elsewhere (e.g. in the courtly tradition) or as uncomprehended formulas learned by rote; nor are they the private interpretations of specialists. They have been worked out by Javanists among friends. Even the most arcane and sophisticated views have stood the test of a relatively public exposure. As I myself found out when I was grilled on Christianity and on what I had picked up among Hindus in other villages, anything 'new' is pored over and dissected, often changing shape in the process. This reshaping is as much practical as intellectual. The mystic-*bricoleur* is not concerned with constructing elegant castles – unlike the courtly mystic or hermit, he lacks the leisure for pure speculation: his makeshift contraptions must do service in daily life. My aim, then, is not to present a seamless esoteric philosophy or to create an illusion of consensus or consistency; I wish to explore the variety of views against a background of common assumptions and premises, and, above all, to show how complex religious and philosophical ideas are formulated and acted upon by the villagers themselves.

Although much of my material is gathered from Sangkan Paran members, who form a majority of self-conscious Javanists in Bayu, the ideas presented here have diverse origins. Adherents draw on a range of knowledge wider than that transmitted by the sect. (The word 'sect', despite inappropriate connotations of reformism and exclusivity, may serve here as a convenient shorthand for 'mystical association'; Javanese equivalents include *paguyuban* and *pirukunan*.) A few have followed the santri path and later changed direction; some have belonged at various times to other mystical groups; all of them draw on a general knowledge of Javanist lore and philosophy acquired during a lifetime's association with others of their kind: fellow-travellers, shadow puppeteers, magicians, readers of lontar (Javanese literature), and disciples of miscellaneous gurus. Chapter 7, which develops the present themes, more narrowly concerns Sangkan Paran and its founder Joyokusumo.

The importance of symbols

For Javanists, the world is permeated with symbolism, and it is through symbols that one meditates on the human condition and communicates with the divine. As the *Serat Centhini*, a nineteenth century Javanist classic, has it:

> If you wish to penetrate through to reality, penetrate something which is a symbol thereof.   (quoted in Zoetmulder 1995: 245)

Javanists – and here I speak of rice farmers, not court poets – are much concerned with notions of meaning and esoteric expression. To the occasional irritation of their plain-speaking santri neighbours, their talk is of conundrums (*sanépa*), symbols (*lambang*), signs (*sasmita*), allusions (*pasemon*), and the less obvious facets of meaning which we denote with words like nuance, drift, purport, and so on. True understanding, a sensitivity to these oblique, between-the-lines meanings, is said to come through insight (which can be granted spontaneously or developed like a skill), not through cleverness or erudition, still less through the rote-learning which characterizes Islam. The novice is rarely told to 'think about' a mystical truth, rather to 'feel it for him/herself' (*rasakno dhéwé*), to 'read', 'filter', 'dig', 'connect', 'feel', or 'become aware of' what is missed by simple reflection. The diction may call to mind the concrete idioms characteristic of santri discourse but such usages are intended to reach beyond the language of ordinary thinking to realities which involve the person's whole being. Parallel to the young Muslim's training in Koranic recitation, the Javanist apprentice is told to 'read/recite (*ngaji*) his or her own body'.

The symbolic conception of the world sometimes approaches a form of idealism in which empirical realities are mere symbols of inner truths, and action in the world is a kind of acting out or rehearsal of these truths. The history of Java, its geography, even the modern constitution, are condensed into puns and metaphors referring to human ontology. The legendary king of Blambangan, Ménak Jingga, and his wife, Sita, become reproductive symbols (*jingga* = red, *séta* = white). Tawang Alun, founder of a later dynasty, signifies the primordial void that preceded man. Even the location of Banyuwangi at the extreme east of the island seems less a historical accident than part of a symbolic masterplan. *Wétan*, east, 'means' *wiwitan*, 'beginning', 'origin'. And where better to contemplate First Things than in Alas Purwo, the 'primeval forest' (*purwa* = origin, east) at the extremity of the Eastern Salient? In the next chapter I recount one such symbolic pilgrimage to Purwo.

Javanism thus contrasts with santri orthodoxy in its predilection for symbolism and in its determined anthropocentrism. And Islam itself, like every other tradition that falls within the Javanist compass, is moulded to human form, in a literal sense humanized. The nine Javanese Muslim saints (*wali sanga*) are defined as the worldly forms or symbols of the nine bodily orifices, the gateways to the inner world and pathways of the senses. The four archangels 'are' sight, hearing, smell, and speech. They guard our welfare, angel-like, and they have 'wings' in that they span distances. More controversially, as we saw in chapter 2, Adam and Muhammad are universals of which their historical forms are merely particular symbolic instances. Even the Koran is a secondary, outward thing derived from a 'true' original; and that original is not the Preserved Tablet of Islamic dogma, the inaccessible treasure of a remote God, but the human form itself, the 'wet Book' (*kitab teles*) of the living body. To 'recite' from this book is to ponder its origins or to reproduce its text by sexual intercourse. There is an oft-quoted injunction: 'Do not recite in a pondhok: recite in Ponorogo.' 'Ponorogo' is both an East Javanese town famous for its occult sciences and a play on words (Old Jav. *pana* = know, *raga* = body). Learning therefore means the pursuit of self-knowledge – not in a psychoanalytic or popular existentialist sense of realizing one's individuality, but in the opposite sense of realizing one's intrinsic universality, recognizing the triviality of differences.

In interpreting symbolism, I was often told, 'one does not need to go outside of oneself' (*sing kadek metu*). To look for enlightenment 'outside' is to go astray, to mistake the symbol for the reality. This is, allegedly, the habitual error of santri. The 'fallacy of misplaced concreteness' is exemplified, for mystics, by the sanctuary at Mecca, the *ka'ba*, Islam's holiest shrine and the direction of worship. The point is well made by a former headman, who related to me a version of how Isma'il came upon the Black Stone which became part of the building. Isma'il had sought God in the wilderness for seven long years, climbing mountains and wandering through jungles, but despaired of ever finding Him. Finally he lay down on a boulder and slept. In his sleep he heard a voice: 'Why do you seek God far away. Where you are sleeping there is God's place.' Isma'il sat up and rubbed his eyes, stared at the boulder in astonishment, and declared it to be the House of God. Henceforth this became the *ka'ba*.[1] Joyokusumo, who may be the author of this moral tale, liked to say to hajis who came to pay their respects: 'You've been to Mecca. Now where is *your* Mecca?'[2]

In the eyes of Javanists, and especially those schooled in mysticism, Muslims direct their devotions idolatrously outside themselves, failing to look inwards to the indwelling God. Symbols deserve our respect but no more than that. If one bows down to the flag or kisses the Black Stone one is making an idol of it. One has become a polytheist. A theological error thus arises from a category mistake. As the story of Isma'il suggests, the true point of orientation, the geometrical origin, is the self. This is why, when the pilgrim circumambulates the *ka'ba*, his direction of ritual orientation (*kiblat*) moves with him; it is no longer at a remote point (say) north-west. When one is close to the centre, the sanctuary of God, one bears one's own *kiblat*. As the *Serat Dermagandhul* has it (in Drewes' synopsis):

Wherever man may be, he himself is the centre of his universe, the real *baitu'llah* unto which he has to direct himself; only outwardly his *kiblat* is Mecca.

(Drewes 1966: 353)

In Javanist thinking the notion of anthropocentric space is fundamental, serving as a model of perceptual and moral relativism and as a basis for speculation. Characteristically, it was first conveyed to me in the form of an enigma, and one which I had to act out. I was seated opposite

two village elders at a slametan and while we drank coffee after the meal
they took turns in questioning me.

'Which way is east?' said one. I pointed ahead.

'Where is the limit (*wangkit*) of east?' said the other.

Sheepishly I pointed ahead, then, knowing by their smiles that this
must be wrong, said: 'There is no limit'. This too was wrong. The limit of
east, since I was facing in that direction, was my back. Likewise the limit
of west was my front, in the sense that everything forward of this point
would be east. We went through the cardinal points. South was to my
right, so the limit of south was my left side. The limit of north was my
right side. The limit of above was the soles of my feet; the limit of below
was the top of my head. Each of these planes, or rather their boundaries,
would change as I moved. And for my companions sitting opposite, the
limits of N, S, E, and W would be reversed.

All the directions originate from you. Think of the five-coloured porridge. North
is black, east is white, red is south, yellow is west. Where is the multicoloured
blob? In the middle.

A practical philosophy

As the above example shows, complex ideas can be expressed in simple
terms, and the novice can be oriented by practical examples. The esoteric
lore contained in manuals and cryptic oral traditions is said to be
meaningless, therefore useless, unless one has first grasped certain basic
principles and these must be 'proved' (*dibuktékaken*) for oneself. Literary
and orientalist approaches to Javanist traditions take the opposite view,
explaining esoteric formulations by erudite references to other esoteric
texts and mystical systems (e.g. Kraemer 1921, Drewes 1966). Typically
there is little or no attempt to explain how such texts are used and
understood, how they are assimilated by people with different cultural
backgrounds. Yet this is important not merely for the sake of ethnographic completeness, but because Javanist knowledge is above all a
practical philosophy. It lives less in texts and in their interpretation than
in discussion and practice. Unlike Islam, there are no official 'guardians'
of a scripture or arbiters of tradition, no pressure towards orthodoxy.
The conception of tradition, the passing on of knowledge and its
reception, is therefore quite different. Consider the following remarks of
a farmer in Bayu.

What does it mean to understand (*faham*) something? If you merely know
something through your senses, that is not yet one hundred per cent. For
example, you hear something but cannot identify it, so you cannot be certain of

it. Likewise, if you know something by reflection or teaching, that is still only half. True understanding is to prove (*mbuktékaken*) one's knowledge, to fit it (*ngocokaken*) to reality. Then one knows it is true. True (*bener*) means fitting (*cocog*) with oneself. But for something to be really true it must be cocog with your companion as well; it must be witnessed. If you know something it is not enough merely to know it. You must put it into practice; it must be expressed (*lair*, [come] out).

This pragmatic, quasi-empirical emphasis contrasts with the santri notion of truths as something enshrined in scriptures, beyond human interference. The goal of Sangkan Paran, for example, is 'superior life, perfected death' *urip utama, mati sampurna*, and this is achieved not by enlightenment but by enlightened action. Practice makes perfect.

The priority given to practice in Javanist thinking gives it a peculiarly worldly, undogmatic tenor, grounding metaphysical discussion in human experience (Geertz 1960; Stange 1980). This will be apparent in the debates from which I quote below. Nevertheless, despite this consistent emphasis, there are different angles on the fundamental questions, as we shall see.

Man and God: first orientations

In an anthropocentric universe the relation between man and God suffers a radical readjustment from that posited by orthodox theism. In my conversations with Javanists, two perspectives on this problem were commonly adopted. One is primarily religious in that it begins with a conception (or sometimes an experience) of God as dwelling in man. The other is primarily philosophical in that it begins with an analysis of experience and comes to a conclusion that the experiencing self or some animating principle within the self is, in some sense, divine. Before considering these ideas as they emerge in debate, it may be helpful to set them against Zoetmulder's preliminary definitions of pantheism and monism in the introduction to his magnum opus on Javanese mystical literature (1995 [1935]: 2–3).

It is immediately apparent that pantheism is just a certain form of monism in which, when establishing the oneness of all that exists, one proceeds from God and reduces everything to Him. The other form, i.e. the one in which God either does not appear at all or remains at a secondary level, is then monism in the more restricted sense in which it is conventionally used. As the most characteristic point of difference between this latter monism and pantheism we can therefore note that in pantheism the world merges with God, the world is in some way a part of His being; in monism God merges with the world, the world is the only absolute BEING, which, because of its absoluteness, may perhaps be indicated with the name God, but with regard to which there is no place for God-adoration or for religion.

As many of Zoetmulder's quotations show, these perspectives are by no means mutually exclusive; writers frequently alternate between monism and pantheism as here defined. Partly this is a matter of ambiguous literary expression, partly of genuine ambivalence. Moreover, as Zoetmulder points out, though such ideas can be distilled from accounts of mystical experiences, they are not, for the most part, originally presented as theories.

In less elevated terms similar notions, with their attendant definitional problems, are encountered among village Javanists. 'Pantheists' start with the idea that God is in man/everything, and that therefore without God nothing exists. 'Monists' reverse the priority: God, the unifying principle, is in man, therefore without man there is no God (or anything else). While there is some overlap and ambivalence of expression, it was the latter, anthropocentric, formulation which was most consistently put to me by Javanists.

A debate

A common starting point in religious debate is the world immediately given to the senses, the homely cup of coffee and plate of bananas invariably placed in front of one.

Take this banana [said Tomo, munching]. Where is its sweetness? In me or in the fruit? It is in neither, or rather in both. It's in the eating, the tasting. The taste (rasa) and the fruit come together and are gone together. If you ask where has the sweetness gone, I can't point to it. It's the same with God and the world. They exist together or not at all. God is in rasa.

Rasa is a complex word, somewhat analogous to the English word 'sense'. It means taste or bodily feeling, but also emotional feeling and awareness, inner meaning, and (in different mystical systems) various refractions of God in a human faculty or centre of consciousness.[3] Pak Tomo exploits these senses here to clinch a point. But his case rests on more than a pun. The different meanings of rasa are connected, physical sensation being but a crude, material form of the subtle inner life, a sign that there *is* inner life. As one elder said, with an irreverence characteristic of many Javanists: 'God moves about: where you itch, there is God; where the mosquito bites, there is God.' Human beings (*manungsa*) are 'united in feeling' (*manunggal ing rasa*), as folk etymology has it; and this feeling is not merely the itch or the taste but what underlies it, the divine life which mysteriously enables the senses to function.

Like taste, colour is not in the object or in the eye but in the act of seeing. If one is not actually looking at something, one cannot really assert that it has colour, 'one cannot *name* it'. This curious formulation (naming = asserting something to be) recalls the idea just mentioned: 'For something to be really true it must be cocog [fitting] with your companion as well as with your own perceptions; it must be witnessed.' Speech is the witness of the senses: if you cannot see something you cannot name it, therefore it does not exist. The same idea recurs in formulations of the God-in-man doctrine. 'If humanity did not exist neither could God, for who could name him?'[4]

Unsurprisingly, such matters are never settled and argument goes back and forth until some provisional solution is reached, only to be reopened on a future occasion. One night, after lontar-reading practice, three of the readers were amicably debating the point. Tomo made his usual statement that man and the earth (i.e. everything) came or comes into existence at the same time. Misji objected: what if everyone died – would the world continue to exist? No, said Tomo. At least he wouldn't be so bold as to say there could be anything. For who would name it? Without man there could be no proof of anything existing. Several of the lontar readers who were listening seemed to agree. But Misji, less given to abstraction, persisted: the world must continue, because a man's fields survived him – at least he hoped they did for his son's sake! This too won murmurs of agreement. Warno had nodded at this commonsense objection; but he was troubled by the idea of a world without humanity (how firmly the connexion is implanted!) and said that conditions would lead to mankind emerging again.

The world comes into being with man (*dumadi jagad bareng ambi manusa*). The conditions for existence now are the same as they were for Adam, the first man. He first *saw* the world and he was given the power to *name* things (*kwasa ngarani*). So if the world exists so must man.

At this point, on cue, someone brought in some plates of food, like visual aids in a lecture. Tomo said: 'Which existed first, us or the plates of food?' There were only two possible answers and they were both wrong. Tomo continued:

They exist together (*bebarengan anané*); and so it is with everything we perceive. There is a seen and a seer, a named and a namer. The one cannot be independent of the other. But the seer and the namer is mankind. Only man knows this; only mankind is clever.

Then, with a vague gesture towards the unenlightened beyond the door, he added: 'But only the clever!'

On another occasion a similar group was discussing the creation. (They were mainly Sangkan Paran people, but they were thinking things through for themselves rather than drawing on a particular doctrine.) There was general agreement that humanity, for the reasons given above, was, in a pantheistic sense, self-created (*dadi dhéwék*) rather than fashioned by a transcendent God. And the same applied to all living things.

'Who made the rambutan?' said Kaso, pointing to the dish of fruit on the table.
'As far as I'm concerned, the rambutan made the rambutan,' said Warno, helping himself to one.
I said: 'So what is God's role in all this?'
Warno began: 'Everything that has being (*ujud*) has a maker; and so, supposedly, must man. Likewise, name and being cannot be separated. Warno and me cannot be separated: I could not be named if I did not exist. But the name God and the being of God, that's difficult. Where is it? What is it? Take this cassava. It will grow into a plant with leaves. So where are the leaves now? Inside it, in a manner of speaking. But what happens if I don't plant it? It will not grow. Why not? Because it needs the elements, the warmth of the sun, rain, the earth's nourishment, the air. These give it life. You could say these *are* its life. Life cannot be separated from the elements; they create life and sustain it. Life and what gives life are one: *and this we call God.*'
'Why not simply call it life?' I suggested.
'You can call it what you like. It doesn't matter at all. The Arabs call it Allah, Javanese call it The Almighty (*kang kwasa*) or Life (*urip*).'

This formulation – remarkable in its simplicity and force – brings us to the heart of Javanist thinking.

God, life, sex, and everything

A biologist, whom I pressed for a definition, suggested that life, though not reducible to anything else, might be defined as the ability to reproduce. Javanists would agree that the mystery of life is contained in reproduction. Analogies of growth and transformation are usually taken from plant life (the tree contained in the seed, etc.), but the deepest mystery, and the absorbing focus of symbolism, is sexual reproduction. Sex is not only an image of union, but of fertile union. This is why sexual symbols such as the red and white porridge are always referred to 'mother and father' rather than simply to 'man and woman'. 'Mother and father' implies sex plus generation. More than this, the parental terms imply an Ego, their child. As the product of mother and father, Ego is a complex whole comprising both male and female principles (analogous, the biologist might say, to mother's and father's genes).

Were the red and white to refer simply to man or woman (husband or wife), however, Ego would be but half.

So where is the mystery in this? In that there is no external cause to set the process in motion, no God standing outside as prime mover; indeed, for some Javanists, sexual reproduction 'disproves' a creator. There is no transcendent God, yet man and woman cannot claim to create the child unaided: they are mere intermediaries (*lantaran*). How do we know this? Because not every act of coition bears fruit, and conception is not a deliberate or conscious act, an act of will. 'Your daughter is pretty', said Sugeng. 'Did you choose the colour of her eyes? Did you make sure she had two symmetrical ears and arms?'

Something extra is needed beyond male and female: whatever it is that brings life, and this comes unbidden from nowhere. 'It comes without origin and leaves without destination' (*teka ora sangkan, lunga ora paran*). Its true nature cannot be probed, only deduced. This is why it is called *ga'ib*, hidden, mysterious. Likewise the unfolding of being (*gumelaring dumadi*), the development and growth of an organism, is mysterious. 'One drop [of semen] is enough', said Sunar. 'One doesn't need to ask: Where does the leg come from, or the hand? All is complete inside the seed. That is *ga'ib*'. The same point is conveyed in a rather beautiful passage from a Sangkan Paran manuscript:

> If the *banyu rasa* [rasa fluid] which comes from Father and Mother is endued with life, then it becomes living *banyu rasa* located in the realm of obscurity (*jagad samar*), that is in the belly of the mother, gradually emerging by the power of Life, ever stronger, its parts unfolding: what is watery growing thicker, what is soft growing harder, what is small growing bigger, what is slack growing tighter, what is short growing longer, and so on. Hence: Life is power/capability (*kwasa*) without will (*karsa*); without raw material it forms the baby. Such is the law of the seed and the plant, the law of the mystery of nature. This may not be denied.

The reverential tone and solemnity of this passage are unmistakable and go some way to answering Zoetmulder's contention, quoted above, that a theory of this kind is incompatible with religion. Indeed, similar ideas are found in the *Suluk Anak*, quoted extensively by Zoetmulder himself (1995: 186–7). He comments:

> This is the enigma of that Life which parents give to their child: something of themselves which becomes a thing belonging to another while remaining the same. It is the enigma of remaining *one* through all changes, which can be ascertained not only in man himself from youth to old age, but also in Life viewed as a single whole which presents itself in various forms and through its oneness encompasses and absorbs all contrasts ... He who knows this discerns the one life and the one BEING in all plurality.   (1995: 188–9)

Bayu's mystics, untrained in scholastic theology and mostly unfamiliar with the classical Javanist literature, do not put it in quite this way. A sense of the unity of existence is conveyed in simpler terms. As one mystic said to me:

Life is one (*siji*), but it divides up into many (*ngawiji-wiji*). It's like water. It exists in many places but it's the same thing. If you are asked to fetch water, you don't ask 'Which water?'

For the ordinary Javanist, as opposed to the scholar, sexual reproduction is of absorbing interest not because of the light it may shed on the scholastic problem of how the one relates to the many, but because, less abstractly, it invites us to ponder how life is transmitted, more particularly how *we* transmit life; and it prompts us to meditate on the fact that there is anything at all. Sex is a focus of interest for itself rather than as a metaphor of other processes.[5]

Microcosm/macrocosm

A second approach to the God–man relation is through the concept of microcosm/macrocosm (*jagad cilik/jagad gedhe*). This concept, which is widely used by Javanists of all persuasions, is linked to the reproductive theme in various ways. Instead of William Blake's 'world in a grain of sand, and eternity in an hour' we have the world in a drop of sperm, and eternity in the moment of conception when life is transmitted (a conceit expressed in the onomatopoeic sequence: *tètès* (drop), *tès!* (the 'sound' of ejaculation), *titis* (incarnate)). The whole process of gestation is one of adjustment between the inner environment of the foetus 'meditating in its cave' and the outer world. As it grows, its constituents curdle and solidify. When they are in balance with the outer elements, inner matching (cocog) outer, the child is born (*lair* = born, outer).

A more arcane but ingenious way of formulating a genetic link between microcosm and macrocosm is by means of the male and female prototypes, Adam and Eve. This was explained to me by one of the Sangkan Paran seniors in Bayu. Adam, by this interpretation, means emptiness, the void (*sepi*).[6] Hawa (Eve) means (i) *hawa*, climate, thus the elements; and (ii) passion, sexual desire (*hawa nepsu*). The sexual union of Adam and Eve is thus analogous to the confluence of elements in the primeval void, the coming into being of the world.

But this is, admittedly, a recondite view. So what does the ordinary Javanist understand by a relation of microcosm to macrocosm? Is it a relation of common substance or form? Since much depends on the answer to this question I spent a good deal of time gathering opinion (the subject is, in any case, unavoidable).

Four views are discernible.[7] These views are not mutually exclusive, but people tend to emphasize one or another.

1. In a poetic sense the human body is the mirror of the world. It has its own seas and mountains, sources of light (the eyes), and so on. Historical and cultural figures are mirrored in the human constitution.

2. Man is the pattern after which the cosmos is built. Putting it another way: man is at the centre of a patterned cosmos and the key to its design. Numerology reveals or encodes correspondences between microcosm and macrocosm in a symbolic classification (see Pigeaud 1983).

3. The body and the world are composed of the same stuff: the four elements (*anasir papat*), earth, wind, fire, and water. This is sometimes put rather abstractly. Thus by 'earth' is meant matter or 'what gives/occupies place' (*mapan*); wind signifies 'what moves things'; fire signifies heat and light; and water stands for fluid.

4. 'The world and man exist together.'

As with the reproductive theme, the role of God is not explicit yet, given a notion of divine immanence, it is paramount. The articulation of God's role is nevertheless difficult and controversial: a matter of endless debate rather than of settled conviction or dogma. Consider the following exchange:

SUHEM. God resides where? If one said that God made man, that would imply he [God] already existed. But what would that mean?

WARNO. It would mean he was hidden, inchoate (*ga'ib*).[8] Think of it like this: this world, its content is the same as the microcosm (*jagad cilik*), is it not? Being is possible thanks to the four elements. Clearly, fire is a tool of rasa [divine indwelling life] with its seat in light; wind, as a tool of rasa, has its seat in breath; water is in the blood; and earth is in the flesh.

SUHEM. Agreed; they are the vessel (*wadhah*). That's clear enough.

WARNO. So the coming together of the four elements is what makes us, what makes you and me. When we die we disperse into the elements, return to our origin.

SUHEM. Yes, that's obvious. But that assumes they already exist. We say that Adam is the result of the four elements; but if Adam has not yet copulated with Eve, then there is nothing [because there is not yet humanity as witness].

AB. Do the elements themselves have an origin or do they simply exist?

JUMHAR. Was God first or man? You might as well ask about the chicken and the
   egg.
SUHEM. As we say: the cock crows inside the egg. They emerge together or not
   at all. I once read on a stone at Candi Sèwu [an ancient Buddhist temple in
   Central Java] 'Begin together, become together, enact together, unfold together: the world's being and man's being' ('bareng miwiti, bareng dumadi,
   bareng nglakoni, gumelaré padha: anané jagad, anané manusa').

Questions about ultimate origins are unanswerable and must end in
paradox. The world simply is; we cannot know how it came into being.
But it is a patterned and intelligible world, not merely a brute fact, and it
stands in a symbolic relation to the microcosm. A village clerk put this
very clearly to me: the macrocosm is symbol (*perlambang*), the microcosm its original pattern (*sejatiné, asliné*), that is, its referent. While
many, perhaps most, Javanists would agree with this formula, people
differ about whether the symbolic relation is given in nature, arbitrary,
or traditional (a tradition (*waluri*) may, in turn, be recognized as
convention or something fixed and eternal), and this affects their
understanding of the God–man relation. If you think that the world is
structured on the model of man, and that God is what animates living
things, then symbolic statements about the microcosm/macrocosm constitute religious knowledge and may be a satisfactory conclusion to
speculation. Others may see such statements as begging the question.
   There is a difference of emphasis and style of thinking here comparable
to the contrast noted by Zoetmulder (1995: 144) between the divination
manuals (*primbon*), with their classificatory, magical bent, and the
philosophical–mystical treatises such as the *Centhini* and *Cabolèk*. The
'classifiers' are usually content to postulate a symbolic connexion; the
'philosophers' want to question its basis.
   Consider the symbolic schemes in which the microcosm/macrocosm
concept is framed. The five-coloured porridge used in the slametan is a
symbol of the human person, the five-day market week, the four
directions and centre, the four primary colours combined in the centre,
the *nepsu* (drives), the elements, even the four Arabic letters of Allah. Its
very form – centre symbolizing periphery – is an image of microcosm-
macrocosm. But what do these correspondences mean? They depend,
apparently, on analogy, and thus on a similarity of relations rather than
substance (see Needham 1980b), but they are not interchangeable as in a
purely formal arrangement. For example, the four elements may be
identified in esoteric discussion with A-L-L-H; but the name of God is
unrelated to the other quartets. Moreover, the associations are expressed

in terms of one thing having its 'seat' (*lungguh*) or being 'located in' (*manggon*) another, suggesting a more concrete relation than analogy. For example, the market day Paing is associated with red and is located south. This may be accounted for by an ancient, long-forgotten circuit of local markets (Ossenbruggen 1983). More puzzling is why Paing has its 'seat' in the ear (thus hearing), as does *amarah*, the anger-drive. I discussed this point with a group of villagers. One suggested that a person becomes angry by hearing bad things; his ear turns red; and Paing sounds like *kuping*, ear. (The ear is not, as such, associated with south.) Another man said that the correspondences are natural and fixed; they can be recognized but not explained. A third said that all such schemes are human inventions: we may speak of Monday and Tuesday but in reality there is only day and night. Since man needs a system of reckoning (*itungan*) to co-ordinate activities he takes these figures from human anatomy. Hence the seven- and five-day weeks correspond to the orifices of the head and the faculties, respectively, but they could just as easily derive from some other schema.

This view, expressing the arbitrary character of the symbol – with man as the arbiter – seemed to divide the group. One elder objected that symbols must match (cocog) reality. They were either right or wrong: one couldn't waffle or invent. The associations of yellow, west, and pleasure, or of black, north, and eternity were fixed, in the nature of things (*kodrat*). We, as bearers of tradition, are mere intermediaries, and cannot alter these correspondences; 'only a *pujangga* could do that'. (A poet-mystic, such as Ranggawarsita, has divine inspiration and therefore has access to eternal truths.)

These disagreements about the motivation (but not the content) of symbolic associations concern routine knowledge. But a similar temperamental division, between classifiers and sceptical enquirers, persists into the higher zones of Javanist learning. Among adepts of all the sects and cults I encountered I found those who delighted in mastery of arcane correspondences, seeing them as the very essence of kawruh (Javanist wisdom), and others who saw them as no more than a means to an end, or perhaps as a way of encoding what is already known. A common point of difference is over the importance given to mantra and spells. One veteran mystic carries in his breast pocket a key to the fatihah, the opening verse of the Koran, which links each syllable with a part of the body. He recites this litany every day.[9]

What distinguishes such arcane correspondences from the ordinary stuff of Javanist lore is that they serve as an object of meditation rather than an end in themselves. They are meant to be assimilated, 'felt' rather than simply memorized or manipulated in spells. (Though some mystics seem to forget this.) Meditation upon symbols involves a movement from outer to inner, from the relatively coarse (kasar), material world, the macrocosm, to the subtler, refined (alus) realm of the microcosm, thus a spiritual progression. Any act of symbolic interpretation (e.g., in a slametan address), if carried out correctly, may involve a similar process, whether or not listeners are aware of the fact. But mystical discourse is especially attentive to the spiritual scale, never losing hold of the idea that though the outer world reflects the inner they are not to be confused or equated.[10] Unless this distinction of levels or degrees is grasped – as santri generally fail to do – the notion of an indwelling God is apt to be miscontrued as a simple identity of God and man.

Ambiguity in the conception of God

A common scheme for representing stages of spiritual development, and, by analogy, scales of other kinds, is derived from Sufism as it has come down to Javanese tradition (Soebardi 1971: 341–4). Conventionally there are four stages. *Saré'at* (Osing dialect for *saréngat*) refers to the observance of Islamic Law, the shariah. *Tarékat*, a word which also means Sufi Brotherhood, refers to The Way, the path of mysticism. *Hakékat* refers to the hidden reality, the truth. And *ma'ripat* means gnosis, the 'union of servant and Lord' (*manunggaling kawula Gusti*). In common parlance, however, these terms are not used in a strict sense but refer loosely to a scale of understanding or scheme of degrees, so that *saré'at* means the rules and regulations of practical reality or simply the way of doing things, and *hakékat* the deeper significance, the truth. Thus, as one man explained it, the *saré'at* of a slametan is its practical organization; the *hakékat* its inner meaning.[11] One might term this a 'native model' of multivocality.

One's speech and action can thus have layered meanings, both to oneself and to others. A case in point is the treatment of ancestors. Most of the mystics reject the notion of a *personal* afterlife, yet like everyone else they take part in rituals directed, ostensibly, to the ancestors. Pak D, who told me bluntly that 'death is the end of the story', gave a feast at which he 'sent prayers to the departed'. As he explained later, the offerings and prayers were simply a way of remembering the dead, and of recognizing one's origin in male and female, symbolized in one's parents. Ancestor, *leluhur*, to him meant 'what was exalted' (*luhur*), and this was within oneself, not somewhere up in the sky. The dead have no separate existence, he said; they can neither harm nor help us. But it does help us to remember them, to ponder our origins.

Another mystic put the same point in different words.

We speak of the afterlife/eternity (*jaman kelanggengan*), but really it is the living, or rather life itself, which is eternal. The ancestors are nowhere but in us. You need not look outside. At a slametan it is we who eat the food and hear the prayers. In so doing we verify (*mbuktèkaken*) our origins.

I asked him about the abode of spirits, *alam antara* (the 'in-between realm').

This is not a place or a time, but what exists potentially between a man and a woman, their mutual desire (*sir musuh sir*) which leads to conception. *Alam antara* is the instant preceding existence (*dumadi*).

A common analogy used to explain the process of generation and death is the life of a plant. It dies but grows again. Where has the tree gone? Into the seed. The seed becomes the stem; the bud becomes the fruit, and so on. Our life continues in our children after we have gone.

Occasionally, however, something more than commemoration seems to be involved, as the following example shows. Pak Muni and friends were invited to read the Javanese version of the story of Joseph and his brothers at the circumcision of his nephew in a neighbouring village. As the recitation drew to a close at dawn the operation could not go ahead because the boy had become feverish. The readers performed a divination using the lontar manuscript, first putting a question to it: was the fever from within, or was it due to some disturbance outside? The words which the diviner read from the lontar seemed to hint at the bewilderment of the boy's deceased father. He was confused, perhaps, because the ceremony was being held at the house of the step-father instead of at the grandparents' house where the boy now lived. So Muni went to the father's grave to 'send prayers' and took some earth from it to rub on the boy's body. The whole event was then transferred to the boy's house and, seeing that he was now 'well', the circumcision went ahead.

Similar cases involving initiated mystics are easily come by and for the most part are no different from the experiences of ordinary villagers – the school caretaker who recovered from a stroke only when rubbed with soil from his mentor's grave; the irrigation official who tended his relative's grave after he had been 'visited in a dream'. Incidents such as these, which typically have to do with misfortunes and worries or premonitions, suggest an active intervention by the dead in the world of the living. Although it is possible to justify the corrective steps taken in terms of 'acting out' or 'proving' inner realities, fulfilling vows, or even shrewd psychology (in the case of Muni), the immediate context suggests otherwise.

A similar ambiguity commonly arises in speaking of God. The extremely impersonal conception of the deity which Javanists use in mystical discussion sometimes gives way to ordinary expressions of faith or dependence characteristic of popular religion. Javanists may thus speak of 'appealing to' or 'acceptance by the Lord' or 'Maker' in a way which contradicts the notion of a pantheist God-within. Whenever I mentioned this contradiction I was always told that the personal idioms were merely a 'way of speaking' and that reality was quite otherwise. Indeed, such ambiguity is a common feature of Javanese mystical literature. But the context of the utterance often makes these retrospective justifications sound unconvincing. As with the notion of ancestors, it seems that people are able to operate with different conceptions of divinity. Crudely, we might distinguish between an emotionally satisfying theism and supernaturalism on the one hand and an intellectually satisfying pantheism on the other. Supernaturalism can be justified, if necessary, by appeal to idiom or social context and thus accorded a relative truth. As one mystic put it to me: 'Do spirits exist? Yes and no. They exist if you believe they do.'

I have outlined the major characteristics of Javanism as I found it in Banyuwangi. Despite the great variety of opinion, which I hope has survived the translation from conversation to print, certain general features can be discerned which define a Javanist style or orientation, by which I mean a characteristic set of strategies and ways of thinking about things. ('Worldview' is, perhaps, too totalizing a concept, suggesting an exclusive group with a particular mind-set and a closed system of ideas. What is at issue here is a certain conceptual flexibility which allows Javanists to switch to other 'styles' as social context demands, much as one switches speech levels in standard Javanese.) Among these characteristics are a predilection for symbolism; a this-worldly, pragmatic orientation in which pantheism subserves a homegrown philosophy; and a conception of reality as multi-layered, therefore inherently ambiguous. In the final part of this chapter we shall see how this 'style' informs the practical problems of ethics.

Javanist ethics

Unsurprisingly, given the metaphysic sketched out in previous pages, Javanist ethics – as consciously elaborated in mystical discussion – is far from being a straightforward matter of pursuing the good, the beautiful, and the true (if such things ever can be straightforward).[12] Its grounding in an analysis of experience is complex and subtle. The goal of correct thought and action, however, is simply identified as slamet, the state of well-being and freedom from hindrances. There is no fundamental difference, from this standpoint, between remembering to look both ways when crossing the road, performing a kind act, and fulfilling a vow to hold a slametan. Common sense precautions, virtuous behaviour, and ritual observance operate within the same ethical framework. Is this, then, a simple prudential morality? On the face of it, yes. But this is to characterize it by its desired effects. If we look at the underlying reasons and values a more interesting picture emerges.

The moral basis of misfortune

In Javanist thinking, as it was presented to me, two words which have similar dictionary definitions, *blai* (Osing spelling of *bilai*, misfortune, bad luck) and *apes* (to have bad luck), are made to bear an important distinction. As Pak Noto explained:

If you make someone angry and they hit you, that's *blai*. If you fall into a hole because you're not looking, that's also *blai*. But if you drop down dead that's *apes*. With *apes* you don't know where it's coming from. In fact it's the consequence of some forgotten mistake or wrong. Its origin is in yourself but not in an obvious way. Why in yourself? Because you didn't ask for it [like the slapped face], nor were you given it: it just happened. We all know that things happen, but if you keep having accidents, evidently they must be something to do with you.

Blai is always related to action which notionally involves intention, niyat. Paradoxically, this can include carelessness, since careless actions are avoidable. But *apes* strikes without warning and is unrelated to the victim's intention at the time. It is only with hindsight that one can (sometimes) discern one's original error. What previously seemed arbitrary then appears as just deserts, revealing the law of karma. Karma thus results indirectly from the exercise of will; hence the etymology: *karma* < *karepé manusa* (the will of man). There is no deflecting such misfortunes and no way of ameliorating them. 'All one can do', said Pak Noto, 'is ask forgiveness of one's siblings born on the same day', that is, hold a slametan with the dishes of red and white and five-coloured porridge.

Pak Noto, being a Sangkan Paran member, took the explanation further. The 'four siblings' – sight, hearing, smell, and speech – are God-given faculties whose origin and workings are mysterious. We have them on trust, as it were, and it is our duty to use them correctly. The initiate is sworn to purify his faculties and warned that 'betrayal' of them will lead to misfortune (*apes*). Betrayal means to 'see this red cigarette packet and say it is white', to falsify one's perceptions. Inside, one's rasa knows the truth and rejects the act; it cannot be cheated. An act of deception is thus always a self-deception; it violates one's own 'rules', that is, one's personal constitutional order. Eventually the act rebounds in an unexpected form. Thus rasa, the controlling centre of consciousness, acts as a kind of conscience and instrument of punishment. One's 'guardian spirits' – the four siblings or faculties – like friends taken for granted, then cease to protect one's welfare and misfortune soon follows. The slametan is a symbolic effort to restore order and an opportunity for self-scrutiny, but it must be accompanied by a resolve to do what conduces to slamet (well-being).

Purity and danger

Again, this sounds like a simple call for prudence and caution; but more is implied. Javanist ethics emphasizes the matching of inner and outer, thought or word with action. Honouring one's word is not just a matter of social expediency or prudence: to break one's word is to be untrue to oneself (*sulaya ambi awaké dhéwék*) and therefore to defile what is pure, for the human voice, like the other faculties, is an instrument of the divine inner life. As one mystic put it to me: the faculty of speech (*pangucap*) is given to us, sufficient and unblemished; it is not of our making. To misuse it by abrogating one's word is to bring on the Maker's curse.

A promise thus commits oneself and one's welfare. When Pak Maksum's son recovered from an eye injury he held a slametan as he had vowed. The address, spoken by a Javanist neighbour, included the following statement:

Busairi can now see. He [Maksum] had said 'Let him be well; if he recovers I will hold a slametan.' Therefore tonight let it be witnessed that the vow is fulfilled (*disaur*). His body owes no debt to his soul. Let the soul not press a debt (*nagih*) against the body.

Vows are particularly compromising, and one has to be especially careful about speech in holy places, such as shrines or haunted spots. But any clear statement of intention, such as 'I will be home in two days' or 'I am going to the shrine tomorrow', whether or not it affects others, is similarly binding. 'Once an intention is expressed, it must be carried out.'

If 'honouring one's word' (*ngajèni nang omongé*) means being bound by it, this should not imply an internal struggle. Although committed, one should act as if freely, not out of compulsion or fear. A gift should be given, a vow fulfilled, or a responsibility accepted willingly and with good grace, otherwise it is worthless. Conversely, to do what one says is a sign of power, proof that one's word is mandi, efficacious.

The harmonizing of word (or thought) and deed is especially important in religious acts and is part of what makes such acts stand out from ordinary behaviour. Thus, in the slametan, as in the spell, the spoken intent is carried out in the very performance; the words become action and are by definition mandi. Javanism shares with Islam an emphasis on purity of motive, on approaching the sacred in a fit state. Hence a common emphasis on intention, niyat, and the provision of rules which cancel a ritual if something untoward interrupts concentration or performance. The chicken dedicated in an important slametan must be 'pure' (unblemished, with white beak and claws) and is cooked by a woman past menopause. But the host's heart must be pure too. Likewise, when scattering flowers on a grave, one's prayers are not received unless one 'sends a pure heart' (*kirim ati kang suci*). As a Bayu woman explained to me:

Illness often comes from eating something dirty, because what is clean doesn't agree with what is dirty. Holy things are sullied by contact with impure things. The *halal* rejects the *haram*. It's the same with people: politeness rejects rudeness, good conduct rejects bad.

As physical beings in the material world we must prepare ourselves for contact with the spiritual, create a proper container or *wadhah* for spiritual knowledge. Hence, in meditation, the thoughts are refined and the senses stilled in order to pass into the ethereal, alus, realm. From this point of view, alus (subtle, refined) and kasar (material, coarse) are contraries rather than distinctions of degree. And – at least in discussions of religious observance – they serve as phenomenological rather than aesthetic categories.

Ethics and ethos

As these remarks suggest, being on correct terms with the world begins with self-correction (Ind. *mawas diri*). One cannot expect harmonious relations with the neighbours, any more than with spiritual beings, unless one's own house is in order. This is a matter of adjusting the inner life, speech, and behaviour so as to harmonize with others. In general, in proceeding from self to the world one applies the same set of ideas and principles, because 'big things are made from small things; the teeming world derives from two people'.

Javanist ethics stresses the interdependence of inner and outer, self and others. One cannot be truly slamet unless circumstances – which include the well-being of others – allow it. People often told me that if one neglects the general welfare one's own slamet is diminished. It sounds glib, but behind the easy no-man-is-an-island moralizing lies a serious effort at cultivating awareness of others which makes good practical sense in the village community. *Rumangsa* (feeling, awareness) is sometimes presented as the basis of rukun, social harmony. As it was explained to me, whereas rasa (feeling-intuition) concerns the inner life and personal salvation, *rumangsa* concerns fellow-feeling, empathy. Our sympathy is stimulated by a sense of reciprocity. If someone invites you to a slametan you feel the object of their concern and want to return the favour; you *duwé rumangsa*, feel aware. The ritual form – the feast – is thus closely tied to an ideal social-spiritual state in which people bury their differences and come together.

The slametan represents the ideal; but in everyday life, too, one is expected to share in the joys and sorrows of one's neighbours 'left and right'. Even in questions of etiquette – which is much less elaborate in Banyuwangi than in some parts of Java – similar considerations arise. Unencumbered by the tortuous speech levels that frame Central Javanese encounters, host and guest can attend to each other's needs and 'watch out for the other's well-being'. (For example, the host must talk a lot otherwise the guest will feel unwelcome.) Co-operation and social harmony are thus seen as rooted in positive socially directed attitudes rather than, as H. Geertz (1961: 149) found in Modjokuto, in dissimulation and caution. It is an ethic of mutuality and interdependence wholly at variance with the Western tradition of individualism and mutual indifference and is therefore, perhaps, easily underrated. I once asked a neighbour why he liked to carry his ten-year-old nephew on his back. 'So that he will grow up knowing he can depend on me', he replied.

Relativism

We have seen how concepts of perceptual relativism, epitomized in ideas about space, pervade Javanist philosophy. In the field of ethics a similar relativism is apparent, though it applies only to a portion of moral action. Although it was never put to me in the form of a straightforward contrast, Sangkan Paran's mystics make a distinction between ordinary rules ([per]aturan) or guiding principles and the hard-wired, constitutional ordering of the person which they call *pernatan* (from *tata*, [proper] order). The former rules are conventional and culture-bound, even idiosyncratic – a matter of custom and habit; the latter are innate and are therefore the same for everyone. Some such distinction is, I believe, widely applicable in Javanese ethics. I came across similar formulations (otherwise phrased) among Javanists with different backgrounds including Hindu converts in south Banyuwangi.

Why should the personal constitution be a moral matter? Anthropologists commonly speak of a system which is endowed with intrinsic value (e.g., caste society or a lineage system) as a 'moral order', meaning by this something rather different from an ethical code. 'Moral', in this sense, refers to the sanctity and inviolability of the order, its ineluctable nature, rather than to the sphere of ordinary moral action. In Javanist thinking the person is conceived in similar terms. The sequence of birth and death, the functioning of the senses, and the miracle of reproduction, are not simply neutral facts of life, the raw materials of morality: they are themselves evidence of a moral order. But what does it mean to speak of an objective moral order or design which has no source outside the individual? Unlike, say, a lineage system or a set of ritual taboos which are sanctioned by supernatural agencies, this moral order derives its force, its objective nature, from within; it does not belong to some transcendental scheme. The organizing principle, the object of respect, is, of course, the indwelling God: Life (*urip*). Hence, sex, generation, and perception, as activities which pertain to Life, have intrinsic moral import (aside from their social regulation, which pertains to conventional, man-made morality). The correct exercise of these human functions – correct in the sense of acknowledging their source and cherishing their use – implies a certain attitude of humility and respect towards the inner life, a recognition of its power, which is greater than that of the individual mortal self. As one mystic said to me: 'Just as a Muslim washes his eyes, ears, and hands before meeting his God in prayer, so we must purify our senses mentally before using them.'

It is difficult to obtain clear explanations of the practical implications of such thinking, or of what exactly is meant by exhortations to 'purify the faculties' or 'honour the body', but some examples have already been considered, such as honouring one's word. Ordinary moral injunctions against killing and stealing are sometimes explained in similar terms. In harming others one harms oneself, either through the working of *karma* or through the reflex of conscience. It is not that such moral prohibitions have a transcendental value as in theistic ethics: their force derives from their relation to the inner constitution.

In contrast to this fixed and absolute order of the person, man-made regulations are variable and relative. Many ordinary Muslims, even some santri, are prepared to recognize a wide latitude of behaviour as tolerable in others, including practices such as drinking or gambling which are contrary to their own principles. But Javanists go much further in undermining value judgements, as the following example shows. I was discussing the relative merits of the the two local shrines with a carpenter, an unaffiliated Javanist named Pak Karto, and got into difficulties over value-words. While I struggled with 'good' and 'bad', his watchword was cocog, which means 'fitting, suitable, right', aptly summing up the relativist's position.[13] I first asked him whether his preference for Buyut Cungking was because he was better than Buyut Cili?

K. I don't often visit Buyut Cili, but 'better' is not the right word. The word 'good' depends on whether something is fitting (*tembung apik iku manut cocoge*). If you try one thing and it's not cocog for you, you'll probably say it's not good; and if the other one works you'll say it's good, but in fact it's just cocog.

AB. In what sense is it cocog?

K. Cocog with your wish, so that your wish is granted. So what we call good is simply what fits. It has to harmonize with what is inside us and that varies from person to person. It's like colours: you can't say red is better than yellow just because you prefer it. I'm cocog with my wife, and so I say she's good, but for someone else she might not be.

A B. Is a prayer at Cungking more efficacious (mandi), then?

K. Again, one is not more mandi than the other. To be mandi is simply to be to the point. If I say I'll come at dawn and duly turn up my promise was mandi. Mandi is a matter of the right words.

This reluctance to judge extends into personal conduct. Conflicts arise because people's habits are different. As Pak Karto explained it, someone is 'wrong' or wrongs you if their actions are not cocog with your own way of doing things, your *aturan*. (This word covers both rules and habitual ways of doing things.) Right and wrong are not in the person but in the habits. Hence, one should never reject another person, only their *aturan*.

Similar comments frequently arise when people talk about morality. A dhukun (healer), deflecting santri criticisms of his impiety said: 'Let's not be too hasty. There is good in what appears bad, and bad in what appears good.' And another Javanist once observed to me (as a generalization, not, I think, as a veiled reproach): 'Clearly, only you yourself can know ["feel"] whether something you have done is good or bad. Others can't tell you.'

The gist of these quotations is that moral judgement is a matter of personal conscience. Whatever other people say – indeed, whatever one protests oneself – rasa unfailingly knows the truth of the matter. This is moral relativism, then, but not nihilism. In practical terms, such ideas foster tolerance – something to be valued above 'right and wrong' in an overcrowded village.

Javanist ethics and Islam

Perhaps surprisingly – given that nearly all Javanists are Muslims – Islamic doctrine was rarely mentioned to me in ethical discussion. This lack of interest can be attributed to the fact that many non-santri, whether mystically inclined or not, do not accept the Koran as the ultimate guide to conduct, and many reject the idea of a revealed religion with a transcendental morality. But there are more specific objections which make legalistic Islam incompatible with Javanist ethics.

(1) The basic schema of Islamic ethics – the categories of obligatory, recommended, neutral, disapproved, and forbidden (Levy 1969: 202–3) – is at odds with the way moral issues are framed in Javanist thinking. For Javanists, obligations come from outside and are therefore considered inferior to internally motivated acts. What comes from oneself and is freely given is superior to what is done to order. Hence, the decision to hold a slametan, perform a kind act, or join a religious organization must come from within. Islamic obligations such as the daily prayers and the Fast, in compelling conformity lose moral force.

For Javanists, the literalism with which ritual obligations, such as the Fast, are carried out detracts from their value and obscures their significance. In order to temper one's appetites it is not necessary to starve oneself; one can make the moral adjustment with little or no change of diet. Indeed, as Pak T put it, if there is a ripe mango on the tree one feels 'obliged to eat it' (*wajib mangan*). Similarly, the obligatory pilgrimage to Mecca is considered a distraction from the interior journey undertaken by the 'true believer'.

In general, the legalistic, normative aspect of Islam is regarded as stultifying and narrow-minded, and its supernatural punishments are not taken seriously. Many non-santri, whether Javanists or not, regard Islamic rules and sanctions as human inventions aimed at social compliance.

(2) Islam – so far as it is known – and Javanism barely overlap in the subject matter of ethics. Javanists do not consider obedience to Islamic prescriptions to be a moral concern, let alone the primary moral concern, since ritual obligations involve neither relations between people (alms-

giving being a partial exception) nor the kinds of self-correction discussed above. Consequently, some Javanese sects have developed parallel rituals modelled on Islam, such as the so-called *salāt sejati* ('the true worship'), which emphasize the moral and contemplative aspects of devotion over the liturgical. Similar contemplative strains within mainstream orthodox Islam (not to mention Sufism) are, as far as I could tell, known only to a few villagers who have studied Islam at a higher level (at a State Islamic Institute). Likewise, the Hadīth literature, which confirms many Javanist norms of social conduct, is not well known to villagers.

(3) The hectoring tenor of Islamic moral discourse (notably in the sermon and dawn broadcast) is found oppressive and disrespectful by non-santri. Even the devout often feel uncomfortable about criticizing their neighbours and distance themselves from the hell-fire broadcasts and denunciations of 'infidels'.

(4) Javanism lacks the idea of orthodoxy (though some sects have borrowed the idea from Islam). The drive for conformity through repetition, harangues, and congregational worship in Islam contrasts with the eclecticism and pluralism espoused by most Javanists. Although different sects have their own distinctive approaches and liturgies, members are usually free to follow other paths as well. One of Bayu's mystics holds office in local branches of both Sangkan Paran and Sapta Darma. He told me he 'goes to Sangkan Paran for its kawruh [mystical knowledge] and Sapta Darma for its meditation postures'. No system is perfect and complete; and none is without merit. One must 'filter' and compare, extract the good, and above all test what one knows against experience. An example (which as it happens does not concern ethics) makes the point.

One evening, at a gathering of Bayu's mystics, a former headman asked me: 'So what, then, for the sake of comparison, do English think? What is the origin of everything? Where is God for the English?' I replied, rather weakly, that English traditionally believed that God made man in his own image.

This was true, in a sense, he said, provided that one did not imagine a divine person prior to and outside his creation. Man is indeed God's image, his material form. 'Your God is from your head to your foot'. But what about Nabi Isa (Jesus)? Was Jesus God or the son of God? He had never quite understood.

Neither had I, I said. But he was supposed to be both.

Again, this could be fitted to Javanese theory, especially if Jesus was seen as a symbol of human ontogeny, with the twelve disciples standing for the twelve constituents of man. God in man, a man-God. It was almost the same.

I pointed out that Jesus was a unique case.

'Ah! There's the error.'

Conclusion

As this anecdote illustrates, Javanist learning may tend towards the esoteric but – at least in the village context – it is neither obscurantist nor remote from ordinary human concerns. The important truths are thought to lie hidden behind everyday forms, embedded in the immediate realities of birth, copulation, and death. Hence, the novice is told that he or she has 'practised' kawruh, as has any human being, but has not yet understood it. Orthodox religion, on this view, is misdirected in its otherworldliness, offering ritual answers to pseudo-problems. As one mystic put it: 'The santri who worries about sin and prays for salvation is like someone who trips on a smooth path or who bumps his head on the air.'

I have tried to capture this spiritual 'worldliness' by presenting Javanism as a practical endeavour, a reflection on experience, rather than as the finished work of experts; hence my emphasis has been less on the esoteric content of mysticism than on the concepts with which people try to make sense of their place in the world. Foremost among these organizing concepts are the notions of microcosm and macrocosm, sexual reproduction as a focus for thinking about origins and human existence, and the human person itself.

The wisdom of the classical Javanist texts is reflected here but often in mirror image. For example, among Bayu's mystics, the joining of male and female, a common literary symbol of mystical union, becomes itself the philosophical focus and recurrent – almost monotonous – object of symbolism. It is other things which are made to stand for sexual union, for example, the joining of the clock's hands at midnight (= coition, conception (when twelve constituents come together)) or the ritual squirting of white porridge by a mother-to-be into her husband's cupped hands (a reversal of male and female roles: the idea is that birth should be as easy as ejaculation). Sex is at the heart of the mystery of existence and a means by which one approaches that mystery.[14]

In such a manner abstract, scholastic questions are translated into human terms, reduced to human scale. Mystical treatises may ponder how the One becomes the many (Zoetmulder takes this to be the central mystical puzzle). But Bayu's Javanists ask: how do the many become the one – how do the elements, colours, directions, Adam and Eve and Vishnu combine in the human form?

A second theme running through this chapter, as through Javanism itself, is the contrast with Islam. As we have seen, the official dominant faith often serves as the point of departure in mystical discussion. Javanists contrast Islam with esoteric knowledge in terms of outer/inner, material/subtle, derivative/original, signifier/signified, prescriptive/self-motivated, and literalist/symbolist. The apparently Islamic tenor of much Javanese mysticism, even at its most heterodox, stems from this pervasive, often invidious, contrast as much as from genuine affinities. One could point to Sufism as a source of such contrasts (roughly Woodward's position), but it is far from being the only influence, and similar contrasts in other traditions suggest a broader, encompassing opposition between mysticism and organized, institutional religion.

The question of how Javanism should be classified is, in any case, a matter for the student of comparative religion.[15] What concerns us here is how practitioners define it and how the dominant religion constrains its expression. We have seen that Islam supplies much of the language, the concepts and categories of Javanism: it is, inescapably, a climate of opinion. Javanists have come to terms with this predicament by modifying Islamic meanings – universalizing them. Islam 'means' slamet; *Muslimin/Muslimat* 'means' man and woman; Muhammad is the body, and so on. It is an old, but effective, tactic. The author of a nineteenth-century *suluk* asks:

What is the meaning of sembahyang (ritual prayer)? ... For what reason does it exist and where did it find its origin? If you do not yet know this, you are not yet a Muslim; you are still a polytheist and infidel ... For those who have true insight, all of the meaning of these allusions is to be found in just a single word. For it is to be found in: you. Allah, that are you; the prophet of God, that also are you; *bismi'llah* are you, *fatiha* are you. (Zoetmulder 1995: 222)

Zoetmulder remarks: 'All of this is located within the Islamic sphere, but the connection with Islam seems to be merely external. Islamic terms are used, but only in order to reject them or to give them an entirely different sense.' By means of such calculated misreadings the exclusivity of Islam is breached and its doctrinal claims are relativized. Among present-day Javanists this shuffling of meanings is made with varying degrees of respect for the dominant faith. For the small minority actually hostile to Islam, fidelity to scriptural obligations is a kind of unbelief since it mistakes the sign for the reality. Such opinions, which cannot be voiced in public, find expression in the *suluk* literature in such ironic inversions

as 'Fasting and almsgiving, *jakat* and *pitrah* are to be regarded as idols
... One is not yet a Muslim if one is not yet an infidel' (Zoetmulder 1995:
225–6; cf. Drewes 1966: 359). Most Javanists of my acquaintance,
however, regarded their position as complementary to institutional
religion rather than opposed to it, and this is borne out by their
participation in the rituals of village Islam. Indeed, many would find a
conscious hostility to Islam both socially embarrassing and personally
disturbing, therefore unconducive to slamet.

The contrast with Islam is important, then, but it is largely formal, a
matter of differing styles. Javanists pursue their interest in the nature of
meaning, ethics, and the constitution of the person, for the most part
independently of Islam.

7

Sangkan Paran: a Javanist sect

Studies of religious and mystical movements in contemporary Java, even
those well grounded in knowledge of local conditions, have mostly begun
at the top, with the most articulate and best-educated representatives.
Only Clifford Geertz – the most vivid of Java's ethnographers – starts
from the grass-roots. The risks of such an approach (risks happily
circumvented by Geertz) are easily identified: an inattention to wider
organizational patterns and a tendency to miss the 'figure in the carpet'
from being too close; but the advantages, though real, are less apparent.
If the anthropologist first comes to his subject in its local context he can
surely understand its relation to other local factors better than one who
approaches it equipped with the 'official' view and finds only deviations.
This may be a poor recommendation for one about to study (say) local
Islam, where some notion of supra-local orthodoxy is always present; but
in the case of Javanist sects the relation of local forms to the wider
civilization is different.

I came to know about Sangkan Paran in much the same way as
ordinary villagers – through background discussion at lontar readings,
attendance at the Cungking shrine (which is popular with members of the
sect), and in numerous conversations over points of Javanese custom.
Like other villagers who go to Sangkan Paran members for advice or
illumination, I generally found that it was these veteran Javanists who
offered the clearest explanations, whether I was asking about the
meaning of slametans, spells, or what Banyuwangi Javanese had made of
Islam. If they were especially clear on these matters, this was because
they had formulated their own thinking on the sect's teachings very much
in terms of such immediate, practical concerns. They had started with
local materials – the red and white porridge, the village shrine, the

ancestors – and found more effective ways of thinking about them, stimulated by what they had learned from the master. Approached in this way, Sangkan Paran appears less as a self-contained ideology – as it might do if one began inquiries in Surabaya or Solo – than as a philosophical flowering of traditional Javanist concerns.

The synthesis of ideas presented in this chapter is therefore not one that could be obtained in quite the same terms by talking to the leaders of the sect, although I am assured that nothing presented below is actually 'wrong' from their point of view. (Some of the more striking formulations which I learned from ordinary members were endorsed by the national leaders, as I was later able to confirm.) I am not concerned with establishing a 'pure' doctrine as contained in texts or official pronouncements. Indeed, no such official view is to be had: unlike other, better-known sects, which have their own dogmas, Sangkan Paran's texts are enigmatic and poetic, open to different interpretations. It is still largely an oral tradition, and its official leaders disclaim the right to a definitive view. My interest is in what villagers themselves think, how Sangkan Paran fits into their lives as peasant farmers and Muslims, and how it relates to the other religious and cultural themes explored in this book.

Though little known outside mystical circles, Sangkan Paran is one of the oldest sects in Java.[1] In character it is closer to a mostly bygone era of mystical movements such as Hardopusoro (Stange 1980: 62, 70–2) than to a later generation of mass organizations like Subud and Sapta Darma. Whereas these latter sects have adopted the methods and style of modern Indonesian associations, with conferences, publications in Indonesian, and well-organized networks of officers, Sangkan Paran, with its cult-like devotion to a charismatic founder, remains more firmly rooted in Javanist tradition. The present-day leadership, like that of any association, is obliged by law to proclaim its aims and principles and to maintain a set of officers accountable to the authorities. But the sect remains loosely structured and lacking a firm ideological identity. This is part of its appeal for the rural membership which values the sect's egalitarian ethos and its tolerance of diversity; but the lack of organizational efficiency also helps to explain why Sangkan Paran has not achieved a mass following. (Estimates put the membership as high as 7,000; but no statistics are kept. Probably a figure of around 2,000 to 3,000 is nearer the mark.)

The origin of the sect and its founder, Radèn Mas Joyokusumo (as I shall call him), is obscured by the legend that has grown up around him.

He is said to have had connexions with the court at Solo, as his title indicates; and, indeed, his anointed successor, the titular head of Sangkan Paran, is a retired court official and grandson of the Susuhunan, Pakubuwana X (reigned 1892–1939). However, biographical details are hard to obtain, probably because for his followers they are a distraction from his symbolic significance. The only facts of a conventional kind are that Sangkan Paran was officially registered in 1912 and that its founder settled in Jati, a hamlet in the plantation district of west Banyuwangi, where he lived until his death in 1956.

The location is significant in several respects. Unlike better-known sects such as Pangestu or Subud, Sangkan Paran has its base in the countryside (Kartodirdjo 1991: 273). There are important branches in Ponorogo, Surabaya, and Malang, and of course the nominal head lives in Solo, but these urban centres do not overshadow Banyuwangi, the area in which Joyokusumo chose to spread his knowledge. The shrine at Jati remains an important place of pilgrimage and is the venue for the sect's annual slametan during the month of Sura. Within the regency, Bayu has the largest representation of any village, with 105 members, about a fifth of its adult population. And the head of the regency branch happens to live in this village. In fact the association with Sangkan Paran goes back many years. Bayu's first members were initiated by Joyokusumo himself in 1948 and continued to visit him regularly until his death. Followers from Bayu served as his pall bearers. Much of the older rural membership thus had direct access to the source and did not stand outside or below an inner core of elite initiates (cf. Anderson 1977).

I stress the local connexion for several reasons. First, to allay suspicions that mysticism as practised in Bayu must be a rustic, garbled version of the courtly variety: the mystics who became my teachers are well-placed, respected figures within the sect. Second, because it adds weight to the methodological advantage of a grass-roots analysis already mentioned. And third, because villagers themselves make much of the local connexion. Bayu's mystics have found a prototype for Joyokusumo in the person of Buyut Cungking (see chapter 4) and see this paradoxical figure as a former incarnation of their own revered teacher. A modern mystical movement is thus grafted onto a much older tradition with its roots in pre-Islamic Java.

Joyokusumo: man as symbol

The founding father, Joyokusumo – followers refer to him as *éyang* (grandfather) or *rama* (father) – was an enigma even for those who knew

him, both an historical figure and a walking symbol. He 'came without
origin, and departed without destination' – an emblem of life itself. Some
say he lacked a navel, like Adam, and could not have been born in the
normal way. And like Buyut Cungking he dematerialized (*musno ilang*)
at death – within hours of burial his grave was empty. People who knew
him say he changed with the phases of the moon: like Ratu Kidul, the
goddess of the Southern Ocean, he appeared weak and wrinkled as the
moon waned, young and strong as it waxed. (The Sangkan Paran
handbook has two photographs, without commentary, of the young and
the old man.) But the characteristic most often mentioned is his left
hand. Whereas his right hand was firm and strong, 'his left hand placed
on your shoulder felt soft like a pillow'. The fingers were flat and even
(*papak*), all of the same length. (This feature is just visible in a studio
photograph of the young, waxing, Joyokusumo.) The word *papak*
alludes to the name of one of his prior incarnations, Radèn Mas Papak
(later known as Pangéran Natapraja; *c.* 1806–52).[2] But in the jargon of
the sect it also signifies femaleness, the flatness of the female genitals. All
humans have a feminine aspect in the left half of the body, and a male
aspect in the right. In Joyokusumo this androgyny seems to have been
made visible, symbolized in the hands. Like the sexually ambiguous
Buyut Cungking he never married; 'he could not marry', as some say.

Neither young nor old, male nor female, without origin or destination:
these parallels alone were enough to suggest a hidden link between the
wandering hermit and the waif, so that people began to say that Buyut
Cungking was the master's boyhood self. At various times he expressed a
knowledge of Buyut's haunts which seemed to confirm the idea, and
when his disciples from Bayu mentioned Buyut, he would say mysteriously: 'I once knew ... ' Local legends of this kind – similar ones can
probably be heard in other rural strongholds of the sect – are given some
credence by the metropolitan leaders: Joyokusumo was known to have
assumed many disguises in his wanderings and to have meditated in the
forests of Baluran and Blambangan. Besides, the leaders too have their
stories. One of them told me how, as the ascetic Wali Koré, Joyokusumo
meditated in a Surabaya rubbish dump. He generated such heat that it
caught fire, but he walked from it unharmed. Another time, outside the
mosque at Ampèl Gadhing, he chanted the mantra *Sir Rasa* causing a
wind which shook the minaret and sent the santri scurrying outside.

Other stories told to me by people who knew him embellish the
enigma. When an orphan was brought to him (later to become his
servant) he suckled it with a finger of his left (female) hand. Occasionally

he performed feats of curing. His assistant used to meditate for days on end immersed in a stream, and once, when his arm was eaten away by crayfish, Joyokusumo restored the flesh with sticky rice. ('Even so', said my hard-headed neighbour, 'the arm remained crooked.') When he died, it was men from Bayu who washed the corpse and rubbed their faces with the water ('not a drop touched the ground; we drank it all'). They tell how the body shrank to the size of a child, and how a rod plunged into the soil after his burial came up clean, indicating that the body had vanished. A few months after the funeral he 'visited' members in Bayu.

I was hoeing in the fields one day and looked up to see a thin old man with a headtie set jauntily on one side. I thought he was a beggar or maybe a madman. What could he be doing there in the middle of the rice-fields? He approached, peering at me, and said: 'What person are you?' I was puzzled by the question and said I was a farmer. He repeated it but I just carried on hoeing. When I looked up I saw him moving very fast over the fields and in no time he had become a speck in the distance. It was then that I remembered the same phrase from my initiation. I ran after him, but he was gone.

Apart from these off-the-record legends of his exploits and former selves there is an official lineage which situates Joyokusumo in a mystical tradition. This *kaluhuran* or *miliran wirid*, as it is called, lists his eleven precursors, beginning with Muhammad, passing through the heretic Sèh Siti Jenar and the Mataram kings, Senapati (reigned *c*. 1584–1601) and Sultan Agung (reigned 1613–46), down to his own predecessor, a kiyai in Gunung Kawi, near Malang. Some of the names are obscure and none (except for Siti Jenar) is renowned as a mystical teacher. There is no mention of the archetypal Muslim-syncretist sage, Sunan Kalijaga, though spells attributed to him are cited in Sangkan Paran texts, nor of Ranggawarsita (1802–73), the court poet whose work Joyokusumo certainly knew and whose ideas his own most resemble. (A digest of Ranggawarsita's *Serat Wirid* made by a Sangkan Paran elder circulates among advanced members of the sect.) A close affinity with the classical Javanist treatise, *Serat Centhini* (1815), is also recognized by the sect, but there is no mention of this work or of any other in the various manuals and litanies handed down by the master.

So what does the mystical pedigree mean? At one level it represents a putative line of transmission comparable to a Sufi *silsilah*. Each figure is supposed to have passed on the teachings complete to his pupil. Joyokusumo was the twelfth and the last such figure to be graced with *wahyu*, divine inspiration. Those he personally initiated were 'grade (*grad*) thirteen'; and they, in turn, initiated the most junior, fourteenth, grade. The first twelve names are sometimes mapped onto a circle, like a clock face, with arrows across the diameter indicating links between them. These links represent lines of reincarnation. For example, numbers two, seven, and eleven are successive incarnations.

At a deeper level the list is not regarded as an historical sequence of real persons at all. The first name, Muhammad Rasulullah, does not refer to the historical prophet but to a mystical ontology. *Muhammad* stands for the human body and thus physical existence, *wujud; rasul* (Ar. 'messenger') stands for rasa, the divine indwelling life; and *ullah* (Allah) stands for the functioning of that life, the capacity or *kwasa* to carry out the wishes of rasa. Other names refer in one way or another to sex and reproduction. For example, the heretical mystic Siti Jenar is said to have derived from a worm, and is therefore interpreted as a phallic symbol. *Gimbal*, in Radèn Bagus Gimbal, means 'clinging together', thus copulation. The number twelve, Joyokusumo himself, is of course symbolic, representing the twelve constituents of humanity deriving from Adam, Eve, and Vishnu, or Mother, Father, and Life.

What looks like a mystical pedigree is thus a kind of mnemonic representing the human organism in its capacity for self-knowledge and reproduction. When the novice recites the pedigree during initiation, he or she is engaged in a reflexive act, not a lineage ritual. The depiction of preceptors as human symbols is consistent with the idea that Javanist mentors can only be mediators of knowledge embodied in the pupil himself or herself; they are not originators of that wisdom. Joyokusumo personally disclaimed the status of *guru*, and unlike some other mystical associations (including Muslim brotherhoods) Sangkan Paran has no organized system of pupils, each loyal to his own guru. Members are not ranked according to their precedence in initiation or their mastery of mystical skills or knowledge: they are all equally *kadang*, 'brothers and sisters'. There is no formal instruction, apart from the initiation, and no training sessions or group activities, apart from the occasional chanting of the litany. The only true teacher, the only master, as I was tirelessly reminded, is in oneself.

The point is worth dwelling on for a moment because it distinguishes Sangkan Paran from well-known sects such as Subud, Sapta Darma, and Pangestu. Sapta Darma, which has a branch in Banyuwangi, teaches a technique of meditation and a doctrine revealed once and for all on a specific occasion. Its members' handbook declares: 'Sapta Darma is a revealed teaching received directly from The Almighty by Harjosapuro in Pare, Kediri on 27 December 1952 at 1 a.m.' The meditation postures practised by adepts imitate the founder's initial revelation, in the same way that the salāt in Islam imitates Muhammad's prototypical act of worship (Sapta Darma prostrations, like those in salāt, are called *sujud*). As in Islam, the authenticity of the initial revelation, or *wahyu*, is of paramount importance to Sapta Darma and establishes the techniques and ideology espoused by the sect (Stange 1986). Other sects show a similar pattern of a founding revelation experienced by an otherwise ordinary man followed by organizational expansion and 'routinization of charisma'.[3] Whatever the stated aims of these sects, the desire to be taken seriously by the dominant faith seems clear and, as Stange (1986: 79) points out, this has tended to mean adopting the categories of Islam. A religion worth the name needs a revelation, a prophet, a holy book, and a method of worship, preferably congregational. A Javanist sect, if it is to be respectable, should boast the same features.

Sangkan Paran lacks all of these criteria and explicitly disavows a religious tag. Its founder may have received *wahyu*, but his followers, like Bima in the famous *Dewa Ruci* story (Soebardi 1975), are told to look within for illumination. For many, the lack of a church-like structure is part of its attraction: unlike the alienated white-collar recruits to Pangestu whom Sartono Kartodirdjo describes, the rural mystics are not in search of a substitute community or a bridge to modernity. Neither, for that matter, are they atavists pursuing a millennial dream. On the contrary, far from seeking a separate corporate identity, their problem is how to maintain their spiritual and moral integrity in the face of the community's demands, for example with regard to Islam.

If the sect is not a religion, as the state defines it, or a protest movement in religious garb, neither should it be mistaken for a cult around the personality of its founder. Despite the devotion of those who knew him, and the attribution of special powers, Joyokusumo was revered mainly for what he taught, not for what he was. His legacy of writings (penned by others) makes no mention of him except as a continuator of a mystical line. Unlike, say, Buyut Cungking, he is not the object of ritual devotion and no one applies to him for magical power, though some seek his guidance in meditation. His paradoxical, symbolic nature – the source of his personal fascination – is of a piece with his teaching.

Sangkan Paran doctrine
Javanist anthropocentrism finds eloquent, if often cryptic, expression in Sangkan Paran. The sect claims not to teach religion or occult science

(*èlmu*), but merely 'knowledge of humanity' (*kawruh kamanungsan*). This is partly a matter of religious politics since Javanism survives in modern Indonesia by keeping a low profile. Under the constitution only the world religions are recognized as *agama*, 'religion'. But the sect's self-styled 'humanism' actually predates the republic: the old handbooks have exactly the same rubric. And most members seem content with the disclaimer. They see enough to object to in official religions not to want their beliefs put in the same category. Religion is for the external, worldly life of citizens going about their business and subject to rules and punishments – the *secular* life, one might say. Alternatively, religion is characterized in contrary terms as devoted to a dubious afterlife. 'Humanism', on the other hand, caters for the inner spiritual dimension, the life within.

The teachings of the sect are contained in a series of progressively more secret writings and in a complementary oral tradition, part of which is also secret.[4] The little handbook issued to members contains a litany (*pujian*), a set of moral prescriptions enjoining self-correction and harmonious relations with others, and a digest of Joyokusumo's ideas concerning the human constitution. This booklet is periodically inspected by the authorities – usually after complaints by santris – and is the official face of the sect. The mystical formulas, praises of God, etc., are variations on standard Javanisms which mean as much or as little as the reader can make of them. Most members have memorized a good deal of the booklet without necessarily being able to give a clear account of its meaning.

A fuller account of the ideas is found in a hand-written text compiled by one of Joyokusumo's closest disciples. But this, too, is obscurely phrased and depends for its understanding on further elucidation. More complicated still are the *Serat Pakem* and the *Adammakna*, two esoteric manuals compiled by disciples for the advanced student. These contain mantras and prayers, schemes of correspondences between parts of the body, letters, numbers, and so on, as well as diagrams of human ontogeny and schemas based on the Sufi-derived doctrine of emanations.[5] Few people I met had actually seen these books, let alone studied them, though many ordinary villagers know something of their contents from oral tradition. Though privately printed versions exist, the examples I have seen are manuscripts, meticulously copied by hand and kept under lock and key.

As the use of this older technology implies, the esoteric doctrine is reluctantly committed to paper and then only in part. The treasured manuscripts are themselves a record of what Joyokusumo said rather than his own composition and they serve as a basis for contemplation and discussion or manipulation in formulas rather than as holy writ. As such they cannot yield their full significance to conventional literary scholarship. In the village, at least, they are adjuncts to what is primarily an oral tradition. But the relation of writing to speech is a complicated matter in Sangkan Paran and a consideration here takes us to the enigmatic heart of its message.

The key formulas which contain the essence of the teaching are communicated verbally, in pitch darkness, during initiation. The novice, wrapped in a funeral shroud, repeats a catechism modelled on the *talkim* (an address to the dead soul which the modin speaks into the grave). Then, guided by his initiator, he 'reads the body' as he traces the passage of rasa through various spiritual nodes in a rehearsal of his death. Each of these nodes corresponds to an Arabic letter and a 'station' on the mystical path. This autograph of the living body is said to be a 'wet book' (*kitab teles*): scratch it and blood flows. It is superior to the 'dry book' (*kitab kering*) of the Koran or any other man-made, derivative, text and requires a different kind of 'recitation'.

How are the letters conceived? As we saw earlier in the discussion of correspondences (chapters 2 and 6), there is ambiguity over the question of whether a colour or direction has its 'seat' in a given organ by sound-association, common substance, or analogy. In the case of body-writing, however, the correspondence is clearly formulated. Letters are said to be the *sandhangan* of the self. *Sandhangan* means (i) clothing, (ii) diacritics used in Javanese script. The self is, as it were, clothed in writing, its material, fleshly form imprinted with sacred characters. But the writing is, as ever, ambiguous. In Javanese-Arabic script (*pégon*) the same letter can be vocalized with /a/, /i/ or /u/, depending on which vowel diacritic (*shakal*) is used. What this suggests is that the self can be one but have various aspects: it can be God, Me, or Life (*Allah-Ingsun-Urip*, of which a-i-u is the mmemonic).[6]

Paradoxically, this intricate and ingenious theory is not to be found in the writings: it belongs to oral tradition. It was explained to me by ordinary village members, not the 'experts' or scribes of the sect. A related idea, which does appear in the manuscripts and has its source in Sufi tradition (Schimmel 1975: 225), is that the body as a whole is 'the letters [making up the name] Muhammad' (*huruf Muhammad*). This is perhaps reversing the original logic: in Arabic script *Muhammad* can be perceived as a body lying down, the initial letter *m* corresponding to the head, the final *d* corresponding to the sole of the foot, the whole word describing 'the figure of man, prostrate before God' (Schimmel 1975: 153). Sangkan Paran makes the further inference: if the word *Muhammad* is a body, the body is Muhammad.

The name and person of Muhammad are thus made to stand for physical existence (*wujud*) epitomized by the human body. The body is the delegate of rasa in a relation analogous to that of God and Muhammad.[7] Rasa is paramount in that it is the source of all activity; but without the body it cannot subsist. Hence, as the mystics often assert, without man there can be no God: the indwelling God (rasa, a manifestation of Life) can have no being without man. The same relation is also couched in traditional Javanist terms of the 'union of servant and Lord' (*manunggaling kawula Gusti*), where 'Lord' stands for rasa or Life, not some transcendent deity.

So much for the ontology of the person, summed up in the relation of *wujud* to rasa. The interrelation of the person and the world is expressed in a third term, *kwasa* (or *kuwasa*, 'power'). In common parlance God is referred to as *ingkang kwasa*, 'the Almighty', but here *kwasa* has a special sense, referring to the capacity or functioning of the organism. A corpse has eyes and ears, but they do not function. One is able to see or hear because of the presence of divine Life; and the activity of seeing is the *kwasa* (operation, actualizing) of the indwelling God. In the mystical pedigree this ontological sequence, *wujud-rasa-kwasa*, is symbolized by the first name in the list, Muhammad Rasulullah, Muhammad the apostle of God. *Muhammad* = *wujud, rasul* = *rasa, ullah [Allah]* = *kwasa*. It is interesting that the third term, *kwasa*, which seems to depend on the other two, is equated with Allah, as it were demoting God to a secondary role. But in the sect's jargon *Allah* 'means' *polah*, activity; it does not denote the God of the Koran. Thus, someone asleep has no *kwasa* (= *Allah/polah*, movements) though he still has Life and therefore has God in the pantheist sense. 'Once he awakes and his rasa stirs he has *kwasa*' (*semasa rasa mlaku, nduwé kwasa*).

It sounds excessively abstract, but my difficulties arise from trying to generalize from the simple examples I was always given.

AB. Give me an example of how *wujud*, rasa, and *kwasa* relate to each other.
T. Water, coffee, and sugar mix and become one. Can you then separate them?
AB. I can see the *wujud*, taste the flavour (with *rasa*). But where is the *kwasa*?
T. You see the coffee, want to taste it, and make your move [taking a sip]. You see a woman's beauty, feel desire [in rasa], and satisfy it – master it (*nguwasani*, from *kwasa*). The action is the action of God, *kwasane Allah*; but existence and rasa are prior to it.

This circuit of perception, feeling, and action takes us back to the ethical conception of man's constitution mentioned in the last chapter. Our senses are the gateways of the passions. Sight and hearing respond to the attractiveness of things and stimulate desire. They are our guardian spirits, protecting us from danger, but they can also cause our downfall. Hence, the proper attitude in daily conduct is one of cautious self-awareness (*éling, waspada*). The senses are accorded special significance as mediating between microcosm and macrocosm, inner and outer worlds. But more than this, they are a source of wonder and evidence of the godhead. Pak Sunar elaborated:

Our senses can master the world. The eye, small as it is, can take in mountains, trees, the sea. The nose can smell everything the world has, fragrant and foul. The faculty of speech (*pangucap*) can master any language – did you need another mouth to learn Javanese? What would you do without it? Imagine going to the market and seeing all the things you'd like but not being able to say anything. You wouldn't be complete. Or smelling the foods and not being able to eat. But neither you nor your parents made these [faculties]. All you have to do is use them.

Since the faculties are God-given (in the special sense already described), we have a responsiblity to use them properly. 'We must not see red and say yellow.' There is a kind of contract or agreement (*perjanjian*) between the ordinary, selfish being and the impartial, inner rasa – the voice of conscience which is also the point of contact with the divine Life. God's side of the contract is explained in terms of his attributes (the terms are borrowed from Islam but are given an unexpected meaning). God's magnanimity (*sifat murah*) is evident in the fact that man is supplied with a full set of faculties; his mercy (*sifat rahim*) is that these faculties can encompass the world, all sensations can enter (*kahanan jaban masuk; isiné alam kabèh wis diwenangakèn nang rika*). God's justice (*sifat adil*) consists in the accuracy and consistency of our perceptions. The properties of things, such as colour, are the same for all of us and consistent for an individual (both eyes see green, and both see green now and later). In other words, one might say, the universe is rule governed.

Again, I should point out that this theory is not taken from the sect's writings or from the speculations of its leaders: I had it from villagers who, presumably, have formulated their views on the basis of what Joyokusumo told them forty years ago. I have not been able to trace the source of the ideas but there is, once again, in the conception of God's justice, a curious echo of Berkeley – though the bishop's God is a transcendent being.[8]

Morality in the ordinary sense is thus not part of God's justice. It belongs to the world of men, of man-made rules and regulations (*adilé manusa*). The fixed quality of things, which is God's justice, contrasts with the subjectivity of aesthetic and moral judgements, good and bad. This is a more precise formulation of the Javanist distinction, noted in chapter 6, between ordinary everyday morality (including that of religion), which is relative, and the absolute moral order of the human constitution. Self-correction or 'purification' in these terms seems to mean something like a deliberate effort to cultivate awareness of the inner life which works through the senses, to 'become aware of *what sees*', and to honour this spring of action, whether it is in seeing, hearing or, paradigmatically, in sex. To comport oneself thus is to have no 'debts' to the body, to honour God's contract, and thus to die perfected.

TOMPO. Think of it like this. If you lend me your shirt and I give it back to you dirty, you'll be angry. The dying man is accepted by God only if he is pure. Why? Because our origin is holy and so must our return be holy. That's why you wear a white funeral shroud when you are initiated and when you die.

A second means of purification is in meditation, when the senses are shut down and consciousness retreats into the depths of rasa. Then, 'if I hear a voice it is not mine but the voice of God; if I see, it is not Tompo's sight, it is God's sight.'[9] Again, I must emphasize that this way of phrasing it should not be mistaken for theism. The mystics are quite emphatic that 'there is nothing outside'. As the litany has it:

Ask yourself who made your life
Ask yourself who made your being
Ask yourself who made your actions/sight/hearing/rasa
I tell you, who made them is who bears them.

The personalistic idiom is due, rather, to the nature of introspection. The life within is experienced as an absolute, something mysterious and awesome, but hidden within rasa and ultimately inaccessible – except for the occasional flash during meditation. Rasa may be equated with Life, but more often it is simply stated that what has rasa has Life/God. It is towards God as manifest in rasa that the personalistic attitude is adopted, whether the experience is conceived in terms of conscience, intuition, or surrender to some profounder consciousness known only to adepts.

The sect in society

Authors on Javanese history have often pointed to the connexions between religious enthusiasm and political upheavals. The classic examples are the Java War of 1825–30 (Carey 1987) and the millennial protest movements that recurred throughout nineteenth-century Java (Kartodirdjo 1966, 1973); but recent history furnishes equally compelling examples. As Stange (1980: 143) observes, 'periods of crisis generate waves of renewed spiritual motivation ... Times of crisis, whether at the individual or collective level, definitely generate intensified quest for meaning.' In the revolutionary period (1945–9), political engagement frequently went hand in hand with spiritual awakening and religious commitment. Militant Islam is usually cited as the example, but, despite its otherworldly cachet, mysticism also played a part in resistance against the colonial oppressor. Sumarah, a Javanist sect described by Stange (1980: 123–55), presents a particularly clear case.[10] In the 1930s and 1940s its leaders explicitly identified their mystical quest with Indonesia's independence, even to the extent of heading their letters with the republican warcry, *Merdeka*, Freedom! (Stange 1980: 135). Among the burgeoning membership of Sumarah's youth cohort it was evidently conflict and danger which helped to awaken mystical yearnings. The revolution, in turn, was able to enlist the spiritual energies of the sect.

In older sects, like Sangkan Paran, which had co-existed for many years with colonial rule (sometimes going underground), no such direct involvement in political history can be traced, though many of its followers took part in the war against the Dutch and drew strength from their mystical experiences. One of the national leaders of Sangkan Paran, now a retired colonel, told me he experienced his first contact with Joyokusumo in 1947 while on duty with the republican army in East Java. He had been meditating at the grave of Brawijaya IV, the Majapahit king, and was confronted by a tall, dignified figure in formal dress who said to him, 'Wake up!' Instinctively he made an obeisance, then the apparition vanished. Two years later he went to Jati and recognized Joyokusumo as the man of his vision.

It was during this same revolutionary period that the first generation of Bayu's members was initiated. At a time of deprivation and extreme insecurity, when travellers were as much at risk from bandits as from Dutch soldiers, groups of half a dozen villagers used to make the arduous journey to Jati where they would sit at the feet of Joyokusumo. What he offered, at this watershed in Indonesian history, was not so much a message for the times, as a more effective way of thinking about the timeless wisdom embodied in ancestral tradition. If the quest for meaning took a mystical turn – for these pioneers at least – this was largely because Javanist mysticism addressed itself, in general terms, to age-old problems that had then become acute: not just the perennial questions like 'Who am I?' and 'Where am I going?' but more pressing ones like, 'How may I be slamet?' and 'What is the good?' It was an intellectual solution, a theodicy, that was required: something quite unlike the ritual solutions of village Islam. During the intensely politicized period that followed independence Sangkan Paran also offered a means of distinguishing among a surfeit of ideologies. As the traditional syncretism threatened to unravel into warring cultural factions, the sect showed its new followers what was of supreme importance and what was only secondary or relative.

The rival system, Islam, whether in its traditional or modernist forms, was at a low ebb in rural Banyuwangi – Bayu did not even have a mosque until 1953 – and there was no direct pressure to find new ways of legitimizing traditional Javanist practices. It was, moreover, many years before the bloody inauguration of the New Order made personal creed a matter of life and death. So the rise of mysticism cannot be put down to political expediency: as the mystics themselves tell it, they were drawn by the teachings rather than impelled by circumstances. Nevertheless, there was a process of cultural stocktaking in the early post-war period. Fierce ideological debate filtered down to village level and led to the splitting of many communities throughout Java (Jay 1963). The leading Javanists in Bayu started to see themselves as alien to the radical Islam then being promoted on the national scene and began to reconsider their cultural identity. (They had had a foretaste of Muslim extremism during the Japanese occupation when units of Hizbu'llah zealots were formed by the Japanese and given local powers to fight the returning Dutch (see Benda 1983: 178–9).)

Little of this turbulent history, however, enters into the accounts of the mystics themselves. In their own estimation they were not seeking a refuge or turning their backs on traditional village Islam – indeed, one of the first members from Bayu was a modin. The emphasis in reminiscences is always on the appeal of the teachings and of the master himself. Joyokusumo's quiet dignity and humour made a deep impression on those who met him. 'You felt compelled to bow, whoever you were, bupati, haji or peasant.' Many had dabbled in other sects and were impressed by the comprehensiveness of his vision. One veteran of the first generation of members compared Sangkan Paran to other sects as follows.

Imagine a man – someone who has never seen an elephant before – let's say someone who doesn't yet know what kawruh is about. He touches the elephant blindly and feels its ear. 'Ah! The elephant is like a banana leaf', he says. True enough, at least as far as the ear is concerned. Someone else feels the trunk. 'It's like a snake,' he says. The next person touches its leg. 'Wah! It could be a tree!' And the last grabs the tail. 'The elephant is tiny'. All of them are right. But to understand what the elephant is you must go from head to foot. Only Sangkan Paran knows the whole beast.[11]

As the memory of Joyokusumo fades, it is the legacy of his teachings which continues to inspire new members. Indeed, a leader in Surabaya spoke of his discovery of the Sangkan Paran handbook as a kind of conversion, and his own tale of ethical transformation and spiritual rags-to-riches has, in turn, inspired others. However, unlike the more practice-oriented Sapta Darma and Sumarah, with their mystical exercises and meditation sessions, Sangkan Paran remains primarily an ethical and philosophical system – 'applied metaphysics', as Geertz (1960: 310) characterizes Javanese mysticism in general.[12] In fact, only a minority of members in Bayu claims to meditate regularly, though most have meditated at one time or another (*semèdhi*, like fasting and isolation in haunted spots, is part of the Javanist's stock-in-trade). To borrow their own scale, then, they are one step above the santri, as *hakékat* (pursuit of the truth) is above *sare'at* (conformity to basic rules); but they are, for the most part, this side of *ma'ripat*, gnosis.

Nevertheless, Javanist science being an empirical one (empirical, because no one is required to 'believe' anything, only to 'feel it for himself'), understanding and spiritual experience are assumed to go hand in hand. Indeed, the function of kawruh, mystical teaching, is to enable one to orient and strengthen oneself prior to the mystical encounter, and then to make sense of what one 'brings back'. Lacking such guidance one is likely to 'seek heaven and create hell'. While we watched the santri streaming up to the mosque one Friday, summoned by the loudspeakers, my mystical companion observed with a sigh: 'When you do not understand things they appear very far away. But when you understand you begin to see they are close.'

The sect in village life

Although the master's teachings seemed comprehensive and compelling to many, the sect was sufficiently undogmatic and loose in structure to allow for the kind of ecumenical approach which characterized ritual life in Bayu. Intellectually and morally it was a definite advance over slametans and spells, but it did not mean giving them up or rejecting one's santri neighbours. Sangkan Paran members continued to take part in the usual activities, saying prayers at slametans and joining in – sometimes leading – Muslim chants at funerals.

For women, Sangkan Paran had an added attraction in that it offered a more stimulating, less subordinate, role than was available in traditional village Islam. There was no comparable segregation of the sexes and women were not excluded from any of the teachings or activities. The familiar counterparts of male piety and female ignorance are not mirrored in Sangkan Paran. Although men take the leading roles in discussion and organization, women are initiated as full members. There are several elderly women in Bayu who are said to be as knowledgeable as their husbands, and I was often coached in the basics by a husband and wife together. Most members in Bayu, in fact, joined as couples. The importance of the marital bond is such that a man may not become an initiator (*penerus wirid*) unless his wife is also a member. The enhanced role of women, compared to Islam, is closer to the pattern of everyday life in Java, and therefore more congenial; but it also reflects the Javanist emphasis on the complementarity of male and female and the central significance of sex, whether as a symbol of union with the divine, or as a focus of contemplation on human origins.

From the initial handful of recruits, membership in the village grew quickly through family and neighbourhood ties before settling at around one hundred – about one-fifth of the adult population. The majority of members in Bayu belong to that broad class of middling farmers who count themselves as having 'just enough to live on' (*cukupan*). (There are also two former headmen, two irrigation officials, and a few traders.) East Bayu, which is populated mainly by landless peasants and labourers, has very few members, just as it has few santri. Only the very poor lack the leisure to pursue their spiritual concerns in either direction.

What limits the number of recruits, however, is not class or even ideological predisposition, but rather the sphere of association of members, which is much smaller than the total number of non-santri in the village. Unlike Islam, Sangkan Paran does not proselytize or broadcast its views. It is a cardinal principle that motivation must come from the individual. Consequently, only a member's family and close associates have the opportunity to learn about it, and then only in general terms unless they take the step of joining. The residential pattern of membership is therefore one of isolated clusters, with a preponderance in west Bayu. I met many Javanists from other parts of the village who had never been approached by a member and did not feel bold enough or sufficiently motivated to take the initiative. Most non-members, even those whose thinking runs along similar lines and who look up to the mystics, know little or nothing of the sect's teachings.

The case of the lontar: reading between the lines

Nevertheless, there are limited opportunities for the circulation of ideas. Apart from informal socializing, which is such an important and pleasurable part of life in Bayu, there are two forums in which non-members can learn something of Sangkan Paran (again in general terms). These are slametans and lontar readings.[13] Discussion over some element of ritual often prolongs a slametan, especially when it figures in an elaborate event like a housewarming or seven-month pregnancy celebration. Then Javanists hold the stage. But slametans tend to involve the same clusters of neighbours and kin who have 'heard it all before'. Lontar sessions, in contrast, recruit from all over the village, bringing together novel combinations of Javanists and traditionalist Muslims. During the night-long performances, readers often discuss points of interpretation in the story, the tale of Joseph and his brothers. Since nobody fully understands the archaic language, commentary is free to range well beyond the literal meanings of the text as Javanist readers make connexions with other kinds of knowledge. For example, a phrase forbidding the breaking of an agreement, often cited as a key precept, is related to the 'contract with God' mentioned above, that is, the proper self-regulation of the sentient person. The Islamic aspect of the story – and this is, ostensibly, a devotional Islamic work (Arps 1992: 179, 378) – is often downplayed or absorbed within a larger, Javanist framework. Thus the hero, Nabi Yusup (the prophet Joseph), is taken to be a symbolic person representing humanity. In explanation of this idea, Arps (1992: 393–4) refers to the cyclical pattern of the recitation: it concludes by returning to the opening pages, as man returns to his origin. This much is broadly acceptable, even to santri: in similar fashion a complete reading of the Koran ends as it begins with a recitation of the Fatihah. But Javanist lontar readers also make use of wordplay to discover allegorical meanings outside of the mainstream. *Nabi* 'means' *bibit*, seed; *Yusup* 'means' spiritual lustre (*cahya*), the light or life-spark which quickens or possesses (*Yusup* > *nusup*) the living body. And the lontar itself is but a 'mediator' (*lontar* > *lantaran*), directing the reader's attention inwards to the ultimate source of knowledge.

These hints of a Javanist subtext are, however, no more than that: the story cannot bear a thoroughgoing point-for-point allegorical interpretation. And the Javanisms which can be gleaned – albeit somewhat arbitrarily and out of context – are commonplaces. As the manuscript makes its slow progress around the circle of readers, the really interesting discussion can usually be found somewhere among the cigarette smoke at the opposite end to the recitation.

Javanist glosses on the text and other, tangential, speculations are accepted mostly without quibble by readers of a more orthodox bent. Like slametans, lontar readings combine conviviality with a serious ritual purpose – the quest for slamet – and in both cases there is, necessarily, a tacit agreement not to contest meanings in a partisan manner. It is Javanists, nevertheless, who tend to predominate since they are the most knowledgeable, though not always the best, readers. Others are therefore obliged to listen good-humouredly while they indulge in the collective ruminations they call *gosok-gosokan*, an amused, often sardonic 'rubbing together' of ideas. During one such session I was seated next to an ex-modin and was able to observe his reactions.

Sucipto, the old village chief, began wondering whether Adam and Eve were married, and if so in what sense. Since there was no *penghulu* in paradise to marry them there could be no formal marriage (*nikah*); but evidently they were married/ mated (*kawin*) in a broader sense, were they not? Jakis thought not: the purpose of marriage was to regulate inheritance: since there was no one to inherit, and no property, there was no need of marriage. Another reader, Sukib, suggested that pairing was God-given, and pregnancy a sign that a pairing was *sah*, approved, since pregnancy without God was impossible. (Marriage, by contrast, was a human invention.) Hence the Balinese marry *after* pregnancy has occurred – he knew this because he had worked as a carpenter in Bali. Sucipto replied that this proved that *kawin* and *nikah* were very different things. Javanese had to perform *nikah*; that was their custom. But the Balinese method was preferable; in fact, it was 'better than all right' and he would tell his wife about it. Someone ended the debate by observing that Adam and Eve were not the father and mother of all, but merely mediators of Life, so discussion of their marital status was beside the point.

Throughout this rambling discussion, my santri neighbour, who had served for many years as a marriage modin, kept silent, staring straight ahead and apparently concentrating on the recitation going on at the far end of the room. Perhaps he could have offered an opinion, but I suspect not. Beyond insisting on a literal interpretation of scripture (or the lontar) there is not much that santri can say in reply, unless it is to grumble at Javanist meaning-mongering. But politeness would forbid direct criticism.

Traditionalist Muslims less compromised than the marriage modin will often nod or make some vaguely sympathetic comment during such divagations. But when I asked in private what they made of Javanist interpretations of the lontar they tended to express ignorance of them, which seems to confirm the Javanist view that relatively esoteric matters can safely be discussed in public because they pass over the heads of the uninitiated. Indeed, Sangkan Paran adepts will often continue debating when a neighbour walks in (to stop talking would be impolite), confident that in an hour or so he will doze off over his coffee and forget what he has heard.

These examples suggest that, despite the weak position which Javanists hold under the law, and despite the successful efforts at Islamization in recent years at all levels of society, rural Javanists remain sure of themselves, confident of their superior knowledge and its ultimate triumph. Indeed, many are surprisingly unworried by the pious trend among the young. As one mystic said to me: 'They will realize their error when they are older, and in any case numbers don't matter. The Pandawas [of the Indian epic] were few, the Korawas were many.'

But in practical terms, this optimism looks misguided. In the new climate of national piety, contrasting patterns of socialization which give santri a head start are being turned to lasting advantage. They begin with infants, whereas Javanists await maturity; they encourage imitation and involvement in order to accustom a child to Islamic ways, whereas Javanists prioritize understanding; and they actively recruit, while Javanists hope that people will come of their own accord. With the rise of a more aggressive, state-sponsored Islam and a greater institutional strength at village level, youthful differences in orientation are hardening instead of being evened out in the affairs of village life. Javanism, unable or unwilling to meet the challenge, looks set to lose out. A generation of Javanist elders – men and women with land and position, and therefore influence over their children – has failed to press home a tactical advantage. Instead they have responded to santri gains with ironic detachment or quiet dismay, or with a principled neutrality. Their children, now in their thirties and forties (New Order children), may find santri piety objectionable but, unlike the elders, they have no answer to it – they have nothing with which to resist its advance.

Many Sangkan Paran members do not, of course, see their predicament in these terms. Indeed, the all-embracing language of the sect, its symbolism and prophetic tone, make it difficult even to discuss such problems in a practical way. (This may be less true of modern sects like Sapta Darma.) As one senior figure put it to me:

Sangkan Paran is knowledge of humanity and as such cannot be separated from humanity; it cannot die. That knowledge can always be drawn upon, even after we have gone, because men remain the same. Besides which, 'people who know' leave behind a seed that must sprout in a future generation. Now we are beaten in numbers (*kalah rame*), but not defeated. And what does it mean to win? If you want a crowd, go where the clamour is, but you won't find understanding there.

Only among Hindu Javanists did I encounter a sharper sense of what is being lost and of the necessity to pass on Javanist ways to a younger generation; but, as we shall see in the next chapter, these same Hindus are well versed in the cut and thrust of religious politics; their very survival has depended on their political skills.

Conclusion

Javanism, as exemplified in Sangkan Paran, exhibits a curious mix of rational scepticism and enchantment. A similar contrast, amounting almost to a contradiction, was encountered in the previous chapter concerning the conception of God. On the one hand, God is reduced to an idea within a philosophical scheme; on the other, people talk of dependence on and acceptance by God: an idea, then, versus a person. In the case of the sect there is a striking contrast between the rigorous debate over doctrine – the determination to put everything into question – and the magical allure of the founder's legend. Again, the contradictions can be – and are – resolved by an appeal to symbolism: every act, every characteristic of Joyokusumo was symbolic and can be referred back to the teachings. It is the teachings, ultimately, which command respect; but the symbolic personage of the founder embodies them and gives them a peculiar force.

The blend of rationalism and enchantment reflected in some of the quotations in these chapters emerges strongly in the following account of a journey, which may serve as a coda to this discussion.

Epilogue: the forest of symbols

Shortly before my departure in May 1993 I made a trip to Alas Purwo, the forest on the Blambangan peninsula at the easternmost tip of Java. With its legions of sprites and ghouls, its steamy grottoes and maze-like false trails, its tigers (heard rather than seen) and its overgrown Hindu ruins, Alas Purwo is a forest straight out of Javanese mythology. I had been prepared beforehand about what to expect, the experience as it were scripted in advance for me by various accounts. My main informant was Pak Toro, a wiry octogenarian who had recently been there with his grandson. His entertaining narrative, itself a meandering tour of Javanist tropes, prompted a group of like-minded villagers to organize a trip.

For Pak Toro, as for most adherents of the sect, a visit to Alas Purwo was something of a pilgrimage. There was a story about Joyokusumo connected with the forest. The Dutch were said to be afraid of Javanese knowledge, and when the court of Kartasura fell into decline in the eighteenth century the exponents of kawruh fled or were exiled. Joyokusumo – at that time a prince – put aside his crown and escaped to Alas Purwo. There he peeled off his face revealing a tiger within. When the time was right to spread his knowledge he returned to human form. But shortly before his death in 1956 he told his followers – Pak Toro among them – 'When my time comes, look for me in Alas Purwo.'

Like the other members of the sect, Pak Toro regarded the sayings of the master, especially the *pujian* chant, as a cryptic guide to the forest. For example, to orient himself in relation to the Bat Cave he had spoken the phrase: *sir lor, daté ana kidul* (mystery/desire is north, essence to the south); and to find the Palace Cave he had used: *sipat kulon, wujudé ono wétan* ([divine] attribute west, Being to the east).[14] What particularly impressed listeners (and there were many, as he went from house to house embroidering his account) was his meeting with an old crone who inhabited a hut in the middle of the forest. He had greeted her with a Sangkan Paran formula and she had embraced him and called him 'My child'. From his report it was unclear (not only to me) whether she was real or was some kind of apparition, perhaps a tutelary spirit of the forest or an emissary of Joyokusumo. She had told him her husband was shopping in the market. 'Market! What market?' Pak Toro had said, looking round at the jungle. After further puzzling exchanges he had made his way to the Bat Cave and was able to 'verify' the truths of kawruh. He realized at once that the cave was 'mother's womb'; the dripping roof signified father's sperm; the rough scrub at the entrance was pubic hair. The way inside was slippery, and the bats clinging to the walls signified coition ... But it wasn't all sex. The path to the cave was overgrown and you had to crawl under fallen bamboo trees and fight your way through: 'a metaphor of the historical struggle', said Pak Toro.

I heard other stories in the next few days. Two men from Cungking had gone to Purwo to meditate and had found themselves in a ghostly town, complete with bus station and army barracks. On their way back they had bathed in a stream and their pockets filled with fish. Not until they had consumed this manna were they able to leave the forest. Pak Slamet, a Hindu leader from Banyuwangi, told me he had been lost in

Purwo for three days. His companions, who had become separated from him, later said they had 'found a village'. It was hard to believe, said Pak Slamet, but how could you doubt honest men – such experiences were granted to few.

With expectations high, twenty-seven villagers – mainly Sangkan Paran members – aged between seventeen and eighty, crammed into a Colt pick-up early one morning for the long drive south. It was nearing midday when, crumpled and exhausted, we reached the observation post at the entrance to Alas Purwo. From there it was an easy walk through sparse woodland to Grajagan Bay, an arc of white sand ten miles across, fringed with forest on one side and pounded by enormous waves on the other. Under a looming grey sky the pilgrims made their way in little clusters around the bay, stopping now and then to examine some object thrown up by the surf or to rest for a moment and comment on the vastness and loneliness of the ocean. It was recognizably a village outing: the women laden with picnic baskets, the men with knapsacks and the trilby hats they wear to the fields each day; everyone barefooted. At some landmark invisible to me, we struck off into the forest and followed an obscure path until we came to a clearing. There, just as Pak Toro had described it, but unexpectedly real, was a long hut with smoke rising from its thatched roof. One by one the pilgrims filed into its gloomy interior to greet the old woman – no apparition – many of them kneeling before her in formal obeisance. It was something of a miracle that anyone should live so far from society in a forest haunted by spirits, and all agreed that she must be a remarkable person. So no one was surprised at her hints of noble connexions or at her vague mystical-sounding allusions. But a brief interview was enough to dispel the mystery. When she led us outside to look at the tree 'guarded by Sèh Siti Jenar', Pak Suhem shook his head sceptically (though he later slept under it). And when her husband arrived bearing firewood ('Back from the market', as some jested quietly), and proved no more enlightening, there was a general feeling that Pak Toro had been overawed by a couple of eccentrics.

A little disappointed, we ate our picnics outside, our voices small against the boom of the surf, and then bathed in a freshwater lagoon beside the sea, men among women 'like brothers and sisters'.

After an uncomfortable night on the floor of the hut (some slept under the stars), we set off at dawn for the caves through a dripping bamboo forest. It was hard going, every muddy overgrown trail leading nowhere. Unable to see more than a few yards in any direction, we were soon lost.

As at every break, picnic baskets were opened and clove cigarettes lit. Pak Arjo took out a photo of Joyokusumo and murmured a prayer. Pak Ali claimed to recognize a tree we had passed three times, and asked who had brought boiled eggs: eggs are round, so your path will be a circle; only halved eggs are permitted in the forest. Barely had he finished explaining when two ragged men emerged from the undergrowth, 'as if guided by Joyokusumo'. They would not identify themselves – some even doubted their reality – but they shook hands silently with each pilgrim and pointed us in the direction of the Padépokan Cave.

It was a deep crevice formed by a giant breach in a cliff above the forest. The ascent to its entrance was likened to the passage of rasa from the left foot along sacred points of the body as life departs the dying person. We were putting the teaching into practice, said Pak Arjo. On the way out, we retraced our steps along the same route instead of crossing diagonally to the Bat Cave, the movement symbolizing sexual intercourse ('you have to go in and out the same way', said Ma Arjo).[15] The path was entangled by fallen bamboo and difficult to find, 'half-erased'. This 'proved' another association. An alternative name for the cave is Emper-èmper, one of the twelve demonic figures of the Cungking cult. On the ritual beaker of Buyut Cungking, Emper-èmper has a half-erased hand.

We came to the Bat Cave. Within its pungent depths people spoke in hushed voices. Some lit incense and murmured prayers; others left small offerings of flowers and coins for the guardian spirit. There were traces of previous visitors: incense sticks, petals, ashes. Pak Suhem, with the air of a cathedral guide, led us in small, crouching groups to a rock formation which projected from the floor 'like hands in supplication'. Then, one by one, amid the squeakings and flutterings of unseen bats, we crawled in darkness to the end of the cave and drank from a pool, splashing faces and hair. It was the climax of our journey, the end of a well-trodden mystical path:

> within this cave of mine
> There is indeed a hidden spring –
> The name by which it's known is 'rasa water',
> In former times the property
> Of God, the Stainless One.
> The man who with this rasa-water bathes himself,
> Incomparable pleasure feels,
> Beyond all others in the world.   *Suluk Gatholoco* (Anderson 1982: 78)

So says Perjiwati to Gatholoco, the man-penis who enters her cave at the end of his mystical quest.

On the way out of the forest we passed through a zone of savannah populated by wild oxen – high horns, white rumps, tails flicking – guardians of the boundary. Two of the villagers uttered a mantra then walked through the herd as though they were domestic cows.

As we drove back, mudstained and footsore, people spoke of what they had experienced and what they now felt, as after a night of meditation. There were small things to 'take away', but nothing extra-ordinary. Three of the party who had become detached from the group had spent the night in the forest and heard the roars of tigers, but luckily they had survived and we had found them back at the pick-up; one man had come upon a quartz rock and was said to be 'granted' his treasure; we had been lost and were fortunate to be found. But that was all. Pak Suhem, who had slept under Siti Jenar's tree after meditating half the night, had had a dream. He dreamed that his feet were placed one on top of the other as he slept. A piece of wood leaned against his soles and a boy climbed up the wood and picked a fruit from the top. When the boy descended the fruit vanished. It was a presentiment that next day we would have no mystical trophies, nothing to 'bring away'. But this was no reason to be disappointed, said Pak Suhem. More important than any personal revelation, the whole party had 'proved' what Joyokusumo had said; fitted experience to words. As one man put it, the forest was there to be read. The king of the forest himself, the tiger (*macan*), was an emblem of reading (*macaan*). *Alas* meant basis; *Purwo* meant origin. So to penetrate the secret places of Alas Purwo was to know one's origins. There was no need to look for supernatural realities, no need to 'go outside'. The forest may be haunted by spirits (*para alus*) but it was, above all, a place where one could leave the world behind and enter the subtle (alus) realm of the life within.

8

Javanese Hindus

A temple festival

In May 1992 I attended the festival of Saraswati – goddess of learning – at Sugihwaras temple in Glenmore, a plantation district in the west of the regency. There are said to be ninety-nine Hindu temples in Banyuwangi, some half-dozen of which are especially important as they are built on sites associated with the pre-Islamic kingdoms. At these sacred points, on Javanese soil, the faithful gather to celebrate the major festivals of the Hindu calendar.

The temple in the hamlet of Sugihwaras was built in 1968 at one such site. Ancient objects had been found there – a dagger, statues, shards. These were said to be relics of Majapahit, the great Hindu-Buddhist state of Java's golden age. The accuracy of the identification was not important – the objects could have derived from the court of Blambangan – but a tangible link with the past had been found and a temple was begun. This was not the first religious building in the hamlet: two beautiful old stucco mosques and a langgar, now little used, testified to a once thriving religious community. But now the settlement was sparsely populated, lost in the vast plantations of Glenmore and reachable only by a dirt road. An unobtrusive place, then, in which to stage a Hindu revival.

I was to hear the word Majapahit many times during the festival, and with a similar monotonous frequency at other events in the Javanese Hindu year. 'Majapahit' was brandished both as a claim to substance – important for a minority religion – and as a touchstone of authenticity. The Javaneseness of the new Hinduism is very important to its followers. They have given up a religion which they see as alien and want to be reassured that what appears new is really quite familiar – once the dust of centuries of Islam has been brushed away. Conversion is therefore not a question of an abstract preference for one religion over another: the new garment has to be 'fitting' (cocog), and if it is fitting this must be due to a fundamental rightness, an affinity deeper than mere preference. Stories of conversion ('awakening' would be a better term – at least as people themselves see it) emphasize the point. Pak Suroso, one of the leading lights of the Hindu movement in Banyuwangi, went so far as to see his sense of familiarity with the new creed as proof of reincarnation. It was more than a return to the ancestral ways: he felt an instinctive aptitude for the mantras and ritual gestures which only reincarnation could explain. In similar vein, a village temple priest confessed he was astonished how easily he could master the prayers in Sanskrit and Old Javanese: it was, he said, more like remembering than learning.

But what was he remembering? The religion of Majapahit – a highly elaborate blend of Sivaism, Buddhism, and Javanese elements serving a cult of divine kingship – is surely remote from the new Hinduism, with its textbooks and local committees.[1] Moreover, very few people know much about Majapahit beyond the name. The popular conception of pre-Islamic Java is mostly derived from wayang plays and historical dramas set in medieval kingdoms predating Majapahit. But historical obscurity does not mean historical irrelevance: to the contrary, a blank record allows a greater licence in rewriting one's cultural genealogy. Blambangan, the early Sivaite kingdom of the Eastern Salient whose capital was somewhere south of present-day Banyuwangi, is an even greater mystery, known only from its ruins and from the legend of Menak Jinggo, its half-mad king who challenged the might of Majapahit. Yet, in my conversations with the new Hindus, the name Blambangan, too, was often invoked as part of their heritage. This was history in the making.

The festival of Saraswati was my introduction to Hinduism in Banyuwangi and I had little idea about what to expect. Pak Suroso, the regional leader mentioned above, was my affable guide and host. A headmaster originating from Central Java, like many others in the leadership he had come to Hinduism via Javanese mysticism and an interest in the wayang. His was an urbane, cultured, and rational faith, tolerant of diversity and – despite many bureaucratic clashes – conciliatory towards Islam. His wife is Hindu, but his children belong to three faiths – Catholicism, Hinduism, and Islam – the daughters having followed their husbands' religion 'for the sake of the children'. But he is proud of this ecumenism: 'We are an Indonesian family', he says. As we made our erratic way on his moped towards Glenmore, interrupted by frequent repairs and pauses for refreshments ('I want you to try the fried eels at this stall'), he kept up a running commentary over his shoulder on the similarities between the world religions, the distinctions between Balinese and Javanese Hinduism, and (swerving to miss a truck) the necessity of interfaith harmony. As we bounced over potholes and dodged traffic, there were quotations from the Baghavad Gita in Sanskrit and Javanese, choruses from temple songs, examples from the wayang, and snippets of Javanese lore. Whatever the ordinary peasant had made of his new faith, Pak Suroso had it all thought out.

By the time we arrived at the temple some three or four hundred of the faithful had already gathered. They had come in truckloads from all over the regency. There were Balinese immigrants from the plantation at Kalibaru and from the Balinese quarter of Banyuwangi, Javanese from the Rogojampi area, and – the largest contingent – Javanese settlers from the south, the stronghold of Hinduism in Banyuwangi. A few Balinese had even made the journey across the straits from western Bali. The bland, tightly organized, and ritually simple – at times even secular – style of the festival was in keeping with this rootless, multi-ethnic congregation; and it was evident that, although many people knew each other from similar occasions, this was a community of faithful in only the vaguest sense.

The details of the ritual, the aspersions and prayers[2] (which I did not understand at the time but later came to recognize as standardized) need not concern us here: what was interesting was how the occasion was constructed – not invented, since this was far from being the first such celebration, but adapted to the setting, made into an Indonesian occasion.

At about 1 p.m. a score of temple priests (*pemangku*; no ordained Brahmana priests, *pedanda*, were present) from all over the regency led the congregation in a long procession from the temple to a water tank in the rice fields. 'In deviation from Indian Sivaism', Hindu ritual in Java, as in Bali, is centred around the making and distribution of holy water (Gonda 1975: 50). The discovery some years before of relics near the tank made this a suitable place from which to draw water for use in the temple ritual. And the little jaunt to the fields also made the Hindu event a Javanese one, bridging the centuries back to *jaman buda*, the glorious pre-Islamic past. Nevertheless, it was a Balinese, rather than Javanese, scene that met the eye (what did the Sivaites of Majapahit look like?): priests in white robes and headcloths; a retinue of decorative parasols and banners; a xylophone ensemble; and a route lined with the drooping bamboo offering poles that distinguish Balinese festivals.

On arrival, three men waded waist deep into the tank and brought out brimming bowls of water. These were consecrated by the senior priest, seated on the bank, who then led congregational prayers. Offerings were then set adrift in the tank (Saraswati is also the goddess of river water) and participants returned to the temple bearing the precious bowls, xylophones jingling in the background. As they approached, the priests scattered offerings – including a newly beheaded chicken, still flapping – in their path and waved sticks of incense. Then the priests broke into a dance and, accompanied by a number of women (the wives of senior figures), flitted and whirled their way into the temple, making a circuit of its precincts. It seemed a conscious, if improvised, effort to embellish and *customize* the entry: I had never seen anything of the kind in Bali. After this impressively exotic spectacle, however, we were back on familiar ground: speeches, microphones, the paraphernalia of modern religion in Indonesia. A committee person read out the agenda (*protokol*) from a pulpit, beginning with 'Number one: reading out of the *protokol*.' Then the head of the Banyuwangi branch of Parisada, the umbrella Hindu organization – himself a Balinese – mounted the podium and gave a twenty-minute speech in Indonesian on the meaning of the Saraswati festival 'when God lowered down knowledge'. It was a phrase no Muslim could quarrel with; indeed, Muslims have their equivalent holy day celebrating the Night of Power when Muhammad received the Koran. Nor was the name of God – Tuhan, the Lord – objectionable: it was common to all Indonesia's faiths, not least the Pancasila state ideology. What Saraswati symbolized, he went on, was the importance of education and school. Education was crucial for development. Later in his speech he had another message for us. We should remember that the Hindu faithful, the umat (he used the Muslim term), indeed the nation, were coming up to a very important moment, the regional assembly elections, and we should do our best to make it a success. He remarked that one of the 'VIPs' who had honoured us with his presence was a member of the government party and a regional assembly deputy, and that as Hindus we should give him our full support. (While he was speaking, his young son hovered round with a camera, the VIPs pointing out the best vantage points.)

With no sense of discontinuity, the Glenmore subdistrict officer, a Muslim, then took the microphone and lectured us on development and the need to beautify the regency with flower beds (the regent's pet scheme), stressing the superior qualities of bougainvillaea (the regent's favourite flower).

There was one further speaker. A young man, introduced as 'Doctor-andus S. who has trained at a Hindu institute in Bali', gave a sermon lasting nearly an hour. It was delivered in a mixture of Indonesian and Javanese, in a furious rant, and was amplified to distortion. There were snatches of song, not very convincing shows of confessional piety, and well-rehearsed moments of passion – sudden artificial shifts of tone which prompted little bursts of dutiful applause from the congregation (enthusiastically augmented by children's screams). I had seen similar, though more polished, performances by Muslim kiyais. It was evidently a standard format: what constituted a religious occasion – or, for that matter, a political one – in modern Indonesia. But apart from these brief signs of life when faces were lifted and hands clapped mechanically, the rows of patient and by now drowsy worshippers, seated crosslegged on the sunbaked compound, took little interest in the proceedings. No one to whom I later spoke could tell me anything at all about the sermon; it was simply part of the ceremony. Equally, no one seemed to mind the hectoring and patronizing tone or the display of overconfident youthful piety. One expected no more and no less.

The ritual proper lasted some twenty minutes – long enough for the priests to move among the seated rows sprinkling water. Most people simply had a few drops flicked over their heads, but the priests themselves and the VIPs (the English word was always used) had, in a addition, a little holy water poured into their hands, from which they took three sips before passing the hands over the head in a gesture similar to that concluding slametan prayers (cf. Goris 1960b: 111). Finally, wetted uncooked rice was distributed and dabbed onto fore-heads and temples.

The festival was over and the congregation dispersed.

The creation of a Hindu umat
Unsatisfied by what I had seen (as, I suspect, were some of the congregation), I returned to Pak Suroso for advice. I shouldn't jump to conclusions, he said. The Hindu 'umat' in Banyuwangi numbered tens of thousands but only a few hundred had attended the temple festival.[3] Clearly, practical Hinduism was carried on at a different level: it had grown in response to rural divisions and was largely a village affair. So, armed with a list of communities which boasted a Hindu presence, I toured the area, finally settling on a coastal village south of the town of Rogojampi. This village (pop. 2,091), which I shall call Krajan, was especially interesting in the light of my previous researches in the Osing

area around Banyuwangi. It was a mixed village of native Osing and settlers from other parts of East and Central Java: Madiun, Ngawi, Nganjuk, Mojokerto, and Blitar. The Osing and the incomers had gone through the same political trauma in the 1960s but they had experienced the wave of Hinduization in notably different fashion. A comparison between these two subcommunities and with the villages I already knew well might, I thought, signify much about the relation between Osing culture and the wider Javanese world.

The Osing part of the village, known as kampung Osing, is a compact, distinct block of some hundred households, different in appearance and character from the rest of the village. Most of its inhabitants – unlike the rest of the village – make a living from fishing. They are the poorest of a poor village in which 75 per cent of the population are landless. The few Osing peasant-farmers were recently forced off their land to make way for a prawn farm. (Much of the coast is now given over to this burgeoning industry in which ex-President Suharto's son has a controlling interest.)

The contrast with the surrounding habitation is striking. Instead of the densely packed side-by-side housing of kampung Osing ('so crowded that if you want to take a leak you are confused as to where to go', as one Blitar man put it), the houses of the immigrant Javanese are widely spaced, each with its own fenced compound and shady orchard. The difference in use of space makes for a different pattern of socializing. The overcrowded, intermarrying Osing form a single, bounded community (subdivided into overlapping slametan neighbourhoods) in which lives are lived out in public and quarrels – said to be frequent – ramify in minutes from one end of the kampung to the other. Despite the overwhelming presence beyond its boundaries of immigrant Javanese, kampung Osing has maintained its distinctive customs, notably the slametan form common to the villages around Banyuwangi.

In contrast, among the immigrant Javanese, only a handful of houses are within wandering distance. One needs a bicycle to travel beyond the fifth or sixth neighbour. People are much less aware of what is going on outside their immediate neighbourhood and are unaffected by quarrels that do not concern their interests.

It was in this sharply differentiated setting that the bloody events of 1965–6 unfolded. Few families were untouched by the violence. Kampung Osing remained solidary – there were no religio-political divisions since everyone was nominally Islamic and in a similar economic position: at the bottom. But outsiders came in to rampage and there were a number of victims. The worst violence, however, was among the immigrant Javanese, riven as they were by class interests, political affiliation, and religious orientation. My host, who was then a Nationalist Party activist and a nominal Muslim (now a Hindu), lost six relatives, some of whom were thrown down a well by Muslim youths. Sixty people are said to have been killed in this way alone. In the atmosphere of terror, accusation and counter-accusation proliferated, mosques and langgars were (or were said to have been) desecrated, and property was burned down.[4]

The years from 1965 to 1968 were a trauma that very few will discuss. But as violence gave way to the all-pervasive surveillance that became a hallmark of the New Order regime (Tanter 1990), indoctrination and 'rehabilitation' became the new methods of control. Despite the fact that religious difference had fed political strife and provided the spark that set fires burning all over Java, the government's remedy for the traumatized nation was more religion (Lyon 1977: 95–6). Javanism, whether in its mystical or popular forms, was not an option: only the recognized official religions were allowable. Accordingly, nominal Muslims – the supporters of the communist (PKI) and nationalist (PNI) parties – were to be coached in the basics of Islam. In Krajan, as in many other villages in the south of the regency, villagers were forced to attend Koranic training sessions in the mosque and to perform the ritual prayers. (Significantly, this did not happen in the Osing villages around Banyuwangi.) Many found this a great humiliation, but what particularly galled was that the instructors had been among the leading persecutors and murderers during the troubles. A number of the nominal Muslims therefore set up their own langgars where they could be undisturbed – and, presumably, inactive. However, the new langgars were soon desecrated, and denunciations continued. At this point the first approaches to Balinese Hindus in neighbouring villages were made. On these secret visits, Krajan's reluctant Muslims – especially those who had dabbled in Javanist mysticism – were surprised to find they had much in common with the Balinese. The first conversions occurred in Sumbersewu where the Muslim indoctrinations had begun; and wherever the 'Mass Guidance' programme was implemented a wave of defections followed. In Krajan, after a month of Mass Guidance over two hundred households had come out for Hinduism, including half of kampung Osing. The Hindu leaders themselves could not have devised a better method of recruitment. The Islamic drive was called off.

There was no formal procedure for becoming a Hindu: one simply declared one's allegiance and added one's name to a list. Identity cards at this time remained unchanged, showing the religion of birth. But there was pressure from Muslims to make a more public show of affiliation; moreover, a number of converts wanted to signal their new commitment in unambiguous terms, so an ordained priest (*pedanda*) was brought over from Bali and a mass 'baptism' (*pembaptisan*) was held.

In most respects the pattern of polarization, persecution, failed compromise, re-evaluation, defection, and recruitment to Hinduism by neighbourhood blocks was similar to that of Central Java (see Lyon 1970, 1977). Lyon concludes her study of the Hindu 'revival' as follows (1980: 214):

The turn to Hinduism was not a matter of conversion in the sense of taking on a new faith; rather, Hinduism provided a metaphor, a new organizing principle, for a new perspective on traditional beliefs and customs and so resulted, for a portion of the membership at least, in a re-examination and recontextualization of tradition.

Lyon also emphasizes the political character of the conversions – the use of PNI networks and methods of recruitment; the role of key PNI figures whose political base had been removed by the New Order and who sought a new way to exercise influence; and the emphasis on external, group identity: 'it is membership, the outward profession of belonging to Hinduism which counts' (1977: 110–12). In Banyuwangi, although Javanist PNI figures played their part, recruitment was often initiated at grass-roots level and (at least in Krajan and neighbouring villages) there was no subsequent recruitment drive following the initial wave of conversions. The problem, to the contrary, was how to maintain numbers when the more obvious threats to life and security had diminished. Neither did the official Hindu body, Parisada Hindu Dharma, play a major role in the early stages as it did in Central Java: its influence came later when converts began to struggle with the problem of what Hindus were supposed to do. In most cases I encountered, it seems to have been personal contacts with Balinese that were crucial. Krajan had the advantage of the example and support of nearby Balinese settlements such as Glondong, which had its own Bali-style temples and an active religious life. Equally important, the protection of Balinese army officers in the region prevented a Muslim backlash in villages such as Tembokrejo and Blambangan where converts continued to face hostility from Muslim activists.

By 1992 a generation of new Hindus had come of age, knowing nothing of the old order and with little idea of the complex politics which

lay behind their parents' conversions. The intervening years have seen a
decline in numbers, down from 200 families to 120, out of a total of 480
in the village as a whole. The most significant loss was kampung Osing.
Conversion in this case had simply been an expedient. Nominal Muslims
became nominal Hindus and, as soon as the pressure was removed,
reverted to what they had always been. As several people put it to me,
the eventual winner was *adat Osing* (custom). But there were also
intrinsic stresses in the structure of the community which made a division
into two camps intolerable. Kampung Osing was a physically uniform
block, internally criss-crossed by intermarriage and a dense pattern of
resulting kinship ties. Culturally, it was an island in a sea of 'western'
Javanese immigrants. Differences which could be overlooked in the
scattered settlements of the incomers could only lead to friction among
the intensely sociable, competitive, and overcrowded Osing. Patterns of
slametan attendance were disrupted as neighbours were embarrassed by
differences in prayers. The Osing form of slametan, in which the incense-
burning and invocation are performed publicly, only served to emphasize
divisions. The new Hindus were dismayed that they were no longer
invited to sedhekah, commemorative feasts, as their Sanskrit chants were
inappropriate; and, on the other hand, they felt oppressed by the
frequency of temple festivals in the short (210-day) Javanese-Balinese
year. Deeply conservative and for the most part uneducated, they were
unwilling to rethink their traditions in new terms: the Sanskrit mantras
and new-fangled Balinese ways appeared as alien as anything the modin
had demanded of them. In this respect it is significant that there were few
adherents of mystical sects among the Osing – few who could 'recontex-
tualize' tradition or make imaginative links across denominational lines
(cf. Lyon 1980: 214). In 1992 there were a mere handful of Hindus left in
kampung Osing. One of them died while I was there and was given a
Muslim burial.

Reversions among the majority settler population have been due to
individual predicaments and decisions rather than a general drift. One of
the Hindu leaders in Krajan described the state of play between the rival
faiths as a 'cold war'. Each side opposes any efforts at proselytization
and there is a truce on this score, but at crucial moments an individual
may be forced to make a choice. Mixed marriages often lead to a
reversion to Islam (much less often one of the partners adopts Hinduism)
– either 'for the sake of the children' or due to pressures from relatives.
There are many variations on this theme. The younger brother of my
host in Krajan, a lifelong Hindu, married a Muslim girl by abduction (a

common form of marriage) and the settlement with her parents involved his conversion to Islam and a proper Islamic wedding ceremony. In another case it was the bride's father who was obliged to renounce Hinduism. The wedding was to be Islamic and the girl wanted her father to be her *wali* (representative), as is usually the case. He could not refuse her this minimal paternal act. Even where both partners want a Hindu wedding a Muslim parent may refuse to co-operate.

Other reversions illustrate the way in which cultural and religious affiliation is entangled in social and economic circumstances. Pak T, who is head of the hamlet, reverted to Islam because of pressure from his wife's son. He himself was landless and had come to live with his wife. Access to the land of his wife's family depended on their continuing good will. Completing his metamorphosis he has now become, albeit reluctantly, a regular mosque-goer: the new headman, a haji, demands full attendance from his staff. Another poor man in a similar marital arrangement was given a large plot of land by his wife's father on condition that he renounce Hinduism. Such reversions, while statistically insignificant, have a demoralizing effect within the Hindu community and contribute to its sense of being an embattled minority.

Even death does not mark the end of the struggle. In families of mixed faith there are often disputes over the burial arrangements. Pak Johan, the oldest Hindu in kampung Osing, was given an Islamic burial. He happened to die in the house of his nephew who claimed that his dying words were a declaration for Islam. In other cases Hindu burials have been followed – at the insistence of the bereaved – by the usual series of Islamic sedhekah.

Two men are at the front line of this 'cold war': the modin and his opposite number, the *klian adat*, an unpaid official chosen by the Hindu community. Each is responsible for the welfare of his umat and for the paperwork of births, marriages, and deaths. Each regards a birth, joyfully, as an addition to the congregation (his joy tinged with sadness at a bad statistic on the birth-control graph) and each looks with satisfaction on a well-stocked graveyard. In a recent controversy, two graves were dug in opposite sections of the cemetery as the rival camps fought over the destiny of the soul. (The Muslims conceded on this occasion.) In another case, a haji opposed the burial of a Hindu woman in the village's second cemetery, which is mixed. He threatened to dig up the grave if the burial went ahead.[5]

Difficulties at village level are compounded by bureaucratic obstruction. In matters of marriage and divorce Muslims are served by the

Ministry of Religion and its local representative, the Office of Religious Affairs. But adherents of other faiths must report to the Civil Registry Office. This is complicated and expensive. In order to obtain a wedding certificate a couple must provide the identity cards and wedding certificates of their parents, the family card, their own identity cards, and their birth certificates. (These requirements, I was told, differ regionally, according to local policy.) Those who cannot provide all these documents and the accompanying fees (and bribes, to expedite the process), must make do with a customary wedding, which is unrecognized in law. For most people this matters little; but candidates for a job in the civil service must provide a birth certificate, which in turn depends on their parents' having a marriage certificate. Unsurprisingly, some young Hindus take the easy path and settle for an Islamic wedding.

Again, divorce for Hindus is costly and difficult. The judge often makes objections and expects a bribe of at least 100,000 rupiah for his approval.

Practical difficulties of this order might seem petty beside the great questions of faith, commitment, and identity which dominate academic discussion of conversion, but they loom large to the people concerned: indeed, such problems are often decisive in determining allegiance; moreover they stress, to those caught up in them, the very narrow limits of personal freedom in a highly bureaucratic state – a state in which Islam has a majority influence. Indonesia is, nevertheless, far from being an Islamic state: the power of Islam to intervene in personal life is restricted to family law; but this domain it defends tooth and nail. Hence – as the *klian adat* put it – every marriage and divorce has four parties: husband and wife, Hinduism and Islam; and every case has to be fought as if it were the first. Or so it often seems.[6]

But there is another, less circumstantial, reason why births, marriages, and deaths rather than temple ceremonies and Sanskrit prayers figure so significantly in people's accounts of why they are Hindu and what it means to become a Javanese Hindu. For syncretist Hindus (which is to say all village Hindus), as for syncretist Muslims, religion is something which imposes itself most forcefully at the great crises of life. It is at birth or death that the individual is stamped, unprotesting, with a religious identity, and at marriage that he or she is the focus of maximum social pressures (often conflicting ones) to proclaim a religious identity – indeed, everyone seems to have a vested interest in this assertion. The sense of alternatives, of the road not taken, is always present in the minds of converts and their families at such moments.

Bali/Java

What Javanese Hinduism is, or should be, is a matter of opinion. In Krajan one can gather quite different views, depending on whether one speaks to the temple priest, the *klian adat*, the local Parisada representative, the school religious teacher (a Balinese), or ordinary villagers. These views differ again from those of the urban leadership in Banyuwangi – men and women who understand the workings of religious bureaucracies and perhaps something of religious apologetics but who mostly know little of how Hinduism has been incorporated into village life. The differences between these various opinions revolve around the relation between the new religion and tradition.

The new converts were confronted with several models of Hinduism. Their primary example was that of Balinese settlers in neighbouring villages. These immigrants, mostly second-generation settlers from the north and west of Bali, had their own Bali-style temple complexes,[7] their temple priests (there were no ordained Brahman priests in the area), and a ceremonial life reminiscent of Bali, though on a reduced scale. There were celebrations of temple 'birthdays' (*odalan*), occasional dance-dramas, and festivals such as Galungan and Kuningan. Many, but by no means all, households had shrines in their yards for ancestor worship.

Javanese villagers in this area also knew something of religious life in Bali itself. Some had worked on construction projects in various parts of the island; and from the 1970s onwards many (of both sexes) found temporary jobs servicing the tourist industry. They have seen for themselves the elaborate temple festivals, the spectacular cremations, the processions of women bearing pyramids of fruit on their heads, the offerings in houseyards, and the hordes of admiring tourists. Somewhere in the midst of this exotic *mélange* was the Hinduism which their ancestors were supposed to have practised and to which they now wished to return.

Part of the problem about what to make of Javanese Hinduism was, and remains, what to make of the Balinese variety. The background to this conundrum is exceedingly complicated and only a few salient facts need be mentioned here. From 1343 until the early fifteenth century Bali was a dependency of Majapahit (Swellengrebel 1960). The impact of Javanese hegemony was formative, both culturally and politically, though it was uneven across the island (Barth 1993: 18). A fourteenth-century Javanese court chronicle affirmed, nevertheless, that 'the other island, Bali, conformed in all customs with the land of Java' (Swellengrebel 1960: 21). Bali had already been for centuries Hindu, or Hindu-

Balinese, but it was henceforth 'Javanese-Balinese, or more accurately still ... Hindu-Javanese-Balinese' (Swellengrebel 1960: 21). The influence of Majapahit is still apparent in Balinese religion today, from the highest level – the mother temple of Besakih was founded, in legendary times, by a hermit from Majapahit (Swellengrebel 1960: 16–17) – down to the altars or 'god-seats' in clan temples for the Majapahit ancestors (Grader 1960a: 167). The nobility of Bali, in fact, trace their ancestry back to the Javanese colonizers and refer to themselves as 'men of Majapahit'. In social structure another important legacy of colonization was the introduction of the Indic system of *warna* (Goris 1960c: 293–4), cognate with the Indian *varna* (classes or 'estates') and often referred to as 'castes' (see Geertz 1973d; Howe 1987, 1989). By a curious irony, many Javanese Hindus now maintain that the *warna* system is native to Bali, part of its adat or custom, and therefore does not belong in a new, translocal Hinduism.

When Majapahit fell into decline in the fifteenth century and was eventually conquered around 1527 by Muslim forces, Bali received a second wave of Javanese influence as many of the priests and literati fled to the nearby island. Some, including, reputedly, Nirartha, the legendary ancestor of Balinese Brahmans, would have found refuge on the way in Blambangan (Marrison 1987: 4), which remained buda until the late eighteenth century. Indeed, the attraction of Java's last Sivaite realm to the Balinese – at one time or another Blambangan has been claimed by Gèlgèl, Bulèlèng, Mengwi, and Klungkung – has ensured a steady cultural influence which has lasted up to the present.

With the Hindu revival in Java the wheel has come full circle, as Balinese 'return' to construct temples such as the splendid *pura agung* Blambangan at Tembokrejo, near Krajan. The brief history of this temple encapsulates many of the themes of this chapter – the political and religious watershed of 1965, the quest for an authentic past and a Javanese-Hindu identity, the guidance and solidarity of Balinese, and the transition from Javanism and Javanist mysticism to a distinct religion.

The temple was built at a site not far from the ruins known as Umpak Songo, 'Nine Steps' – a stone platform with column pedestals and a flight of steps, thought to be part of the original palace complex of Blambangan. According to a printed history kept by the caretaker, the ruins were discovered by pioneers from Yogya in 1916. The descendants of these settlers, a close-knit group of families who belong to a Javanist mystical sect, used the ruins as a place for collective meditation. Umpak Songo was also visited by mystics from other areas and by Balinese and

Javanese Hindus. After the 1965 coup it became the ceremonial focus of the emerging Banyuwangi umat. Lay priests (*pemangku*) from all over the regency were trained at Tembokrejo, and on 26 July 1969, 101 people were 'baptized' at Umpak Songo by a Balinese Brahman priest. In 1973 the regency branch of Parisada approved a plan to build a temple over the site, but this was, understandably, blocked by the Department of Antiquities. Indeed, it was not until 1978 that work began on the present building, financed entirely by donations. (Golkar, the government party, contributed fifty sacks of cement.) There was great excitement when two ancient wells were found in the excavations – sacred repositories which had lain buried for hundreds of years. These are now used for holy water and have been further sanctified by infusions of Ganges water brought by visitors from India. The *padmasana*, stone seat of Siwa (Shiva), was built over a third well.

The temple of Blambangan – its name was carefully chosen – is now one of the major centres of Hinduism in Banyuwangi and serves as the location for the festival of Kuningan. One of its two priests, a Javanese from Ponorogo who converted in the fateful year of 1966, is a lapsed member of the Javanist sect, Sangkan Paran.

To the great satisfaction of Banyuwangi's Hindus, the Blambangan Temple is now an essential stopover for Balinese on their way to the enormous new temple at Watu Klosek on the slopes of Mt Semeru in East Java.[8] These showpieces of the new Hinduism are the outcome of decades of planning, politicking, and negotiation between Javanese and Balinese about the public face of Javanese Hinduism. They are a visible statement that the new religion has come of age, suggesting that what was once an experiment, a tentative groping for a new religious form, has achieved a mature and balanced realization. In the ordinary village temples, however, the abstract synthesis of Javanese and Balinese cosmologies – made concrete in the great temples – is hardly to be seen. The rough-and-ready compromises of the early period of Hinduization are still all too evident.

Practical Hinduism

The great and obvious difference between the Hindu reform movement in Bali and Java is that in Java – excepting the Tengger region – there was nothing to reform. The new religion had to create space for itself in an entirely different setting. The solution to the problem was, super-ficially, a simple one. Islam had been rejected; the new practices and beliefs were made to fill the peculiarly shaped space it had vacated.

Consequently the transformation of village religion was largely a process of substitution, a matter of finding an equivalent prophet to Muhammad, a different prayer for use in slametans, a Hindu way of commemorating the dead, and so on. The village pioneers had two audiences in mind: their own congregation, who wanted to carry on performing slametans and doing things in the familiar Javanese way; and the rival, ever-watchful Muslim umat.

Thus, while the apprentice Hindus were busy learning prayers and rituals from the Balinese, they were also keen to impress the Muslims that they, too, had a proper religion. In the early days 'emphasis was on a minimal set of elements which would "make" an occasion Hindu in definition' – incense sticks, holy water, petals, orientation east (Lyon 1977: 177–8). But as well as drawing on Balinese models, in learning how to be Hindus the converts borrowed from the example they knew best: Islam. There was a double irony here. It was the programme of forced Islamization which had created the Hindu umat in the first place; but to survive as a legitimate alternative, Javanese Hinduism had to adopt the categories and ritual forms of the hated rival. The parallel with the development of Javanist mysticism in recent decades is clear (Stange 1986: 80); but since Hinduism is *agama*, a public, official religion, not a private spiritual quest, its compromise has had to be that much more systematic and unambiguous. This process of redefinition has taken place on two levels, popular and official, but it has been most conspicuous at the level of official discourse – in the publications and pronouncements of Parisada and the big public festivals.[9] In its official guise reformed Hinduism, unlike traditional Balinese or Tengger religion, lays a great emphasis on the singularity of God, congregational worship, a uniform set of scriptures (including the Vedas, which were unknown to traditional Bali), and – analogous to the Muslim salāt – thrice-daily prayers chanted in a sacred, uncomprehended language (Forge 1980; Hefner 1985: 252–5; Lyon 1980). Geertz (1973b: 184) and Hefner (1985: 253) have also noted an emphasis on personal piety.

Besides these basic ingredients of an *agama* the new religion has acquired Indonesian, rather than specifically Islamic, trappings which signal its legitimacy: committee-style speeches, political pep-talks, visits from dignitaries, microphones and piped music, youth's and women's sections, savings associations, recitation contests, textbooks and school instruction.

At village level, however, the transformation brought about by forcing Hinduism into an Islamic mould has, if anything, gone even further.

Apart from simple concessions to Islam, such as the continuing practice of circumcision or the form of burial – which owes little to Hinduism, whether Indian or Balinese – Hindu rituals have been remodelled in parallel with Islam. For example, the Balinese festival of Galungan is conceived as the Hindu equivalent of Lebaran, the feast ending the Fast. (The Fast in turn is paired with Nyepi, the Hindu day of silence.) Galungan – or Lebaran – in Krajan is a day when people pray collectively (from 7 a.m. to 9 a.m.) in the temple/mosque, hold slametans, visit relatives and ask their forgiveness, and morally speaking turn over a new leaf. These parallels are explicit. One of the reasons given by Osing converts for their reversion to Islam was that, compared to Lebaran, Galungan was 'not lively enough'.

But there are also subtler mutations which lend a distinctive ethos to Javanese village Hinduism. Taking their cue from village norms of egalitarianism and the equality of men in ritual – norms emphasized in Islam – Javanese villagers have created a religion in which the basic rites can be performed by any individual. Knowledge is not evenly spread, to be sure; but the possibility of general participation in domestic and public rituals – slametans, commemorative feasts, weddings, temple worship – mirrors the populism of village Islam. Thus, there is no separation of priestly and popular religion as in Bali or the Tengger highlands (Forge 1980; Hefner 1985). The temple caretaker-priest is not an elevated figure but is similar in function to the Islamic modin. He is a prayer-leader, a source of counsel, and an exemplar rather than an intermediary with God. The ordained priesthood, with its specialist knowledge, its esoteric rituals, and its semi-divine status (Balinese *pedanda* are possessed by Siwa and are 'Siwa' to their client families), is absent in Banyuwangi. Lacking the 'caste' hierarchy of Bali and, *ipso facto*, the Brahman priesthood, Javanese Hindus have made a virtue of necessity. They point out proudly that they themselves are quite capable of making the holy water for Sanskrit prayers (*trisandhya*), or of conducting a slametan. The *pemangku*'s presence is strictly necessary only in temple worship.

This democratization of a hierarchical – indeed, hieratic – religion has its source in two distinct impulses. On the one hand, there has been an effort, led by Parisada, to disseminate knowledge and encourage mass participation among ordinary Hindus. Thus, weekly study groups practise Sanskrit chants and hand postures, visiting speakers address the temple congregation on the morality of the Gita, and schoolchildren learn about the Indian origins of the faith. On the other hand, there has been popular concern to incorporate adat – the heritage of the collectivity – into religion.

These laudable and conscientious efforts are generally assumed to be complementary, but, apart from the levelling effect mentioned above, they hardly converge. As a result, village Hinduism is every bit as fragmentary as village Islam – a congeries of disparate notions and practices linked solely by the routine of performance and the common identity of the actors themselves. Before we consider some examples, it is worth considering for a moment how this unintended result of so much planning has come about.

The Hindu organization, Parisada, grew in response to the need to rethink the role of religion in a modernizing Bali, as well as to lobby for government recognition (Geertz 1973b), but its priorities in Muslim Java were rather different. As Forge observes (1980: 227), in Java 'the balance between internal reform and external proselytization was early set in favour of the latter'. In rural Banyuwangi the role of Parisada has tended to be one of organization and practical guidance: committees, officers, how to do this or that. Doctrine has played a very small part in the transformation of religious life in the village. Chants are memorized rather than explained; prayer postures and hand movements are practised without reference to their symbolism; and Hindu cosmology has been framed in familiar Javanese terms broadly shared by the syncretist Muslim population. On the other hand, the Parisada manual, *Upadeca*, conceiving of religion in a narrow, rationalized form, has little to say about Javanese traditions. Consequently, while villagers follow Parisada's prescriptions concerning canonical worship to the letter, they have largely been free to discover their own solutions to the problem of how to integrate religion with daily life. In time-honoured fashion, they have absorbed the new ways without fundamentally altering their cherished traditions. Rather like the fat man who eats a lettuce salad for the sake of his conscience and then gorges himself on dessert, they have taken the streamlined, rationalized religion propounded by Parisada and simply added it to the panoply of traditional practices instead of replacing or reforming them.

Perhaps an opportunity has been missed. As in Tengger (Hefner 1985: 252–3), the deeper affinities between the local religions of Bali and Java were hidden by the imposition of an 'essential' Hinduism prised from its cultural background. This was ironic given that what first attracted Banyuwangi's reluctant Muslims to Hinduism was the similarity they perceived in the ways of their Balinese neighbours. The common ground

– a shared Indic mythology in the wayang, a sense of community with the ancestors, a classificatory bent (which even overlapped in content, e.g. the 'four siblings' and the colour schemas), a sacred geography with its power-points and place spirits, and, not least, a close kinship in the performing arts[10] – remains unexplored in the austere monotheistic creed of the new Hinduism. Naturally, Majapahit, with its tantric cults and its Sivaite and Buddhist priesthoods, was even less admissible, unless as a slogan or a rallying cry for denominational unity.

The feeling of incongruity and obscurity which struck earlier observers of Javanese temple worship (Lyon 1977: 180) has therefore hardly diminished. No doubt this is one reason why the regular congregation has dwindled to a fraction of the total Hindu community. (Attendance at Krajan's temple varies between about twenty and fifty.) Nevertheless, away from the temple with its prescriptive ritual and Sanskrit liturgy, villagers have succeeded to a degree in integrating the old and the new.[11]

The sequence of life-cycle rites remains almost unchanged. The slametans held at intervals during pregnancy and infancy are celebrated in the usual way, with the addition of a Sanskrit prayer. These and other slametans are simply assimilated to the category of rites that reformed Hindus (following Balinese practice) call *manusa yadnya*. The general aim, as in mainstream Javanese Islam, is understood to be the quest for *kaslametan*, well-being, security. Indeed, even temple worship (like worship in the mosque) has the same goal. With a typical Javanist touch, the priest informed his congregation one evening that the meaning of *pura* (temple) was *sepura*, forgiveness. Thus, one came to the temple – as to the mosque – to ask God's forgiveness and request His blessing. In similar fashion, commemorative feasts (sedhekah) are equated with analogous Balinese feasts which reformed Hindus call *pitnya yadnya*, and are understood in familiar Javanist terms as a means of hastening, or symbolizing, a return to one's origin.

If the form and purpose of slametans among Javanese Hindus remains essentially what it always was, there are, nevertheless, substitutions in the slametan address which lend a distinctively Hindu flavour to custom. Resi Wiyoso, a Hindu sage, gets the bananas normally offered to Muhammad (both are bringers of religion and are therefore interchangeable); and root vegetables are dedicated to the underworld serpent, Antaboga, instead of *nabi* Suleiman. I also heard mention of Betara Wisnu (Vishnu) as 'guardian of wells' and Betara Bromo (Brahma) as 'guardian of the hearth' – oddly minor roles for the Creator and Preserver of the Universe, but designations which would not sound out of place in a traditional Muslim slametan. Sanghyang Widi Wasa, the Supreme Being who has eclipsed the Hindu Trinity in Javanese Hinduism, substitutes Gusti Allah.

These minor innovations – an expression of the 'all religions are one' philosophy of Javanism – betray both the cultural conservatism of the new Hindus and the dominant position of the slametan in village religion. Concerning other rituals, however, there is a more experimental, eclectic attitude and a conscious revivalism bordering on antiquarianism. Whereas Muslim Javanese have tended, in recent years, to perform agricultural rituals in a perfunctory manner, knowing they are 'old-fashioned' and disapproved by pious youth, and no doubt sensible that industrial fertilizers, pesticides, and the rice goddess do not really belong together; in contrast, Hindus, have actually expanded the range of rituals. Thus, while Muslims allow Dewi Sri to languish unattended in the ricefields, the Krajan temple priest invites her to his orange-picking, along with Mother Earth and the danyang (place-spirit). Another Javanist-turned-Hindu told me how he had spotted a magic square in one of the elaborate Balinese calendars most Hindus now possess and has adapted it to his planting ritual.

2 9 4
7 5 3
6 1 8

In the top rice terrace where the irrigation channel enters (the *wangan*, which is also accorded special attention in Osing ritual), he plants nine bunches of shoots, each bunch about 15 cm from the next, with two shoots in the top left hand corner, four in the top right, and so on, according to the number scheme. He burns incense and announces to the place spirit that he is 'going to plant Mbok Sri' (the rice goddess), then he utters the following formula:

Om [the Hindu invocation]. You, the sage (*resi*),
Arise, the sun's rays are red
Remove the pests from the rice
Om. Plant!

after which he places offerings around the plot. A number of other farmers have now adopted the same technique, impressed by his improved harvest and the number symbolism of the magic square which has Javanist as well as Balinese resonances.[12]

These instances illustrate the sort of individual initiatives that are possible, especially at the margins of village religion. With the folklorist's eye for the arcane detail, local experts are forever picking over the various traditions at their disposal in search of correspondences, allusions, and new applications. The priest told me he was amazed at how much of Java he could find in the Indian scriptures. There was even a mantra for the five-coloured porridge![13]

But it is in the area of eschatology that the most serious rethinking of tradition has occurred. The compromise Javanese Hindus have made between their own cultural heritage – which includes, of course, Islam – and Hinduism in its various manifestations, marks a genuinely creative synthesis – a synthesis of which the somewhat glib equation of sedhekah with *pitnya yadnya* (a Parisada idea) is, perhaps, the least part.

The showing of respect to the deceased is, of course, a feature of the traditional Javanese pattern, though one which is frowned upon by reformed Islam (Federspiel 1970). Muslims generally restrict their observances to occasional thanksgiving feasts at which they 'send prayers' to the dead and to the annual grave-cleaning rites that precede the fasting month. Such rituals, and the shadier dealings of healers and mediums, concern the recently deceased and the parental generation of spirits who are thought to retain some influence over the living. Ancestors, in the stricter sense of remote progenitors, are hardly given a thought, unless they figure among the village founders who may be venerated as guardian spirits. The notion of 'ancestor worship' in the Balinese sense (Grader 1960a: 167–8) is therefore alien to the traditional Javanese context. Among the new Hindus, too, interest in the dead concerns only one's near relatives. History is shallow: most people cannot name ascendants beyond the third generation. Thus, there are no clan temples or deified ancestors, as among the Balinese.[14] And it would be inappropriate to erect a household temple or shrine such as is usual in a Balinese compound. (Many houses of Balinese settlers also lack this feature.)

Reverence for the dead – not to speak of 'worship' – is, nevertheless, a more explicit feature of daily life among Javanese Hindus than among Muslims. Usually a particularly cherished relative is singled out. My host in Krajan burns incense and says prayers every week on the day his wife died. A neighbour performs the same service every thirty-five days for her father and grandfather (who both died on the marketday/weekday combination, Monday-Paing), putting out a plate of flowers, their favourite cigarettes, and two cups of coffee – offerings typical of the sedhekah rather than the equivalent Balinese ritual. Some people also say prayers to a general category of ancestors (*leluhur*) on Thursday

evenings, or on Friday-Legi, though this is not, apparently, very
common. All such rituals are conducted privately inside a bedroom or
inner chamber.

These departures from Javanese tradition seem modest enough, and
one might expect the new Hinduism to offer no more than an elaboration
of the usual pattern with a few Sanskrit prayers thrown in for good
measure. In fact, the synthesis has gone much further. Balinese categories
of the dead have been simplified and harmonized with the stages of
Javanese eschatology and mortuary ritual (Goris 1960a: 84). Thus,
Javanese Hindus have adopted the distinction between the unpurified
dead (*pirata*) and those who have been partially purified by cremation
(*pitara*) without, however, reviving the rite of cremation which was once
common to Java and Bali. Instead, the usual sequence of Javanese
Muslim commemorative feasts at three days, seven, forty, one hundred
days, one year, two years, and one thousand days – feasts which,
however, are no longer referred to as sedhekah – is regarded as having
the same effect. The last such commemoration, *nyèwu*, is the point at
which the dead soul becomes a *pitara* and ceases to have any claim on the
living. (There are no further purificatory ceremonies, nor is there a
category of deified ancestors.) A further point of compromise is that this
final transition is phrased in the formal address (*ujub*) in familiar terms as
'returning to the era of eternity' – a formula which retains the fertile
ambiguity among Hindus that it has among Muslims. Some people
conceive of an abode of the dead or, perhaps, heaven; others envisage
extinction. The temple-priest, sticking more closely to the Parisada line,
speaks of dissolution – karma-permitting – into the All or world-soul
(*atman*).

Thus, in the Javanese scheme, cremation is no longer integral to the
cycle – it speeds up the dissolution of the bodily elements but it cannot
alter the destiny of the soul, which depends on the person's karma. One
man explained the difference between Balinese and Javanese as follows:
the Balinese believe that funeral rites procure salvation automatically; in
fact, they are a symbolic expression of the wishes of the relatives, of their
hopes for a reunion of the soul with God. You cannot compel salvation;
that depends on your karma. 'It's like this: someone may show you the
way to Rogojampi, but if you haven't got a ticket how will you get
there?' The sequence of feasts is part of the long process of justification,
but one can never assume that the soul's progress is perfectly in step with
the ritual. Like the Calvinist unsure of his election, one has to look for
'signs'.

The *klian adat*, Pak Gatot, told me about his wife's tragic death and his worries about her fate in the afterlife. She had given birth to a healthy child but the placenta would not come free. The midwife had sent Gatot to look in the garden for medicinal herbs and *jara'* leaves. 'It was then that I felt a chill – *jara'* leaves are a symbol of death. Then I felt a twitching in my arm (*keduten:* an ominous spasm). It happened three times. I knew she would die.' As the official responsible for Hindu funerals he had often experienced such symptoms in advance of bad news. His wife died of blood loss on the way to hospital. After the burial he prayed fervently that her soul 'would find a good place'. Then, around the time of the third funeral feast, he had a series of dreams which he saw as a revelation (Ar. *ilham*). In the first dream he was struggling to light a pressure lamp – the harder he pumped the weaker the glow. He looked across to a neighbour's house and saw his wife putting a match to a similar lamp. It immediately burst into dazzling light. In the next dream he was coaxing his aging moped along, eventually breaking down, when his wife sailed past on her smart new bicycle. Both dreams signified that her path was smooth and 'illuminated' while he had been left behind, struggling in the material world. Nevertheless, he was still doubtful about her fate until his third dream. In this he was offered a cigarette by another villager, Pak Nyoto. Because the cigarette was half drawn out of the packet he looked carefully at it and noticed the brand name: Sampoerna. *Nyoto* means 'evident', 'proven'; *sampoerna* means 'perfect'. He interpreted the dream as indicating that his wife's soul had been purified or 'perfected' and had 'reached a good destination'.

A 'good destination' means, in this case, reunion with God or, perhaps, reincarnation. Pak Gatot is content with the reassurance offered by his dreams without being entirely clear about their import; but he has named his daughter after his deceased wife and sees many resemblances between them which, evidently, cannot be due to upbringing. His vagueness on this score is characteristically Javanese. The doctrines of karma and reincarnation, familiar from the wayang, form part of the stock of eschatological concepts available to all Javanese villagers, whether Muslim or Hindu. Many people hold some vague notion of spiritual transmission – evident in birthmarks or skills inherited from grandparents or greatuncles – without going so far as to conceive of a dead soul taking up residence in a newborn descendant. (Javanist mystics, as we have seen, have a more abstract conception of the spiritual links between generations.) But the new Hindus are freer than Muslims in their speculations; and they have access to a body of teachings which, unlike Islam, does not contradict their background knowledge.

Balinese practice, once again, forms the point of departure. Whereas Javanese Hindus tend to conceive of reincarnation (if they conceive of it at all) as a process indifferent to the sex of the linking relatives, Balinese are said to stress transmission through the male line. Thus, a dead soul might pass to a son's child but not to a daughter's child. Some people explain this patrilineal bias in terms of what they take to be a Balinese folk theory of reproduction. Others explain it in terms of the Balinese system of inheritance which, unlike Java, is exclusively through males.[15]

The details can be worrying – especially if reincarnation is restricted to family members, as Balinese and Javanese seem to agree. One man pointed out that more people are born than die, so there cannot be enough souls to go round. The *klian adat*'s assistant, as the man responsible for the family planning register, had the opposite worry: that birth control would lead to a queue of souls awaiting vacant bodies. In any case, we are evidently in the area of speculation, even faith, rather than dogma. Given the lack of an institutional context for reincarnation beliefs there is no need for consensus. As the Parisada spokesman in Krajan put it to me: 'One sometimes has an inkling, but it's difficult to prove. Really, you must have the conviction (Ind. *keyakinan*) and then the signs will follow.'

As will be apparent by now, the Hindu movement in Java, whatever the political nature of it origins, has indeed resulted in a rethinking of both tradition and religion on the one hand, and of their interrelation on the other (Lyon 1980: 214). Apprised of the fact that their slametans and offerings were really a part of religion all along, that adat was simply the form that religion adopted in a given setting rather than a set of practices in tension with it, Javanese Hindus have been preoccupied with the problem of how to make that conceptual whole a reality. In other words, while the Parisada leaders – urban men with busy schedules and compartmentalized lives – wanted to build a bounded, 'transportable' religion (Forge 1980), villagers were engaged in the opposite endeavour: to recreate a religion in a village context, to restore that sense of wholeness and embeddedness which they perceived in the religion of their Balinese neighbours and which contrasted so painfully with their own sense of alienation from orthodox Islam. Paradoxically, this venture has given the new Hinduism one of its most striking characteristics: its air of deliberation. For what does not come naturally must be carried out deliberately; intention enters into routine and opens up a distance between the actor and the action being performed. The most everyday matters – planting a seedbed, saying a prayer, naming God, greeting fellow Hindus – have about them an air of self-conscious purposiveness. And anything outside routine is undertaken in a spirit of improvisation: what must I do to make this a Hindu performance? This characteristic is one among several reasons why Javanese Hindus contrast their own religious style with that of the Balinese in terms of intellectualism versus ritualism. (Another reason is that many converts were Javanist mystics who are addicted to such reflexivity.) Thus, as I was often told: Balinese like to make beautiful offerings, but Javanese are thinkers; they do not adopt a custom unless they know the reason behind it. (As we have seen, this is not strictly true, at least regarding temple worship.) As the temple-priest put it:

Religion has three aspects: philosophy (*filsafat*), morality (*susila*), and ceremony (*upacara*). All three are necessary for a complete religion, like the three parts of an egg, the yolk, the white, and the shell. But the Balinese genius is for ceremony; ours is for philosophy.

Hindu practice among Javanese differs, therefore, from that of Balinese in the spirit in which it is undertaken. It is action based on commitment rather than routine. This may be a characteristic of conversion in general, but Javanese recognize the fact and incorporate it into their sense of what is distinctive about their faith.[16]

Lest this commitment be mistaken for the zeal of the born-again evangelist, I want to end with two comments which place Javanese 'conversion' in a different perspective. I was probing for personal motivation and what is usually referred to as the 'psychology of conversion'. Aside from the party politics, the terror, the mass defections, the bureaucratic struggles, and so forth, what did it feel like to abandon one's religion of birth to take on another? Didn't one put down roots in a certain soil and grow attached to a certain way of thinking, a particular prophet, and so on? After all, belief in the Prophet's mission is not simply an idea – it commands loyalty, even adoration, in the faithful.

It was difficult to get this idea across, except by analogy. One young man responded that, just as God was 'the same' for all faiths, so Muhammad was 'the same' as Resi Wiyasa and Jesus Christ. Another man protested that they were obviously different kinds of people. Yes, but they were the same in relation to God, returned the first man. He couldn't see a problem.

The priest understood my point and said that it was true that Christians found conversion to Hinduism difficult or even impossible, such was their devotion to Jesus. A Christian woman in Krajan who had married a Hindu refused to convert, despite the best efforts of her family.

But Christianity isn't a Javanese religion. Think of it like this: you Christians can't get a divorce, at least it's very difficult. But we Javanese marry and divorce as we please. Pak Tulik here has had six wives. How is it that one can love a woman, marry her and then divorce so easily? It's the same for us with religion. We can make the 'divorce' easily.

The quality of devotionalism, which one finds among santri, is, indeed, lacking in the syncretist religion of Javanese Muslims and Hindus alike. Hence, without much difficulty, Muhammad and Jesus can be made to appear 'the same'. But the divorce analogy was both apt and intriguing – and not one that, as the priest realized, I could have picked myself. A related analogy came up in a later conversation with neighbours on the same topic. I had asked whether it was difficult to make the adjustment, not just to different ideas and terms but, psychologically, to deny one's previous beliefs and feelings of attachment to a way of thinking and to shift them to some new object. My neighbour said (roughly):

The way you are putting it sounds like someone who foolishly disowns his parents. But in reality it is more like the case of a child who has been adopted and always assumed his adopters were his real parents – I could tell you lots of examples. Then, one day, the real parents appear and tell him the truth. Can he continue to resist it? No, he must go with the true parents.

Divorce, adoption, and conversion. I had stumbled upon a quite different angle and – as is often the way – right at the end of my stay.

Hindus among Muslims
I began this book with the slametan, showing how, in the close and intensely gregarious community of an Osing village, ideological diversity can be accommodated in a single ritual form: pantheists, monotheists, and frank supernaturalists can happily sit down and pray together, saying the same things while thinking their different thoughts. It seems appropriate, therefore, to end with a slametan (or equivalent) in an area of mixed faith in order to see how far an ambiguous idiom can be stretched and to determine the limits of consensus in a community divided by faith and political history – in other words, to put the miraculous flexibility of the Javanese ritual to the ultimate test: can it unite Hindus and Muslims? The short answer, as far as the Osing form of the slametan goes, is a resounding No. Ecumenical slametans in kampung Osing proved impossible and, partly for that reason, the Hindu converts, having weathered the political storm, reverted to their old

ways. But what of the settlers, the people whom Osing refer to as 'western Javanese'? Their slametans have a different form: compartmentalized, less demanding of consensus or full involvement, brief and business-like (in these respects closer to the Gayo *kenduri* described by Bowen (1993)). An Osing slametan, it will be recalled, while not exactly a seamless whole, is a closely integrated performance which maximizes participation and consensus, or at least the appearance of it. It is a highly focused event – two rows of men directed towards an altar-like arrangement of offerings, listening attentively to the address and pointing out omissions, assenting to each dedication, speaking prayers in unison, then sharing the slametan food and, face to face, enjoying or enduring each others' company. It begins with the ceremonial lighting of incense in front of witnesses, thus sanctifying the formal address which follows (the incense conveys the message to the ancestors or God). In contrast, the settlers perform this most sacred moment alone, in private, before any guests arrive. The offerings are placed in an interior room out of sight. The whole tone of the event is thus altered, lowering the temperature of the occasion, as it were, and secularizing or diluting the power of the speech. Seated in a rough circle, with minimal formality and no necessity to face one's neighbour, the guests eat *before* the slametan begins – at least, that is how Osing see it. A small plate of food is hurriedly consumed before the festive dishes proper are brought out and the explanatory speech is made. The festive dishes are then divided up and taken home to be eaten.

This loose, episodic structure seems designed to minimize contact, to eliminate friction. If the solution to ideological diversity among the Osing is a systematic ambiguity, here, where the divisions are more radical, the alternative strategy is adopted: a segregation of elements, a seclusion of the sacred, a non-committal, seeming co-presence. These characteristics are exploited to the full in mixed-faith gatherings. Indeed, the slametan pattern is a fitting image of the cautious, slightly aloof, but still neighbourly relations that obtain among Hindus and Muslims – at least so far as their religious identity is concerned. Moreover, when the opposite faith is present, the characteristics I have highlighted are emphasized even further – the event is more disjointed, interrupted by comings and goings, the guests form an inconstant, fluctuating audience, and the slametan address is further toned down, avoiding specific Hindu or Muslim references (Widi, Siwa, Allah) in a blander-than-ever ecumenical style. Only the slametan prayer obtrudes as a sign of division among the guests. But here too the manner – a rhythmical, rapid delivery in an uncomprehended tongue, interspersed with *Amin*s or *Rahayu*s from the guests – reassures those of the opposite faith with its familiarity: it surely *means* the same thing!

The feast I shall describe was the ceremony commemorating the second anniversary of the death of Bu Eti, an ordinary Krajan woman who had adopted Hinduism in middle age. The host for the occasion was her son-in-law, Parmin, himself a Hindu. The guests were all neighbours: nine Hindus and five Muslims. As in a Muslim sedhekah there were no women present. I arrived with a group of Hindus and we made our entrance, as is normal, *after* the host had burned incense and spoken an appropriate formula. We were seated in rows in the front room of the house facing east. The Muslims' arrival was timed for a later stage. As the most knowledgeable person present, Pak Gatot, the klian adat, officiated. He first prepared the holy water, consecrating it with a Sanskrit mantra, and lit the incense sticks which were then passed back to the rows of guests. Each person, quietly and individually, spoke a preparatory prayer, manipulating flowers in a set routine similar to that beginning worship in the temple. Then Pak Gatot led joint prayers, again borrowed from congregational prayers in the temple. There followed a long chant for the dead, the *puja pitara*, which was performed three times in a low monotone. The last repetition was uttered while holding a flower. Pak Gatot concluded this part of the ceremony by passing back wetted rice which the guests dabbed onto their foreheads and temples.

At this point, synchronized with the end of *maghrib* (sunset) prayers, the Muslims entered. The east-facing rows broke up and a ragged circle was formed, Hindus among Muslims. Each guest was presented with a plate of rice with a bit of chicken on top and a bag of food, his *berkat* (Ar. 'blessing'). Pak Parmin, who as host had been hovering discreetly in the background, now stepped forward and informed the *klian* of his 'intention' (niyat) in organizing the gathering. Then Pak Gatot spoke the formal address (greatly abbreviated here):

We are here to safeguard and preserve sister Eti who has returned to the era of eternity, it being now her second anniversary. May her path be brightened, her grave broadened, her return unimpeded; and may her children and grandchildren be resigned and untroubled (*iklas*). May she be united with the will of God (Gusti) in heaven ...

Furthermore, Man Min [i.e. Uncle Parmin] and his family, [on their behalf], let prayers be sent to all their ancestors, male and female, wherever they may be installed [*wonten pundi papan kurungipun:* ambiguous code for 'reincarnated']. Let this be witnessed by everyone. May Man Min and family, who are alive in the material world (*alam bebrayan*), be safeguarded day and night, throughout the seven days and the five market days. Furthermore, let them be protected by the danyang [place spirit] who watches over us.

Ending with an apology and begging forgiveness for any errors, he then began a prayer with the invocation: 'Om! Brahma, Wisnu, Iswara ...', and the guests, hands one on top of the other in the Hindu position, chimed in at the end of each line with *Rahayu*. The Muslim guests sat quietly and a bit awkwardly with hands folded in laps. The festive food was then brought in, divided up, and added to the *berkat* to be taken home. After a brief smoke and chat the gathering broke up, Hindus and Muslims going their separate ways.

9

Conclusion

I have presented a picture of Javanese religion which conveys, I hope, both a sense of its complexity and of the intimate interrelations among its forms. As we have seen, each element in the kaleidoscope has its own distinctive hue, its characteristic tone, style, and manner. We began with the blandness and ambiguity of syncretic forms – the common denominators of village religion – and then considered, in successive chapters, the raucous banality and evasions of popular folk culture, the stifled quest for significance in cultic symbolism, the anxious literalism of Islamic ritual, the allusiveness and irony of mystical discourse, and finally the makeshift inventiveness of Javanese Hinduism. Each variant embodies – sometimes only suggests – a different conception of the world and one's place within it; and each gives voice to that conception in its own way. What brings them together is a common social context in which no single element can be fully comprehended without reference to the others. This is a structuralist insight, but it takes us beyond the purely formal; for, as we have seen, the complexity of cultural expression (evident in borrowing, ambiguity, avoidance, suppression, and irony) is closely tied to the exigencies of Javanese village life: the need for rukun, the privileged position of Islam, the reach of state power, and the latent threat of chaos.

In emphasizing the expressive differences between, say, Javanist mysticism and practical Islam, or between neighbouring spirit cults, my intention has not been to aestheticize Javanese religion, which would be to trivialize it, but to show how political and social tensions affect religious expression, variously shaping, stimulating, and muting it. By looking in detail at the way religious ideas are formulated in practice and acted upon, or resisted, we can begin to answer an important question posed by Talal Asad (1983: 240), namely, 'How does power create religion?' And we can do so in a way which does not lead inevitably and reductively back to the blind play of material forces. This means taking ideas seriously: positioning oneself in the midst of debate – as one has to in the field – instead of standing on the sidelines, observing and analysing, as though the argument were of no real consequence either to our hosts or ourselves. There is no neutral ground in this debate: a fair account is simply one which renders all points of view. And this, I believe, is how people in Bayu would see it.

Three years after leaving Bayu we returned for another spell of fieldwork. It was to be a lively year in Indonesia – election years usually are – and not too much, perhaps, should be made of the changes we observed. Nonetheless, certain trends had become more visible and there were developments which would have a lasting impact. In front of our old house now stood the green board of Nahdlatul Ulama (NU), the traditionalist Muslim association. The vanguard of Bayu's pious were now part of an organization with some thirty million members. Hitherto the only such sign, at the other end of the village, had belonged to the mystical sect, Sangkan Paran. NU had run a recruiting drive throughout the district and had opened branches in several villages. Bayu could now boast some twenty members. Their leader was Haji Sanuri, the motorbike dealer, who since performing the pilgrimage to Mecca in 1993 had set up as a village sheik, complete with scarf and flowing robes, glowering expression, and terrible warnings to backsliders. Despite his lack of Islamic learning, Sanuri's assiduous cultivation of local religious leaders had assured his nomination as an NU officer; but within the village his intemperate character seems certain to limit the expansion of membership. Indeed, during the year some recruits fell away, embarrassed by his behaviour. The more respectable santri, including the modin, have remained unaligned.

Nevertheless, the existence of an NU cadre in Bayu meant that Muslim activists could henceforth expect strong outside support in disputes. The need for compromise would diminish: numbers and connexions would now count for more. In a year of intense organizational activity in the religious sphere, Javanists had failed to respond to the challenge and their hand had been significantly weakened. NU had already lodged complaints about mystical activities during the Fast.

The new zeal for lists and rallies may have been part of the general mobilization and ideological agitation that accompanies election year;

but there were also signs that Muslim gains achieved over many years were now being consolidated. Among the pious there was a new self-confidence and a greater willingness to flout rules of engagement with the less devout which had for so long preserved the village from factional controversy. At the celebrations of the Prophet's birthday in the mosque, prominent santri had cheered when a guest speaker had mocked 'identity-card [nominal] Muslims'. Ordinary villagers took the offence deeply. During the Fast, our neighbourhood imam made a dawn broadcast attacking the headman, saying that only a pious leader could command loyalty. Not willing to risk confrontation just before the elections, the headman had no option but to swallow the insult. After being out of favour for some years, kiyais (traditional religious leaders) were once again popular as guest speakers at weddings and circumcisions. Their amplified sermons preaching 'holy war' against the impious reached every corner of the village and made many ears burn. Some spoke of the corrupting influence of the West as evidenced by television and the 'animal behaviour' of tourists in Bali. One denounced the secularizing effects of a state education and urged parents to send their children to Muslim boarding schools. Not all speakers took an uncompromising line, to be sure. One could still hear tolerant, pragmatic sermons which remained close to Javanese values and reflected a gentler side of Islam. However, against the trend towards a more liberal, ecumenical, and progressive stance among the national Muslim leadership, there was a noticeable hardening of positions among local leaders, a desire for moral retrenchment. This contrast came to a head in riots which took place in Situbondo, the nearest major town to Banyuwangi, as well as in other places across Java. Churches, courts, and symbols of state authority were attacked. Pancasila, the pluralist state ideology, was under fire.

The disturbances were given many conflicting explanations, ranging from social deprivation, as the Muhammadiyah leader suggested, to Machiavellian government plots intended to discredit the umat. There was a strong suspicion that factions within the ruling elite were playing a double game, manoeuvring for advantage in the run up to the aging President's much-anticipated demise. But national Muslim leaders, at any rate, were mostly dismayed and baffled, some even apologizing for actions committed under the banner of Islam.[1] Banyuwangi, which was close enough to the rioting for main roads to be sealed, held back from the brink. Efforts to spread resentment through anonymous phone calls and leaflets failed when local kiyais were persuaded to co-operate with the authorities. During the election campaign, Muslim party activists were rewarded with an unusual degree of freedom. The town square was decorated with party flags. Even the security forces seemed to be acting with unaccustomed gentleness in handling anything that might spark communal violence. Lynchings of alleged sorcerers in Kenjo and Pesucen, two strongly Muslim villages near Bayu, were allowed to go unpunished. In Bayu, a renewed effort by Muslim activists (now acting as NU members) to unseat the headman was treated with great circumspection by the authorities, whereas three years earlier a rebellion by the same malcontents had been quickly crushed. All these incidents were seen, or at least were optimistically represented by government spokesmen, as signs of the 'heating up' which precedes an election rather than as the stirrings of deeper religious currents. But no one was taking chances. The district military chief arranged a public meeting between Sangkan Paran members and prominent Muslims at which he urged tolerance. And he twice spoke in the mosque about communal strife (*primordialisme*), raising the spectre of 1965, that fateful and bloody year which inaugurated the New Order.[2]

Such were the wider political circumstances of 1996–7, in what turned out to be the twilight years of the Suharto era. But within the community tensions surfaced in ways which could not be directly attributed to religious politics or factionalism, betraying deeper anxieties about cultural change. One particular event stands out as both symptomatic of the moment and – given the nature of the cultural compromise described in this book – entirely characteristic of the setting. For reasons which will by now be clear, the majority of Bayu's population disdain any show of religious rivalry or antagonism and could only respond with ambivalence to the resurgence of Islam. It would be oversimplifying to say their loyalties are divided: rather, they have internalized the compromise between Bayu's different orientations, giving place – if not equally – to practical Islam, Javanist philosophy, and the ordinary rituals of village life. To be forced to choose between these theoretical rivals, or to repress one in favour of another, would not be easy.

The event which exemplified this cultural predicament was a wedding – or rather two weddings held in quick succession, the first being almost a rehearsal for the second. I was privileged to observe the celebrations at close quarters and knew most of the participants well. (My daughter served as a bridesmaid.) In both cases, a young man from a family indifferent to Islam married a pious girl from another village. Such unions are not uncommon and do not usually excite controversy. But in both cases, female members of the husbands' families took exception to the fact that the in-marrying woman insisted on wearing a headscarf, sometimes even a veil (*jilbab*) – tokens of piety and difference which the in-laws could not live with.

Three years earlier no adult women had worn the veil except at prayer-time. (Girls attending the *madrasah* in Banyuwangi usually wear the veil to school.) Now there were three or four young women who had started to wear the veil on trips outside the village or on public occasions when strangers were expected in Bayu. It was as if the village was a large household and one could act freely within it, as among family; but in contacts with outsiders the protection of the veil was needed. The new brides had not understood this code and made their hosts feel like strangers in their own homes.

The first wedding was opposed by the grandparents – old-fashioned Javanists and devotees of the Cungking cult who found santri piety unbearable within their own circle. They boycotted the event and the grandmother threatened to disinherit her daughter and grandson. (Later she relented.) Every stage of the event was marred by disagreement. Haji Sanuri, the groom's uncle, tried to prevent his brother-in-law from hiring a female dancer (gandrung). Such entertainments were immoral and contrary to Islam, he declared. The host told him not to worry: he would be hiring a kiyai – Kiyai Upak, to be precise (the nickname of a popular

Plate 10 Guests at a feast dance with the *gandrung*

local gandrung, after her favourite song, Upak Apem); and he reminded the haji to watch his own reputation. But there could be no winners in such confrontations and the wedding left behind a bad taste for all concerned. Soon afterwards the new couple moved to the girl's village where they said they felt more at home.

The second wedding followed an elopement: the young man forced his parents' acceptance by presenting them with a *fait accompli*. His father tried to shrug it off – it was only the boy's first marriage, he joked. But during the month before the nuptial celebrations (which are separate from the Islamic ceremony), the new bride made matters worse with her sharp tongue and reluctance to help in the house. Again, the veil betokened an inability to 'fit in' with Bayu's ways, or so it was said. However, the groom's father still thought he could put matters right and please everyone with a grand five-days' feast at which a gandrung would dance and a kiyai would lecture. On the last evening some two hundred guests – with santri to the fore – gathered to hear prayers, recitations by langgar students and evangelical speeches. The 'kiyai' (actually a preacher) was an exceptional speaker, a tolerant and wise man with a delicately chiding humour of the kind 'mixed' audiences find most appealing. I had listened to him on other occasions and, like many of the guests, was anticipating a treat. But before he began, the host's niece mounted the podium to recite a prayer. She was wearing a veil and dark gown, as is customary on Islamic occasions, and she looked the epitome of angelic, youthful piety. Some commented on the fact that her husband was not in the audience. That same evening he was performing in Delik as an ape-demon in the barong show. It occurred to me that this curious contrast between husband and wife mirrored that of the bridal pair. Indeed, a similar division characterized the whole extended family; Asih's two uncles, both important men in the community, were on opposite wings of village culture – one a modin, the other an arts impresario with little interest in religion. Her grandfather, too, had once been a modin, though at a time when mastery of Islamic liturgy qualified one to deal with other supernatural affairs. It seemed highly probable that one reason why the family now wanted to host an Islamic evening was to remove the stain of this man's dark history. For the old modin had gone too deeply into magic and had ended as a sorceror. He was said to have had many victims in Bayu and was eventually killed by a mob. But his memory could not easily be erased: from time to time he reappeared as a were-tiger and was now said to haunt the forest of Alas Purwo.

After she had recited her prayer and closed with an Islamic salutation,

Asih turned to get down from the pulpit. But something had caught her eye. She stopped and stared intently into the darkness to one side of the house. Then she seemed to lose balance and tottered forward, as if about to faint, before someone rushed to her aid. A rustling of papers at the microphone covered her exit while the next speaker took her place at the pulpit. The preacher hadn't noticed.

She was carried into the bridegroom's house and laid on a bench, rigid and mumbling, surrounded by anxious, weeping relatives. While the preacher began his melodious sermon, unaware of what was happening in the dingy kitchen nearby (unaware, too, of the extraordinary opportunity for evangelism it presented), the young woman went into trance and was conveying messages from the spirit world to her assembled family – her first request being to remove the veil. As she later explained, she had finished her recitation and looked up to see a huge tiger – her grandfather! – standing in the dark beside the house. He had taken her to sit with him under the big starfruit tree at the back. It was her grandfather who now spoke through her. He called upon his son (the groom's father) and reminded him of his responsibilities to his widowed sister (Asih's mother) who had no income and had to fend for herself. He warned his family not to visit him in Alas Purwo, for they would never return. Then he ordered roasted bananas and tea – seven glasses of it – to be placed under the starfruit tree where Asih imagined she was sitting. (This was immediately done.) The seven glasses were for the seven dead souls who now spoke through her.

It was a family reunion, in which the living had the sensation of talking directly to the dead. The interviews were conducted by the girl's uncle, the modin – no longer a mere official but an intermediary with the spirit world (a role in which the deceased modin had himself excelled). He sat beside the murmuring girl, occasionally crumbling incense on the brazier, and patiently questioned each spirit in turn, satisfying their worries and then, one by one, dismissing them. When the girl suddenly went cold and stiff he massaged her limbs and forced the possessing spirit to speak, then threatened to burn down its 'house' (i.e. grave) if it 'took her away'. The spirits were all deceased relatives of the groom's family and all gave voice to the same grievances. They had been overlooked by the young couple. No dishes of food had been laid out for them in the house and they had not been properly informed of the coming wedding as custom demands. It was clear whom they blamed: the bride had walked out of the cemetery before any flowers were strewn, saying it was unnecessary to 'send prayers' to the dead or to request their blessing. The groom had wavered but followed her lead. He now knelt meekly beside his cousin and was chastised for marrying a 'foolish girl'. More than once he was forbidden to move in with her family. Finally, yet another cousin, a man with a degree from a Muhammadiyah university – a doubter by definition – was summoned and made to introduce his baby son to the spirits. Clearly shaken by what he was witnessing, and unable to resist collective family pressure, he too knelt and submitted.

It was a convincing display of cultural resilience – not merely a return of the repressed but an effective lesson, indeed a counter-lesson, staged in a manner which could not be gainsaid. What made it especially powerful, and deeply ironic, was the occasion – a night of Islamic preaching – and the chosen medium – a sensible, phlegmatic woman of irreproachable piety making her public debut as a santri. The point was, of course, that she was not merely a santri. She had put on the veil for the occasion but could not, like her cousin's bride, wear it permanently. What made a simple unqualified turn to Islam so difficult was the fact of diversity – the fact that, like everyone else in the village, she was enmeshed in a web of obligations to people of very different religious complexion, and she, no less than they, embodied that diversity. However strong the claim of Islam, it could not be allowed to exclude other claims: the necessity for social harmony, the demands of the ancestors, and older traditions which a modernizing Islam would throw out. The persistence of a diverse religious life depended on more than mere tolerance or indifference to the activities of others. In the close-knit world of the village it was sustained by an ethic of mutuality. If Asih's hypnotic appeal was, initially, on behalf of her neglected mother, how could she in turn deny her own impious relatives, be they living or dead?

But ancestral power, for all its ability to shock and surprise, cannot compel lasting conformity where other interests are at stake. A week after the spirit possession the young couple had absconded, first staying in the house of a relative, later moving in with the bride's family. When I asked the modin what he thought of this outrage, he merely smiled and said: That's love. Weren't they in mortal danger from the ancestors? No, not really – at least *they* didn't think so. They may have a hard time making a living, their harvests might be poor, but you never can tell. Would the groom's father be shocked? Again, it was just the kind of thing newly-weds do: his best option would be to forgive them and let them have their way. Later they might come back.

Asih, too, seemed to get over her ordeal quite soon. Her neglected mother had received a sack of rice from the groom's father and she was no longer worried on that score. She herself would continue on her chosen path – struggling, like many others, through personal piety to create a more Islamic society; but chastened, too, perhaps, by the enormous difficulties of making a stand. As her story illustrates, the cat's cradle of interests and compromises which holds every villager in its gentle embrace, and which partly defines his or her identity as a Javanese villager, has its own peculiar tenacity.

Nevertheless, the enduring, flexible compromise which we loosely and synoptically call Javanese syncretism is slowly being rethought. And present signs indicate a move towards a more prominent role for Islam. We should not assume that this is inevitable. Past history suggests that a genuine rethinking, stimulated by wider social changes, throws up novel solutions to old problems. This happened in the wake of Revolution, which led to a revival of Javanist mysticism, and again, in 1965–6, with the Hindu renaissance; and the end of the present era of political stability and cultural stagnation may well signal a radical rethinking on all sides. Much depends upon the character of the political order that follows the New Order: its stance on intellectual and religious freedom of expression, on the status of the Pancasila, and above all on the legal status of Islam as the majority religion. Much depends, too, on broader socio-economic conditions which carry unpredictable consequences in the field of religion: urbanization, mass education, the growth of the middle class, and new technologies. At village level, a transition to a purer form of Islam, or a more dominant role for official religion within a variegated field, is likely to be resisted or deflected by committed Javanists and the many merely indifferent who see Islam as only a part of their cultural inheritance. Recent advances in Islam are, in any case, not always regarded seriously by Javanists, who tend to take a longer view. The old headman of Bayu, after learning of the riots in Situbondo, told me with a laugh: 'I'm not worried. It's been happening since Demak' – Java's first important, but short-lived, Muslim kingdom.

But the present struggle to define a new role for religion within rural society is not one in which the old or even the middle-aged can fully participate; indeed it may be a struggle they cannot really understand from the inside: they can only place it in a wider historical perspective. Their relation to Islam, in all its variety, was forged under different conditions and in other times. They themselves are no longer under severe pressure to conform, still less to do what seems 'modern', to strike an attitude towards a dimly understood, despised yet envied West, or to search for a cause against which to measure themselves, having fought their own great formative causes – revolutionary, cultural, left–right, nation-building – long ago. In any case, it is the young, those born in the New Order and schooled in its mythology, formed by its discipline, and disenchanted by its corruption and violence, who will take on these contemporary challenges and will make their own compromises with tradition.

Notes

Chapter 1

1 Sven Cederroth's study of economic development in the Malang area also discusses rural mysticism (Cederroth 1995).

2 The most important work on language in Banyuwangi is by Indonesian scholars. Of special note are the thesis of Suparman Herusantosa (1987) and the unpublished work of Hasan Ali. See also Supardjana 1986.

Chapter 2

1 Hefner's (1985: 104–10) account of Muslim slametans, embedded in an illuminating comparison with Hindu ritual, is similar to Geertz's. See also Jay (1969: 206–14), Sullivan (1992: 90–4), and Veth (1875: I, 322–5).

2 Geertz himself is equivocal. Compare 'The *abangans* are Java's peasantry, the *priyayis* its gentry' (Geertz 1960: 228) with 'the terms *abangan, priyayi,* and *santri* indicate dimensions of cultural variation, not absolute categories' (347) and 'Thus the three groups tend to become socially segregated to a degree' (374).

3 Javanese themselves sometimes express this opposition as *wong jawa/wong Islam* (Javanese person/Muslim) or *agama jawa/agama Islam* (Javanese religion/Islam). Historically, kejawèn referred to the 'cultural realm which constitutes the core of Javanese civilization centering on the Javanese courts of Surakarta and Yogyakarta. In contrast to it the coastal areas are referred to as *pasisir*' (Kartodirdjo 1991: 267).

4 Only Mayer and Moll (1909: 5–6) note this distinction. They also observed that Javanese religious 'synkretisme' was especially evident in these feasts. The Malay term for prayer-meal, *kendurèn* or *kenduri*, is not well known in this area. I heard it used in certain villages among devout, reform-minded Muslims who have turned their backs on Javanese tradition.

5 *Ajat* (Horne 1974, Pigeaud 1982) in literary language means 'need', 'want', or 'requirement'; and 'communal religious meal, slametan'. Prawiro Atmodjo (1987) also lists the meaning: *niyat* (intention). The latter sense seems indicated here, since it expresses a kind of commitment analogous to the Islamic *niya*.

6 See also Hefner's comments on vagueness and the ambiguity of Tengger liturgy (1985: 184–6). Barth's (1993) emphasis on the disorder inherent in Balinese cultural diversity contrasts sharply with the present case.

7 The layout of the five-coloured porridge is the same as that of the colour scheme associated with the four quarters and the centre of the kingdom in fourteenth-century Hindu Java (Pigeaud 1960–3, IV: 57–8; see also Behrend 1985). The set of spiritual siblings is prominent in Hindu Balinese ritual (Hooykaas 1974), suggesting a common Hindu-Javanese source, though some authors see the four-five structure as indigenous (Ossenbruggen 1983; Pigeaud 1983). Woodward (1989: 75–7) discusses various formulations of the micro/ macrocosm doctrine in Muslim theology and the imperial cult.

8 Keeler, in his excellent study of the Javanese shadow play, differs on this point. He argues that *kérata basa* 'illustrate the tendency to assert meaning by imposing associations on and among words quite arbitrarily ... *Ngèlmu* [esoteric wisdom] and *kérata basa* are not really intended to expand a person's understanding. They do not represent an analysis of the world. Instead, they assert control by the imposition of a grid upon data' (1987: 251–3). The puppeteer may indeed possess such poetic licence and the verbal skills with which to deploy it, but among Banyuwangi's mystics knowledge is attained by penetrating to links among hidden realities, not by imposing an arbitary order on the random. Truths are 'passed on', not invented. As Pigeaud (1983) showed, except in trivial wordplay (or, one should add, in the artful play of the *dhalang*), the correspondences and links are putatively real ones, hence their importance in magic and divination. The assonances, puns, and coin-cidences of number (a kind of numerical pun) therefore indicate inner harmonies and are themselves part of the order. Many such puns are traditional; and one who habitually 'makes them up' is apt to be accused of 'waffling'. Woodward's intriguing exposition of palace symbolism (1989: 201–14) makes use of the same ramifying wordplay.

9 Such techniques are manipulative and socially useful. Indonesian political slogans and symbols display a similar zest for combination and political syncretism, employing acronyms (Nasakom = nationalism + religion + communism) or 'magic numbers'. The red and white flag, the Five Principles of the state ideology, and the 1945 Constitution (referred to as *undang-undang empat-lima*) seem, to villagers accustomed to such symbols, entirely 'natural', part of the order of things and therefore legitimate. Key political acronyms which marked the transition to military government, such as Gestapu and Supersemar, derive their power not merely from their connotations but from a sense that, as in *kérata basa*, such linguistic echoes are not simply arbitrary. For a different view see Anderson (1990a: 128, 147).

10 Many Javanese mystics regard santri views as false if taken literally and few perform the daily prayers or attend the mosque (cf. Woodward 1989: 149–50; Zoetmulder 1995: 185–6).

11 A classical formulation of this view is found in Yasadipura's *Serat Cabolèk*, where the 'container' is Islamic Law and the 'content' Javanist mysticism (Soebardi 1975: 53; see also Woodward 1989: 72).

12 These meanings are coupled in other Indonesian languages (Beatty 1992:

277). See also Keeler's insightful discussion of verbal efficacy and vows (1987: 124–34).

13 Woodward (1988: 61–2; 1989: 142–3) and Hefner (1985: 107) follow Geertz (1960) and Jay (1969) on the segregation of santri and non-santri and their complementarity in ritual.

14 I am describing something more precise and systematic than the diffuse significance of community symbols astutely analysed by Cohen (1985: 20–1, 55). The slametan recruits overlapping sets of neighbours and is emphatically not about group identity or boundary markers.

15 Woodward does not mention this derivation, suggesting that 'while it is not manifestly drawn from Arabic textual sources, the [J.] *ujub* is motivated by Islamic religious concerns' (1988: 77). One contemporary use of the *ijāb/kabul* notion familiar to all Javanese is the protocol of the Islamic marriage ceremony. However, no one ever mentioned this parallel to me in discussion of slametans.

Chapter 3

1 I use the term 'cult' here rather loosely to denote the set of practices associated with the village guardian spirit. As we shall see, for good reasons, it has not really crystallized into a cult worth the name.

2 Pigeaud (1938: 134 and *passim*) describes other Javanese barongs. His information on the Banyuwangi barong (1938: 209–11) is from Brandts Buys and Brandts Buys-Van Zijp (1926).

3 The name Lundoyo may derive from Lodaya, the forest ruled by Singo Barong in the *réyog* Ponorogo. According to a tale related by Pigeaud (1938: 432), Lodaya (now a village near Blitar) is the place of origin of all were-tigers in Java.

4 Buyut Cili, Siti Sendari, and Siti Ambari are recognized as local spirits in the *seblang* performance of Olehsari. Some of the names also occur in non-local contexts. A few people know that in the wayang Siti Sendari is the daughter of Krishna. The bird of the final scene, Panji Kolaras, appears in the Andhe-Andhe Lumut, a popular drama of East Java.

5 Adat (from Ar. *ada*) is recognized in Islam as the order of custom and customary law, distinct from the *shariah* or canon law. In modern Indonesian usage the term is current among non-Muslim as well as Muslim groups. For definitions, see Goldziher 1953, Kern 1953; for discussions of Islam and adat, see Geertz 1983, Hefner 1985, Hooker 1983, and Ibrahim 1985.

6 As these practices indicate, the emphasis is on power rather than on the life-giving attributes of the sap, suggesting a corruption of the original concept. In Hindu-Javanese thought the 'waters of life' derived their power from the immanent force of rasa, 'essence', a life-giving substance which is concentrated in plant sap, semen, blood, etc. (Bosch 1960: 59–61). While contemporary mysticism preserves this association between rasa and the life-principle, the word rasa is never mentioned in connexion with the Cili cult.

7 This is one, abbreviated, version of a complicated story – the history of the *seblang* is a hotly contested issue in local cultural politics. A former Olehsari headman, however, confirmed the version I was told in Bayu, namely, that

the *seblang* returned to his village around 1930 after a longish absence. Interestingly, barong and *seblang* are considered to be 'opposed': the barong may not perform in Olehsari.

8 In the same period, *réyog* troupes in Ponorogo were divided among the contending parties – the communists, nationalists, and the Muslim party (Mahmudi 1969). On the background to communal strife see Jay 1963 and Lyon 1970.

9 For an account of post-coup 'theatre as cultural resistance' see Hatley 1990.

10 Banyuwangi had a large PKI following, especially in the plantation and port/ fisheries sectors (Cribb 1990: 149–57). The regent himself was a PKI placement. Cribb (1990: 174–6) gives some details of executions. An intelligence report (Anon. 1986) outlines the army role.

11 The Tenggerese communities of East Java which were culturally homogeneous and highly integrated (even more than the present case) escaped the bloody implosion typical of the lowland, faction-ridden populations. Killings of Tenggerese communist suspects were carried out by outsiders (Hefner 1990: 209–16).

Chapter 4

1 Williams, of course, meant something altogether different by this slogan.

2 Old Jav. *palambang* meant, among other things, poem (Zoetmulder 1974: 147–8), thus a written form. The opposite is implied in the present instance, viz. an unwritten (though not exactly non-verbal) message. Intriguingly, however, word and object may once have been fused – Zoetmulder suggests that *palambang*, poem, may be related to *lambang*, part of the house frame on which the words may have been inscribed.

3 The pair signifies male and female. Burkhill (1935: 1458–9) identifies *sari kurong* as the 'closed buds' of the *Mesua ferrea*, 'a sacred tree of India' known in Java by its Sanskritic name *nagasari*.

4 The situation is superficially complicated by the fact that Cungking now belongs to the *kelurahan* (urban district) of Mojopanggung. However, since the lurah is a resident of Cungking and normally attends the shrine's rituals this fact can be ignored. He appears as *de facto* headman of the traditional village community.

5 On the importance of male/female symbolism in Tengger ritual and mythology see Hefner (1985: 127, 139).

6 No one to whom I spoke could satisfactorily explain the significance of this number. But according to the former caretaker, one is supposed to count the markings on the blade (not the bends), which shift over a period of time and thus foretell the future or diagnose the present state of the nation.

7 In Java, *pangiwa* usually refers to the 'left-hand' line of royal succession, which includes the Hindu gods, in contrast to the *panengen*, the 'right-hand', religious, line of Javanese Muslim saints (Pigeaud 1967–70, 1: 151).

8 Hefner's (1985) study has a photograph of a zodiac beaker, dated 1347 (resting, one notes with disappointment, on a right hand). Regarding other priestly implements, the Tengger priest wears a 'ritual cord (*sampet*) made of batik or bright yellow cloth' (Hefner 1985: 192). Could Buyut's oddly named

garment (*sambut* = Old Jav. 'receive') really be a *sampet* or similar priestly cloth?

Chapter 5

1 E.g. Geertz 1960: 228, 374; but compare pp. 347, 355.
2 Nakamura, in his study of modernist Islam in Kota Gede notes a situational flexibility in socio-economic patterns of association and 'lifestyle' such that 'the two orientations [santri and abangan] are alternative ways of action always close at hand' (1983: 135). But he is not speaking at this point of *religious* behaviour. (Strictly speaking, of course, the terms santri and abangan concern religion.)
3 A young Muslim from town who transcribed the slametan address for me was rather shocked by this explanation and wrote the word *porno* in the margin of the transcript.
4 In Javanese and Sumatran mysticism there are conventionally four stages on the mystic's path to gnosis: J. *saré'at* (or *saréngat*), *tarékat, hakékat, ma'ripat*, (Rasjidi 1977: 26; cf. Schimmel 1975: 99). Javanese mystics use this series in analogies to indicate levels of understanding and meaning.
5 Bowen (1989: 615) argues that salāt prayers (aside from the question of their comprehensibility) are 'not structured around an intrinsic propositional or semantic core' (1989: 615), but gain their meanings for actors in discourse *about* worship or in differences in performance which serve to indicate social distinctions, etc. (612).
6 Cf. Bowen's (1993: 94–101) perceptive account of traditionalist and modernist approaches to the Koran among the Gayo and their different conceptions of ritual speech. See also Baker (1992: 108), who distinguishes between the mental act of comprehension and the practical activity of 'apprehension', a more socially engaged process in which one grasps various aspects of recitation without necessarily comprehending the literal meaning.
7 Bowen (1993: 18–30). Cf. Jordaan (1985: 52), writing of rural Madura: 'Differences in the observance of religious practices by traditionalist Muslims and Muhammadiyah followers led to recurrent and rather fundamental debates about doctrinal matters.'
8 Ar. *ahl al-sunna wa 'l-jama'a*, 'the people of the *sunna* and of the community' (q.v. *sunna* in *Shorter encyclopaedia of Islam*). This term, from which Sunni is derived, generally denotes traditionalist orthodoxy in Indonesia (Dhofier 1980: 23).
9 Noer (1973: 300–8) and Federspiel (1970: 46–81) summarize doctrinal differences. See also Jordaan's (1985: 328–31) diagnostic table of criteria in Madura. Good anthropological accounts of reformed Islam in Java are Nakamura 1983 and Peacock 1978a and 1978b.
10 The hadīth refers to Ar. *sadaka*, almsgiving. Clearly the word sedhekah derives from *sadaka*, but since commemorative feasts in Banyuwangi do not involve almsgiving or invitations to the poor, the hadīth justification is sophistical. I do not share Woodward's (1988) view that the slametan and sedhekah, as performed today, are based on Islamic scriptural precepts.
11 On the political context of the Islamic revival, see Raillon 1985; Hefner 1987

and 1993a; Vatikiotis 1993. For a sample of Indonesian views see the special issue of *Editor*, 13 Feb. 1993.

12 The cultural history of Java turns on this paradox, nicely epitomized by Geertz (1968: 25–9) in his vignette of the saint, Sunan Kalijaga.

13 Koentjaraningrat (1985: 359): 'Most Javanese consider *sunatan* an initiation in which the boy becomes a Muslim.' In many countries, circumcision is accompanied by the ceremonial completion of the Koran, *khataman* (Wensinck 1953b: 255), but in Banyuwangi the *khataman* is generally deferred until the wedding day. Thus, one could argue that induction into the adult faith awaits social maturity.

14 Roff (1984), combining insights of Van Gennep and Turner, emphasizes the tripartite structure of the pilgrimage, with its rites of separation, spiritual brotherhood in *communitas* experienced in Arabia, and the changed spiritual state of the returnee. My point is somewhat different: local constructions and interpretations of the haj compensate for a perceived lack of sanctity, or supplant the orthodox significance of the rite.

15 The classical exposition of this theme is Mauss 1925. I have explored the debt-influence mechanism in the feasts of merit of Nias (Sumatra) where the exchange theme is carried to theatrical extremes (Beatty 1992). In the Tengger highlands of East Java feasting is closely tied to status (Hefner 1985: 222–30). But in Banyuwangi festive competition is mainly restricted to village politicians and hajis, and then only in an unsystematic fashion.

16 Levy (1969: 192), in a comprehensive discussion of morality in Islam, gives the orthodox position: 'In the official expositions of the faith, such as are contained in the books of *fiqh*, no special distinction is made between rules regarding conduct and those which concern ritual.'

17 In Ash'arite orthodoxy 'Verbal utterance of the creed and the fulfilment of the statutory duties, the "pillars" (*arkan*) of the religion (namely, almsgiving, worship, fasting, and pilgrimage) are "branches" (i.e. secondary offshoots) of the belief "in the heart". A man does not cease to be a true believer if he refrains from carrying out the "branch" duties but only if he denies the "oneness" of Allah and the truth of the prophets' (Levy 1969: 192–3).

Chapter 6

1 In this account, the Black Stone [Ar. *hajaru 'l-Aswad*] seems to be confused with the *ka'ba* itself. See Hughes 1935: 154–5.

2 The implied criticism is compatible with a monist strain of classical Sufism. Ibn al-Arabi, for example, 'says that the true *ka'ba* is nothing other than our own being' (Wensinck 1953a: 195).

3 See Geertz (1960: 238–9); Stange (1984: 119); Gonda (1952: 158); Zoetmulder (1995: 182–4).

4 The terms of debate (but not the meanings) stem from Sufism, which is much concerned with the relation between God's Essence, Attributes, and Names (these also figure in Sangkan Paran litanies). One could cite, further, al-Jili whose monism is said to have influenced Javanese mysticism: 'As man is created in the image of God, so the universe is created in the image of man, who is its spirit and life'; 'the world will not cease to be living so long as

humankind continues there' (Nicholson 1921: 121). But Bayu's Javanists reach similar conclusions via a different logic which has more in common – remarkably enough – with Berkeley's *esse es percipi* than with classical Sufism.

5 For more elaborate, allegorical figurations of sex/creation see the arch-Javanist poem, *Serat Dermagandhul* (Drewes 1966: esp. 352).

6 Possibly this idea was originally a play on the Arabic word *'adam*, non-being, which occurs in earlier mystical works, both orthodox (Drewes 1969) and heterodox (Zoetmulder 1995: 105; Anderson 1982: 47). In any case, the derivation is now forgotten.

7 Other possibilities, which I do not consider here, are the Sufi doctrine of emanations (*martabat pitu*: the seven grades of being) and the related doctrine of the Perfect Man, *Insan al Kamil* (see Johns 1957, Nicholson 1921, Zoetmulder 1995: 45–6, 97–114). Some of Sangkan Paran's leaders are familiar with the *martabat pitu*, which are set out schematically in the sect's secret texts. But ordinary members and other Javanists know at most the names of some stages without understanding how the system works as a whole.

8 The word *ga'ib* (hidden, mysterious) was often used by informants in a context suggesting the sense of 'potential' or 'potentially existing'. This is consistent with usage in Javanese mystical tracts such as one quoted by Zoetmulder (1995: 97, 102): 'The "ideas" do not yet exist; this is the state of hiddenness (*aib*).'

9 Cf. the quotation at the end of this chapter (p. 185). The *basmala* provides another stock schema (see Drewes 1925: 84–5).

10 Geertz (1960: 232) presents alus and kasar as terms defining a (mainly priyayi) aesthetic which comprises the arts, etiquette, and mysticism in a single system. Bayu's mystics, unconcerned about art and etiquette, use these terms mainly to express phenomenological distinctions.

11 In the *Serat Dermagandhul* the four stages are said to refer to sexual intercourse (Drewes 1966: 352).

12 For general accounts of Javanese ethics covering the socio-cultural spectrum see Geertz (1960), Magnis-Suseno (1984) (a philosophical study), and Mulder (1992). Mulder (1978) is a useful survey of mystical practices in Yogyakarta.

13 Geertz (1973a: 129–30) discusses the concept of cocog as a key to the relation between Javanese ethos and worldview, ignoring its relativist connotations: 'as in harmony, the ultimately correct relationships are fixed, determinate, and knowable' (130).

14 Not that this theme is lacking in the literature. Cf. Drewes's synopsis of the *Serat Dermagandhul*: 'what the confession of faith really means is sexual union. The same with ritual prayer; the place to perform this (*masjid al-haram*) is woman' (Drewes 1966: 352). The possible tantric origin of such ideas is discussed by van Akkeren (1951).

15 Modernist Muslims hostile to Javanism, such as Hamka and Rasjidi, emphasize Islamic influences and represent Javanism as a more or less heretical schism. One study sponsored by the Ministry of Religion translates the loan-word *sinkretisme* with the Islamic category *bid'ah* (illegitimate innovation)

(Kartapradja 1990: 25). Javanese authors sympathetic to Javanism, such as Hadiwijono, Koentjaraningrat, and Sartono Kartodirdjo, stress the continuities with pre-Islamic culture. Javanism, of course, comes in many varieties.

Chapter 7

1 Discretion obliges me to use a pseudonym. Those interested will be able to identify the sect and its founder from the (otherwise factual) context.
2 On several counts Natapraja (Papak) was an apt choice of ancestor. He had the same physical peculiarity, betokening magical power; he was also known for his expertise in occult science; and he was an associate of the rebel leader, Prince Dipanagara (whose tabard, it is believed, is among the relics of Joyokusumo). I am grateful to Peter Carey for this information.
3 See Hadiwijono (1967) for a survey of the major sects' doctrines, and Sartono Kartodirdjo (1991), Stange (1980) and (1986) for historical background. Geertz (1960: 328–33) saw the *guru-murid* pattern as integral to mystical organization. Stange (1980: 380) suggests that it 'remains very strong … but it has decreased relative to earlier patterns'.
4 As in the previous chapter, for the sake of clarity and brevity, I confine this account to a broad outline of metaphysics and ethics. The detailed content – spells, chants, and symbolic correspondences which are, in any case, mostly secret – need not concern us.
5 Comparable material more easily accessible may be found in the works of Ranggawarsita (see the excellent summary in Hadiwijono 1967: 103–51; also Simuh 1987) and in Rasjidi's (1977) unsympathetic study of the *Pathi Centhini*. The name *Adammakna* is associated (in Sangkan Paran) with *tapel Adam*, which has diverse meanings in Javanist tradition. There is a treatise on the prophets with this name. In Sangkan Paran, *tapel Adam* refers to human origins in the four elements and the male and female principles: the pre-existent Adam (cf. Mellema 1950). This seems to be roughly the meaning in the *Suluk Gatholoco*, Canto X, st. 14 and XI, 59 (Anderson 1982: 47, 80). The annual slametan at Jati is called *slametan tapel Adam*. Popular divination manuals called *Adammakna* sold in bookstalls have nothing to do with the Sangkan Paran teaching.
6 In Ranggawarsita's system a-i-u stands for *Aku iki urip*, 'I am Life' (Hadiwijono 1967: 149). The same formula, purporting to encapsulate the highest wisdom, can be found in the *Serat Centhini* (Zoetmulder 1995: 190).
7 In Ranggawarsita the conception is similar, though the terms Muhammad and Allah are transposed: 'there is no Lord except Me, and I bear witness, in reality Muhammad is my apostle. Truly what is called Allah is my body, apostle [*rasul*] is my mystery [*rahsa*], Muhammad is my light' (Hadiwijono 1967: 138). See also Drewes's outline of the *Serat Dermagandhul* (1966: 353): 'when uttering the second part of the confession man does not testify to the Arabian prophet but to his own body as the shadow of God's Essence, as the "House of God"'. Similar formulas modelled on the Islamic confession of faith figure in the teachings of many Javanese sects. A further variation on this idea is the writing of the Confession in the form of the body of the powerful wayang figure and guardian spirit of Java, Semar, an example of

which embellishes the entrance to the Mangkunegaran palace (P. Carey, personal communication).

8 One way in which western epistemologies could have entered the Javanist stream is through the Theosophical Society which was active in Java from 1883 with the founding of a lodge in Pekalongan. A Netherlands Indies branch was set up in 1905 and had twenty-four lodges by 1930. The founder of the Society, Madame Blavatsky, visited Java three times (Encyclopaedie van Nederlandsch-Indië 1932: VI: 763–4).

9 This idea, deriving from a *hadīth qudsi*, is prominent in Sufi tradition (Schimmel 1975: 43) and in orthodox Javanese works on mysticism (Drewes 1969: 27, 53–5; 1977: 73).

10 Other examples of revolutionary engagement from the world of Javanist mysticism included Suryomentaram, founder of Kawruh Béja (Bonneff 1978), and Adari, a nationalist cult which adopted Sukarno as its prophet and the Pancasila as its bible (Kartapradja 1990: 117, 170–4).

11 The parable, now something of a mystical commonplace, derives from Aesop, via the poet-mystic Rumi (Schimmel 1975: 3).

12 Stange (1980, 1986), in contrast to Geertz, sees Javanese mysticism as grounded in the experience of, or quest for, union with God. This is a fair definition of mysticism in general; but it does not capture the variety of Javanese sects.

13 The subject of lontar reading in Banyuwangi is comprehensively and admirably treated in Bernard Arps' monograph, *Tembang in two traditions* (1992).

14 These terms from Islamic mysticism are given an anthropocentric gloss and framed in terms of the spatial paradoxes mentioned in chapter 6. Cf. the *suluk* quoted in Zoetmulder (1995: 185): 'He who has a true insight ... He returns to his origin; he strikes something on the north side and hits on the south; he calls and is thereby called himself.'

15 Man as penis, cave as vagina: this trope is developed in the mystical poem, *Suluk Gatholoco*, Canto XI (trans. Anderson 1981–2) and figures in the *Serat Centhini* (cited in Hadiwidjono 1967: 135). On Javanist phallicism and its roots in Sivaism see van Akkeren (1951) and Drewes (1966).

Chapter 8

1 On Majapahit see Pigeaud 1960–3. Gonda (1975) offers a cautious survey of what is known about Indic religions in Indonesia and the relation with contemporary Bali. See also Swellengrebel (1960) on the latter. On the traditional/reform contrast in Balinese religion, which has a bearing on the present discussion, see Geertz (1973b) and Forge (1980). Hefner (1985) describes the influence of the reform movement, Parisada, on the traditional religion of the Tengger people of East Java. The work of M. L. Lyon (1970; 1977; 1980) is an important comparative source for the present chapter.

2 Formal worship in temples and private homes follows guidelines laid down by Parisada Hindu Dharma in its publications, especially the widely circulated handbook *Upadeca*. The sequence of actions involved in temple worship is described in Goris (1960b: 110–11). Banyuwangi's Hindus also use an

anthology of prayers and mantras called *Manggala doa* compiled by a Banyuwangi Balinese.

3 Numbers at other festivals I attended averaged 500 or 600. At the festival of Kuningan in 1996 I counted roughly 3,000 worshippers (including many Balinese) seated in shifts in the temple. There were said to be 45,000 Hindus in Banyuwangi in 1969. Parisada does not accept later, much lower, figures which are based on identity-card (KTP) ascription and census returns. Census officers are said to have falsified forms in favour of Islam, and KTPs do not always correspond to true affiliation. For example the children of the (Balinese) Parisada leader in Banyuwangi were issued with Muslim KTPs.

4 According to the anonymous report (evidently an insider's account) in Cribb (1990: 174–6), mass killings in Banyuwangi began on 20 November 1965, three weeks after the coup. By 25 December, 25,000 had been killed. 'On 1 October 1966 another 150 were killed [presumably to celebrate the anniversary of the coup] and more were killed in May 1968, though the number is not known.' Some PKI-dominated villages in the south of the regency were virtually wiped out. The killings were mainly carried out by military units and the youth wings of Nahdhatul Ulama (the conservative Muslim party) and – to a lesser extent – of the PNI. In many cases the murders were marked by horrifying cruelty.

5 There is no cremation among Javanese Hindus. In Krajan the orientation of Hindu graves is the same as that of Muslims, i.e. north–south – a concession to Islam and village harmony.

6 As Lyon shows, practical difficulties of this kind influenced the form of the nascent Hindu organization. 'The establishment of procedures for registering and conducting marriages and ... other rituals became of central importance to Parisada Hindu Dharma, for it was the primary basis of its religious authority, the practical functions upon which Javanese Hinduism as an organization could rest' (1977: 157).

7 Glondong, for example, has a *pura desa* (village temple) and a *pura dalem* (temple of the dead or nether-world). As in Bulèlèng, the northern regency of Bali, the 'navel' temple (*pura puseh*) and the *pura bale agung* are amalgamated in the *pura desa* (Goris 1960b: 107).

8 This temple, inaugurated in July 1992, was visited by 15,000 Balinese in 1991, with a further 50,000 visitors expected in 1992 (*Panorama, East Java tourism*, March 1992). The temple has a special significance for Balinese since Mt Semeru, like Bali's own Mt Agung, is associated with the mythical mountain, Meru, and the god Pasupati, who played a key role in the creation of Balinese religion (Swellengrebel 1960: 16). Completing the spiritual reunion of Java with Bali, water is taken from the new temple for major festivals in Bali.

9 The 'interpretive tensions' between these two levels of reform in the traditional buda setting of Tengger are astutely analysed by Hefner (1985: 250–65).

10 Banyuwangi's dance-drama is accompanied by a Balinese gamelan orchestra which is quite different in style from the sedate Javanese variety. (On music in Banyuwangi see Brandts Buys and Brandts Buys-Van Zijp 1926; Sutton 1993; Wolbers 1993.) The area also has a barong, gandrung dancers and, until

recently, *sangyang dedari*, a duet performed by young girls in trance intended to rid the community of an epidemic (cf. Grader 1960b: 214).

11 Again one is struck by the parallel with village Islam, divided as it is between the canonical ritual of the mosque and the syncretist religion of the household.

12 The numbers add up to fifteen in any direction. My informant could make nothing of this, but pointed out that fifteen comprises the digits 1 and 5, which yield 4/5 combinations and add up to 6 (the time of sunrise/sunset, thus of Surya, the sun god; the six tastes which unite in *rasa*, etc.). The layout suggests the 8/9 Balinese *nawa-sanga* cosmic schema (Grader 1960a: 169–73). Nine stands for gestation, therefore ontogeny. Five is central, as in the Javanese schema of 'siblings-four, self-fifth'.

13 This appears to be a Balinese formula referring to the *kanda empat*, the equivalent of the Javanese 'siblings-four, self-fifth' constellation (see Hooy-kaas 1974). It is spoken in conjunction with an offering of five-coloured porridge (a staple of Javanese domestic slametans) in temple ritual – one of the few elements in the service which resonates with Javanese worshippers. The priest's assistant noted that the first line depicts the 'sibling to the east' as a white tiger. This can only be a reference, he said, to the capital of Banyuwangi's last Hindu kingdom at Macan Putih (White Tiger).

14 Javanese Hindu temples, such as that of Krajan, contain offering columns to the Majapahit ancestors (and in some cases to the Blambangan ancestors); but these deities are conceived as cultural precursors – analogous to Java's nine Islamic apostles – rather than genealogical forebears.

15 See Barth (1993: 35) on the complex relations between descent, kinship, and reincarnation.

16 For a recent overview of conversion theory see Hefner 1993b.

Chapter 9

1 For a sample of opinion see the journal *Forum Keadilan*, 27 January 1997 (which contains an outspoken interview with Muhammadiyah leader Amien Rais); *Tiras*, 24 October 1996, on Situbondo and the alleged role of pondhok-pesantren in the violence; and *Forum Keadilan*, 10 March 1997, on the riots and the Suharto regime's courting of Islam.

2 Organized terror, though not communal strife, returned to the area in the aftermath of Suharto's fall (as this book goes to press). From August to October 1998 more than one hundred 'witches and warlocks' throughout the regency were targeted by squads of masked, sword-bearing 'ninjas' (*Jakarta Post* 5.10.98; Reuters 6.10.98). Many of the victims were Muslim preachers and NU personnel. As in the past, a presumed link between Islamic expertise and sorcery has been exploited for apparently political ends. Many see the hand of the army in the killings. Another case, perhaps, of exemplary violence.

References

Akkeren, Ph. van. 1951. *Een gedrocht en toch de volmaakte mens. De Javaansche suluk Gatolotjo, uitgegeven, vertaald en toegelicht.* 's-Gravenhage: Excelsior

Anderson, Benedict R. O'G. 1977. Religion and politics in Indonesia since Independence. In *Religion and social ethos in Indonesia*, ed B. R. O'G. Anderson, M. Nakamura and M. Slamet. Melbourne: Centre of Southeast Asian Studies, Monash University

    1981–2. The *Suluk Gatoloco*. Translated and with an introduction, in two parts. *Indonesia* 32: 109–50; 33: 31–88

    1990a [1966]. The languages of Indonesian politics. In *Language and power: exploring political cultures in Indonesia*. Ithaca: Cornell University Press

    1990b [1972]. The idea of power in Javanese culture. In *Language and power: exploring political cultures in Indonesia*. Ithaca: Cornell University Press

Anon. 1986. 'Report from East Java.' (Report by intelligence officer, 1965.) *Indonesia* 41: 135–46

Arifin, Winarsih Partaningrat. 1995. *Babad Blambangan* Translation and commentary. Yogyakarta: Ecole Française d'Extrême-Orient/Yayasan Bentang Budaya

Arps, Bernard. 1992. *Tembang in two traditions: performance and interpretation of Javanese literature*. London: School of Oriental and African Studies

Asad, Talal. 1983. Anthropological conceptions of religion: reflections on Geertz. *Man* (NS) 18: 237–59

Austin, J. L. 1970. Performative utterances. In *Philosophical papers*. 3rd edition. Oxford: Oxford University Press

Bachtiar, H. 1973. The religion of Java: a commentary. *Madjalah ilmu-ilmu sastra Indonesia* 5: 85–110

Baker, James N. 1992. The presence of the name: reading scripture in an Indonesian village. In J. Boyarin (ed.), *The ethnography of reading*. Berkeley and Los Angeles: University of California Press

Bali: studies in life, thought, and ritual. 1960. The Hague and Bandung: W. van Hoeve Ltd., reprinted by Foris Publications, Dordrecht, 1984.

Barth, Fredrik. 1987. *Cosmologies in the making: a generative approach to cultural variation in inner New Guinea*. Cambridge: Cambridge University Press
1993. *Balinese worlds*. Chicago: Chicago University Press
Bassett, D. K. 1964. British trade and policy in Indonesia, 1760–1772. *Bijdragen tot de Taal-, Land- en Volkenkunde* 120: 197–223
Beatty, Andrew. 1992. *Society and exchange in Nias*. Oxford: Clarendon Press
Behrend, T. 1985. Kraton and cosmos in traditional Java. *Archipel* 29: 173–188
Bellah, R. N. 1969. Religious evolution. In *Sociology of religion*, ed. Roland Robertson. Harmondsworth: Penguin Books
Belo, Jane. 1949. *Bali: rangda and barong*. Monographs of the American Ethnological Society, no. 16. Seattle: University of Washington Press
Benda, Harry J. 1983 [1958]. *The crescent and the rising sun: Indonesian Islam under the Japanese occupation, 1942–1945*. Dordrecht: Foris Publications
Bonneff, Marcel. 1978. Ki Ageng Suryomentaram, prince et philosophe Javanais (1892–1962). *Archipel* 16: 175–204
Bosch, F. D. K. 1960. *The golden germ*. The Hague: Martinus Nijhoff
Bowen, John R. 1989. *Salāt* in Indonesia: the social meanings of an Islamic ritual. *Man* (NS) 24: 600–19
1993. *Muslims through discourse: religion and ritual in Gayo society*. Princeton: Princeton University Press
Brandts Buys, J. S. and A. Brandts Buys-Van Zijp. 1926. Over muziek in het Banjoewangische. *Djawa* 6: 205–28
Bruinessen, Martin van. 1992. *Tarekat Naqsyabandiyah di Indonesia*. Bandung: Mizan
Burkhill, I. H. 1935. *A dictionary of the economic products of the Malay peninsula*. London: Crown Agents for the Colonies
Carey, P. B. R. 1979. Aspects of Javanese history in the nineteenth century. In *The development of Indonesian society*, ed. Harry Aveling. St. Lucia, Queensland: University of Queensland Press
1987. Satria and santri: some notes on the relationship between Dipanagara's kraton and religious supporters during the Java War (1825–30). In T. Ibrahim Alfian ed., *Dari babad dan hikayat sampai sejarah kritis*. Yogyakarta: Gadjah Mada University Press
Cederroth, Sven. 1995. *Survival and profit*. Richmond: Curzon Press
Cohen, Anthony P. 1985. *The symbolic construction of community*. London: Tavistock Publications and Ellis Horwood
Covarubbias, Miguel. 1972 [1937]. *Island of Bali*. Oxford: Oxford University Press
Cribb, Robert. 1990. *The Indonesian killings of 1965–1966: studies from Java and Bali*. Monash Papers on Southeast Asia no. 21. Clayton: Monash University, Centre of Southeast Asian Studies
Denny, F. M. 1988. Qur'an recitation training in Indonesia. In *Approaches to the history of the interpretation of the Qur'an*, ed. A. Rippin. Oxford: Clarendon Press
Dhofier, Z. 1980. Islamic education and traditional ideology on Java. In *Indonesia: the making of a culture*, ed. J. Fox. Canberra: Australian National University

Djatnika, Rachmat. 1985. Les *wakaf* ou 'biens de mainmorte' à Java-est. *Archipel* 30: 121–36

Drewes, G. W. J. 1925. *Drie Javaansche goeroe's: hun leven, onderricht en messiasprediking.* Leiden: Drukkerij A. Vros

1966. The struggle between Javanism and Islam as illustrated by the Serat Dermagandul. *Bijdragen tot de Taal-, Land- en Volkenkunde* 122: 309–65

1969. *The admonitions of Sèh Bari.* The Hague: Martinus Nijhoff

1977. *Directions for travellers on the mystic path.* The Hague: Martinus Nijhoff

Empson, William. 1930. *Seven types of ambiguity.* London: Chatto and Windus

Encyclopaedie van Nederlandsch-Indië. 1917–40. ed. J. Paulus *et al.* 8 vols. 's-Gravenhage: Martinus Nijhoff

Epp, F. 1849. Banjoewangi. *Tijdschrift voor Nederlandsch-Indië* 11, 2: 241–61

Federspiel, Howard M. 1970. *Persatuan Islam: Islamic reform in twentieth century Indonesia.* Ithaca: Cornell Modern Indonesia Project Monograph Series

Forge, Anthony. 1980. Balinese religion and Indonesian identity. In *Indonesia: the making of a culture*, ed. James J. Fox. Canberra: Research School of Pacific Studies, Australian National University

Furnivall, J. S. 1939. *Netherlands India: a study in plural economy.* Cambridge: Cambridge University Press

Geertz, Clifford. 1960. *The religion of Java.* Glencoe: The Free Press

1968. *Islam observed. Religious development in Morocco and Indonesia.* Chicago: University of Chicago Press

1973a [1957]. Ethos, world view, and the analysis of sacred symbols. In *The interpretation of cultures.* New York: Basic Books

1973b [1964]. 'Internal conversion' in contemporary Bali. In *The interpretation of cultures.* New York: Basic Books

1973c [1972]. Deep play: notes on the Balinese cockfight. In *The interpretation of cultures.* New York: Basic Books

1973d [1966]. Person, time, and conduct in Bali. In *The interpretation of cultures.* New York: Basic Books

1983. Local knowledge: fact and law in comparative perspective. In *Local knowledge.* New York: Basic Books

Geertz, Hildred. 1961. *The Javanese family.* Glencoe: The Free Press

Goldziher, I. 1953. ʿĀda. In *Shorter encyclopaedia of Islam*, ed. H. A. R. Gibb and J. H. Kramers. Leiden: Brill

Gonda, J. 1952. *Sanskrit in Indonesia.* Nagpur: International Academy of Indian Culture

1975. The Indian religions in pre-Islamic Indonesia and their survival in Bali. In *Handbuch der Orientalistik*, Part 3: *Indonesien, Malaysia und die Philippinen.* Leiden/Cologne: E. J. Brill

Goris, R. 1960a. The religious character of the village community. In *Bali: studies in life, thought, and ritual.* The Hague and Bandung: W. van Hoeve

1960b. The temple system. In *Bali, studies in life, thought, and ritual.* The Hague and Bandung: W. van Hoeve

1960c. The position of the blacksmiths. In *Bali, studies in life, thought, and ritual.* The Hague and Bandung: W. van Hoeve

Graaf, H. J. de. 1949. *Geschiedenis van Indonesië.* The Hague and Bandung: W. van Hoeve

Grader, C. J. 1960a. The state temples of Mengwi. In *Bali, studies in life, thought and ritual.* The Hague and Bandung: W. van Hoeve

1960b. Pemayun Temple of the Banjar of Tegal. In *Bali: studies in life, thought, and ritual.* The Hague and Bandung: W. van Hoeve

Graham, William A. 1985. Qu'ran as spoken work: an Islamic contribution to the understanding of scripture. In Richard C. Martin ed., *Approaches to Islam in religious studies.* Tucson: University of Arizona Press

Hadiwijono, Harun. 1967. *Man in the present Javanese mysticism.* Baarn: Bosch and Keuning

Hägerdal, Hans. 1995. Bali in the sixteenth and seventeenth centuries. *Bijdragen tot de Taal-, Land- en Volkenkunde* 151: 101–24

Hasan Ali (n. d.). Sebuah catatan tentang bahasa dan sastra Using. Unpublished typescript

Hatley, Barbara. 1990. Theatre as cultural resistance in contemporary Indonesia. In *State and civil society in Indonesia,* ed. Arief Budiman. Monash University: Papers on Southeast Asia no. 22

Hatley, Ron. 1984. Mapping cultural regions of Java. In *Other Javas away from the kraton,* ed. R. Hatley. Clayton, Australia: Monash University, Centre of Souh-east Asian Studies

Headley, Stephen C. 1979. *Il n'y a plus de cendres: description et histoire du finage d'un hameau javanais.* Doctoral thesis, Université de Paris V

Hefner, Robert W. 1985. *Hindu Javanese: Tengger tradition and Islam.* Princeton: Princeton University Press

1987. Islamizing Java? Religion and politics in rural East Java. *Journal of Asian Studies* 46, 3: 533–55

1990. *The political economy of mountain Java: an interpretive history.* Berkeley: University of California Press

1993a. Islam, state, and civil society: ICMI and the struggle for the Indonesian middle class. *Indonesia* 56: 1–35

1993b. Introduction: world building and the rationality of conversion. In *Conversion to Christianity,* ed. R. Hefner. Berkeley: California University Press

1995. Syncretism. In *The Oxford encyclopedia of the modern Islamic world.* Vol. IV, 149–52. Oxford: Oxford University Press

Herusantosa, Suparman. 1987. Bahasa Using di kabupaten Banyuwangi. Doctoral thesis, Universitas Indonesia, Jakarta

Hooker, M. B. (ed.) 1983. *Islam in South-East Asia.* Leiden: Brill

Hooykaas, C. 1974. *Cosmogony and creation in Balinese tradition.* The Hague: Martinus Nijhoff

Horne, E. C. 1974. *Javanese–English dictionary.* New Haven: Yale University Press

Howe, L. E. A. 1987. Caste in Bali and India: levels of comparison. In *Comparative Anthropology,* ed. L. Holy. Oxford: Blackwell

1989. Hierarchy and equality: variations in Balinese social organization. *Bijdragen tot de Taal-, Land- en Volkenkunde* 145: 47–71

Hughes, T. P. 1935 [1885]. *A dictionary of Islam*. London: W. H. Allen & Co.

Hugo, Graeme J. 1980. Population movements in Indonesia during the colonial period. In *Indonesia: the making of a culture*, ed. James J. Fox. Canberra: Research School of Pacific Studies, Australian National University

Humphrey, C. and J. Laidlaw. 1994. *The archetypal actions of ritual*. Oxford: Clarendon Press

Husson, Laurence. 1995. *La migration Madurese vers l'est de Java*. Paris: l'Harmattan

Ibrahim, Ahmad, Sharon Siddique, and Yasmin Hussain (ed.). 1985. *Readings on Islam in Southeast Asia*. Singapore: Institute of Southeast Asian Studies

Jay, Robert T. 1963. *Religion and politics in rural Central Java*. New Haven: Yale University South-east Asia Studies, Cultural Reports Series no. 12

    1969. *Javanese villagers: social relations in rural Modjokuto*. Cambridge, Mass.: MIT Press

Johns, A. H. 1957. Malay Sufism as illustrated in an anonymous collection of 17th century tracts. *Journal of the Malayan Branch of the Royal Asiatic Society*, vol. 30, pt. 2 (no. 178)

Jordaan, Roy E. 1985. *Folk medicine in Madura*. Proefshrift, Leiden

Juynboll, Th. W. 1953. *Idjab*. In *Shorter Encyclopaedia of Islam*, ed. H. A. R. Gibb and J. H. Kramers. Leiden: Brill

Kartapradja, Kamil. 1990 [1985]. *Aliran kebatinan dan kepercayaan di Indonesia*. Jakarta: CV Haji Masagung

Kartodirdjo, Sartono. 1966. *The peasants' revolt of Banten, 1888, its conditions, course and sequel: a case study of social movements in Indonesia*. 's-Gravenhage: Martinus Nijhoff

    1973. *Protest movements in rural Java: a study of agrarian unrest in the nineteenth and early twentieth centuries*. Kuala Lumpur: Oxford University Press

    1991. Religious responses to social change in Indonesia: the case of Pangestu. In *Modern Indonesia: tradition and transformation*. 3rd edition. Yogyakarta: Gadjah Mada University Press

Keeler, Ward. 1987. *Javanese shadow plays, Javanese selves*. Princeton: Princeton University Press

Kern, R. A. 1953. *Adat law*. In *Shorter encyclopaedia of Islam*, ed. H. A. R. Gibb and J. H. Kramers. Leiden: Brill

Koentjaraningrat. 1985. *Javanese culture*. Singapore: Oxford University Press

Kohlbrugge, J. H. F. 1896. De heilige bekers der Tenggereezen: Zodiakbekers. *Tijdschrift voor Indische Taal-, Land- en Volkenkunde* 39: 129–41

Kraemer, H. 1921. *Een Javaansche primbon uit de zestiende eeuw*. Leiden thesis

Kumar, Ann. 1976. *Surapati, man and legend: a study of three babad traditions*. Leiden: E. J. Brill

    1979. Javanese historiography in and of the 'colonial period': a case study. In *Perceptions of the past in Southeast Asia*, ed. A. Reid and D. Marr. Singapore: Heinemann

    1997. *Java and modern Europe: ambiguous encounters*. Richmond: Curzon Press

Leach, E. R. 1964. *Political systems of highland Burma*. London: Bell

Lekkerkerker, C. 1923. Balambangan. *De Indische Gids* 45: 1030–67

Levy, Reuben. 1969. *The social structure of Islam.* 2nd edition. Cambridge: Cambridge University Press

Lewis, Gilbert. 1980. *Day of shining red: an essay on understanding ritual.* Cambridge: Cambridge University Press

Lyon, M. L. 1970. *Bases of conflict in rural Java.* Research monograph no. 3. Berkeley: University of California, Center for South and Southeast Asian Studies

   1977. Politics and religious identity: genesis of a Javanese-Hindu movement in Central Java. PhD thesis, University of Berkeley

   1980. The Hindu revival in Java: politics and religious identity. In James J. Fox (ed.), *Indonesia: The making of a culture.* Canberra: Research School of Pacific Studies, Australian National University

Magnis-Suseno, Franz. 1984. *Etika Jawa.* Jakarta: Gramedia

Mahmudi. 1969. *Reyog Ponorogo.* Sarjana muda thesis. Universitas Gajah Mada, Yogyakarta

Marrison, G. E. 1987. Eastern Java – History and Literature of Blambangan. Paper given at Sixth European Colloquium on Indonesian and Malay Studies, Passau

Mayer, L.Th. and J. F. van Moll. 1909. *De sedekahs en slametans in de desa.* Semarang: Van Dorp

Mauss, M. 1954 [1925]. *The gift.* Trans. Ian Cunnison. London: Cohen and West

Mellema, R. L. 1950. De schepping van Adam volgens Javaans-Moslimse traditie. In *Bingkisan Budi. Een bundel opstellen aan Dr Phillipus Samuel van Ronkel*

Mulder, Niels. 1978. *Mysticism and everyday life in contemporary Java.* Singapore: Singapore University Press

   1992. *Individual and society in Java.* Yogyakarta: Gadjah Mada University

Nakamura, Mitsuo. 1983. *The crescent arises over the banyan tree: a study of the Muhammadiyah movement in a central Javanese town.* Yogyakarta: Gadjah Mada University Press

Napier, A. David. 1986. *Masks, transformation, and paradox.* Berkeley: University of California Press

Needham, Rodney. 1967. Percussion and transition. *Man* (NS) 2: 606–14

   1980a. Dual sovereignty. In *Reconnaissances.* Toronto: University of Toronto Press

   1980b. Analogical classification. In *Reconnaissances.* Toronto: University of Toronto Press

Nicholson, Reynold A. 1921. *Studies in Islamic mysticism.* Reprinted 1978; Cambridge: Cambridge University Press

Noer, Deliar. 1973. *The modernist Muslim movement in Indonesia, 1900–1942.* Singapore: Oxford University Press

O'Dea, Thomas F. 1968. Sects and cults. In *International encyclopedia of the social sciences,* vol. XIV: 131–6. New York: The MacMillan Company and The Free Press

Ossenbruggen, F. D. E. van. 1983 [1918]. Java's Monco-pat: origins of a primitive classification system. In *Structural anthropology in the Netherlands,* ed. P. E. de Josselin de Jong. Dordrecht: Foris Publications

Padwick, Constance E. 1961. *Muslim devotions: a study of prayer manuals in common use*. London: SPCK

Peacock, J. L. 1978a. *Muslim puritans: reformist psychology in Southeast Asian Islam*. Berkeley and Los Angeles: University of California Press

1978b. *Purifying the faith: the Muhammadiyah movement in Indonesian Islam*. Menlo Park, Calif.: Benjamin, Cummings

Pemberton, John. 1994. *On the subject of 'Java'*. Ithaca and London: Cornell University Press

Pigeaud, Th. 1932. Aanteekeningen betreffende den Javaanschen Oosthoek. *Tijdschrift voor Indische Taal-, Land- en Volkenkunde* 72: 215–313

1938. *Javaansche Volksvertoningen*. Batavia: Volkslectuur

1960–3. *Java in the fourteenth century: a study in cultural history*. 5 vols. The Hague: Martinus Nijhoff

1967–70. *Literature of Java: catalogue raisonné of Javanese manuscripts in the library of the University of Leiden and other public collections in the Netherlands*. 3 vols. The Hague: Martinus Nijhoff

1982 [1938]. *Javaans-Nederlands Woordenboek*. 's-Gravenhage: Martinus Nijhoff

1983 [1929]. Javanese divination and classification. In *Structural anthropology in the Netherlands*, ed. P. E. de Josselin de Jong. Dordrecht: Foris Publications

Pigeaud, Th. and H. J. de Graaf. 1976. *Islamic states in Java, 1500–1700*. The Hague: Martinus Nijhoff

Prawiro Atmodjo, S. 1987. *Bausastra Jawa*. Surabaya: Yayasan Djojo Bojo

Raillon, François. 1985. Islam et Ordre Nouveau ou l'imbroglio de la foi et de la politique. *Archipel* 30: 229–62

Rasjidi, H. M. 1977. *Documents pour servir à l'histoire de l'Islam à Java*. Paris: Ecole française d'Extrême-orient

Ricklefs, M. C. 1979. Six centuries of Islamization in Java. In *Conversion to Islam*, ed. N. Levtzion. New York: Holmes and Meir

1993a. *War, culture and economy in Java, 1677–1726*. Sydney: Allen and Unwin

1993b. *A history of modern Indonesia since c. 1300*. 2nd edition. London: Macmillan

Roff, W. R. 1984. The Meccan pilgrimage: its meaning for Southeast Asian Islam. In *Islam in Asia*, vol. II, ed. Raphael Israeli and Anthony Johns. Jerusalem: Magnes Press

1985. Islam obscured? Some reflections on studies of Islam and society in Southeast Asia. *Archipel* 29: 7–34

Schimmel, Annmarie. 1975. *Mystical dimensions of Islam*. Chapel Hill: North Carolina University Press

Schrieke, B. 1957. *Indonesian sociological studies*, vol. II: Ruler and realm in early Java. The Hague and Bandung: W. van Hoeve

Shaw, Rosalind and Charles Stewart. 1994. Introduction: problematizing syncretism. In R. Shaw and C. Stewart (ed.), *Syncretism/anti-syncretism*. London: Routledge

Shorter encyclopaedia of Islam. 1953. Ed. H. A. R. Gibb and J. H. Kramers. Leiden: Brill

Simuh. 1987. Aspek mistik Islam kejawen dalam 'Wirid Hidayat Jati'. In *Warisan intelektual Islam Indonesia*, ed. Ahmad Rifa'i Hasan. Bandung: Mizan

Snouck Hurgronje, C. 1906. *The Achehnese*. Trans. A. W. S. O'Sullivan. 2 vols. Leyden: E. J. Brill

Soebardi, S. 1971. Santri-religious elements as reflected in the book of Tjentini. *Bijdragen tot de Taal-, Land- en Volkenkunde* 128: 331–49

1975. *The book of Cabolèk: a critical edition with introduction, translation and notes, a contribution to the study of the Javanese mystical tradition*. The Hague: Martinus Nijhoff

Sperber, Dan. 1975. *Rethinking symbolism*. Cambridge: Cambridge University Press

Stange, Paul. 1980. The Sumarah movement in Javanese mysticism. Unpublished PhD. thesis, University of Wisconsin-Madison

1984. The logic of rasa in Java. *Indonesia* 38: 113–34

1986. 'Legitimate' mysticism in Indonesia. *Review of Indonesian and Malaysian Affairs*. 20, 2: 76–117

Stoppelaar, J. W. de. 1927. *Balambangansch adatrecht*. Wageningen: Veenman

Stewart, Charles. 1995. Relocating syncretism in social science discourse. In *Syncretism and the commerce of symbols*, ed. Göran Aijmer Göteborg, Sweden: IASSA

Strecker, Ivo. 1988. *The social practice of symbolization: an anthropological analysis*. London: The Athlone Press

Sullivan, John. 1992. *Local government and community in Java*. Oxford: Oxford University Press

Supardjana, Yoseph. 1986. Unda usuk bahasa Jawa Osing. Unpublished research paper. Faculty of Letters, University of Jember

Sutherland, Heather. 1973–4. Notes on Java's regent families. *Indonesia* 16: 113–47; 17: 1–42

1975. The Priyayi. *Indonesia* 19: 57–78

Sutton, R. Anderson. 1993. *Semang* and *seblang*: thoughts on music, dance, and the sacred in Central and East Java. In *Performance in Java and Bali*, ed. Bernard Arps. London: School of Oriental and African Studies

Swellengrebel, J. L. 1960. Introduction. In *Bali: studies in life, thought, and ritual*. The Hague and Bandung: W. van Hoeve

Tambiah, S. J. 1985. A performative approach to ritual. In *Culture, thought, and social action*. Cambridge, Mass.: Harvard University Press

Tanter, R. 1990. The totalitarian ambition: intelligence organizations in the Indonesian state. In *State and civil society in Indonesia*, ed. Arief Budiman. Monash University: Papers on Southeast Asia no. 22

Turner, Victor. 1967. *The forest of symbols*. Ithaca: Cornell University Press

1969. *The ritual process*. Harmondsworth: Penguin Books

Vatikiotis, Michael R. 1993. *Indonesian politics under Suharto: order, development and pressure for change*. London: Routledge

Veth, P. J. 1875–82. *Java, Geographisch, Ethnologisch, Historisch*. 3 vols. Haarlem: Erven F. Bohn

Vredenbregt, J. 1962. The Haddj: some of its features and functions in Indonesia. *Bijdragen tot de Taal-, Land- en Volkenkunde* 118: 91–154

Weber, M. 1948. *From Max Weber: essays in sociology*. Translated and edited by H. H. Gerth and C. Wright Mills. London: Routledge and Kegan Paul

Weiss, J. 1977. *Folk psychology of the Javanese of Ponorogo*. Yale PhD thesis

Wensinck, A. J. 1953a. Ka'ba. In *Shorter encyclopaedia of Islam*, ed. H. A. R. Gibb and J. H. Kramers. Leiden: E. J. Brill

1953b. Khitān. In *Shorter encyclopaedia of Islam*, ed. H. A. R. Gibb and J. H. Kramers. Leiden: E. J. Brill

Wilson, B. R. 1968. Religious organization. In *International encyclopedia of the social sciences*, vol. XIII: 428–37. New York: The MacMillan Company and The Free Press

1969. A typology of sects. In *Sociology of religion*, ed. Roland Robertson. Harmondsworth: Penguin Books

Wolbers, Paul A. 1993. The *seblang* and its music: aspects of an East Javanese fertility rite. In *Performance in Java and Bali*, ed. Bernard Arps. London: School of Oriental and African Studies

Woodward, Mark R. 1988. The *slametan*: textual knowledge and ritual performance in Central Javanese Islam. *History of Religions* 28: 54–89

1989. *Islam in Java: normative piety and mysticism in the sultanate of Yogyakarta*. Tucson: University of Arizona Press

Zoetmulder, P. J. 1974. *Kalangwan: a survey of Old Javanese literature*. The Hague: Martinus Nijhoff

1995 [1935]. *Pantheism and monism in Javanese Suluk literature: Islamic and Indian mysticism in an Indonesian setting*, trans. M. C. Ricklefs. Leiden: KITLV Press

Index

Cambridge Studies in Social and Cultural Anthropology